a reason for Science

Hands-On Activities   With Scripture Values

LEVEL G

TEACHER GUIDEBOOK

ISBN #1-58938-152-1

Published by The Concerned Group, Inc.
700 East Granite • PO Box 1000 • Siloam Springs, AR 72761

Authors	**Dave & Rozann Seela**
Publisher	**Russ L. Potter, II**
Senior Editor	**Bill Morelan**
Project Coordinator	**Rocki Vanatta**
Creative Director	**Daniel Potter**
Proofreader	**Renee Decker**
Step Illustrations	**Steven Butler**
Character Illustrations	**Josh Ray**
Colorists	**Josh & Aimee Ray**

Copyright ©2003 by **The Concerned Group, Inc.**
All national and international rights reserved. Except for brief quotations in reviews,
no part of this publication may be stored or transmitted in any form or
by any means (mechanical, electronic, photocopy, recording, etc.)

Printed on recycled paper in the United States

For more information about **A Reason For®** curricula,
write to the address above, call, or visit our website.

www.areasonfor.com
800.447.4332

TABLE OF CONTENTS

Overview
A New Paradigm p.5
Inquiry-Based Learning p.5
National Standards p.6
Methodology p.6
    Concepts, Not Content p.6
    Multi-Sensory Learning p.7
    Student-Driven, Teacher-Directed p.7
Components p.7
    Letter to Parents p.7
    Student Research Teams p.8
    Individual Student Worktexts p.8
    Materials Kits p.8
    Personal Science Glossary p.8
Safety Issues p.9
Assessment Methods p.9
Scripture Connection p.9
Creationism p.10

How To Use This Guidebook
Sample Lesson p.11

Weekly Lessons
Life Science p.17
    Lessons 1 - 9
Physical Science (Forces) p.53
    Lessons 10 - 18
Earth Science p.89
    Lessons 19 - 27
Physical Science (Energy/Matter) p.125
    Lessons 28 - 36

Assessment
Weekly Quiz (black line masters) p.163
Quiz Answer Keys p.235

A Reason for Science

*"A sound grounding in science strengthens many of the skills that people use every day, like solving problems creatively, thinking critically, working cooperatively in teams, using technology effectively, and valuing life-long learning."**

*National Science Education Standards, 1999 Washington, D.C.: National Academy Press. (p. ix)

A NEW PARADIGM

A Reason For® Science was designed for children, the handiwork of an infinite God — young minds created with an unlimited capacity to think, to learn, and to discover!

Because of this emphasis on children and how they learn, *A Reason For® Science* is based on a different paradigm from the traditional textbook approach. Why? In an effort to address standards and accountability, many of today's science textbooks seem to get learning backwards. They focus primarily on building a knowledge base, assuming students will later attach meaning to memorized facts. The problem is that few elementary students master information presented this way because they simply never become engaged with the material.

By contrast, *A Reason For® Science* is based on the premise that learning science is an *active* process. It's "something children do, not something done to them."[2]

According to the **National Science Education Standards**, ". . . active science learning means shifting emphasis away from teachers presenting information and covering science topics. The perceived need to include all the topics and information . . . is in direct conflict with the central goal of having students learn scientific knowledge with understanding."[3]

To paraphrase William Butler Yeats, "Teaching is not filling a pail. It's lighting a fire!"

INQUIRY-BASED LEARNING

A Reason For® Science is designed to teach basic Life, Earth, and Physical Science concepts through fun, hands-on activities. Its focus is to make learning both fun and meaningful.

But hands-on activities by themselves are not enough. To truly master a concept, students must have "minds-on" experiences as well! This means actively engaging the material through a variety of activities such as group discussion, problem solving, and journaling. It also requires thought-provoking questions that help develop higher-level cognitive skills. The weekly format of *A Reason For® Science* is designed to reflect this inquiry-based model.

According to the **National Science Education Standards**, "Inquiry is central to science learning. When engaging in inquiry, students describe objects and events, ask questions, construct explanations, test those explanations against current scientific knowledge, and communicate their ideas to others . . . In this way, students actively develop their understanding of science by combining scientific knowledge with reasoning and thinking skills."[4]

Since different students achieve understanding in different ways and to different degrees, the flexible format of *A Reason For® Science* also encourages multiple learning styles and allows for individual differences. Activities challenge students to develop their own unique skills, and encourage them to come up with creative solutions.

NATIONAL STANDARDS

National standards referred to in **A Reason For® Science** come from the **National Science Education Standards**[1]. More specifically, they reflect the "K-4 Science Content Standards" (p.121 - 142) and "5-8 Science Content Standards" (p. 143 - 172).

The Teacher Guidebook includes a list of content standards that relate to each individual lesson. References are based on the NSES alphabetic format, plus a numeric code to indicate the bulleted sub-topic. For example, **C1** in a fourth grade lesson would indicate Content Standard **C** and sub-topic **1**. (A detailed description of this content standard can be found on pages 127 - 229 of the **Standards**.)

As noted above, lower grade and upper grade standards are found in different sections of the book. A **C1** reference for a third grade lesson, for example, would be found on page 127 (characteristics of organisms). By contrast, a **C1** reference for a seventh grade lesson would be found on page 155 ("structure and function in living systems").

METHODOLOGY

Master teachers know that a science curriculum is much more than information in a textbook. It has to do with the way content is organized and presented in the classroom. It is driven by underlying principles, and by attitudes and beliefs about how learning occurs. It is expressed in the practices and procedures used in its implementation.

In other words, textbooks don't teach science — *teachers* do!

That's why it's important for you to understand how this curriculum is designed to be used, and how you can enhance the learning process in your classroom.

Concepts, Not Content

The needs of children in elementary school are very different from high school students, especially when it comes to science education. The presentation of the Periodic Table provides a good example. High school students may find it useful to memorize each element, its atomic weight, and its position on a chart. By contrast, elementary school students must first understand the concept of such a table. What is it? How is it used? Why is it arranged this way? Has it always looked like this? How (and why) has it changed over time? Such an approach leads to a foundational understanding of a concept, rather than a body of memorized "facts" that may change over time.*

As Nobel prize winner, Dr. Richard Feynman, once said, "You can know the name of a bird in all the languages of the world, but when you're finished, you'll know absolutely nothing whatever about the bird . . . (that's) the difference between knowing the name of something and knowing something!"

---

* For example, less than 30 years ago many students were still being taught the "fact" that matter only has three states (solid, l Alfven won the Nobel prize for identifying a fourth state of matter (plasma). There are many such examples in education — includ able charts themselves, which are being replaced in many colleges by a new 3D computer model that offers new insights into relationships bet

Multi-Sensory Learning

In addition to focusing on concepts instead of just content, **A Reason For® Science** uses a multi-sensory approach to learning that supports multiple learning styles.

Visual events include watching teacher demonstrations, studying diagrams and illustrations, and reading summaries. **Auditory** events include participating in group discussions with team members, listening to teacher directions and explanations, and hearing the unique sounds associated with the activities. **Kinesthetic** events include tactile interaction with activity materials, hands-on experimentation, and taking notes, writing answers, and drawing diagrams in individual Student Worktexts.

Omitting any of these components can significantly weaken the learning process, especially for children with specific learning disabilities.

Student-Driven, Teacher-Directed

As long-time educators, the authors of this series recognize that many elementary teachers don't consider themselves "science people." Therefore, this series avoids unnecessary technical jargon, and deals with complex interactions in simple, easy-to-understand language that's reinforced with concrete, hands-on activities.

The Teacher Guidebook is designed to give you the confidence that you need to teach science effectively. In addition to the usual answer keys and explanations, it includes several sections just for teachers.

"Additional Comments" offers tips and techniques for making each lesson run smoothly. "Teacher to Teacher" provides expanded science explanations to increase your understanding. "Extended Teaching" presents a variety of extension ideas for those who wish to go further.

During the first year, we strongly recommend that you try every activity a day or two in advance. Although most activities are relatively simple, this added practice will give you a better feel for any potential problems that might arise.

Most of all, remember that one of the primary goals of this series is to make science FUN for the participants. And that includes you, too!

COMPONENTS

The following are some of the key components in this series:

Letter to Parents

Positive communication between home and school is essential for optimum success with any curriculum. The "Letter to the Parents" (page 3, Student Worktext) provides a great way to introduce **A Reason For® Science** to parents. It covers the lesson format, safety issues, connections with national standards, and the integration of Scripture. Along with the opening sections of this Guidebook, the parent letter provides information you need to answer common questions about the series.

Student Research Teams

A Reason For® Science was created to model the way scientific study works in the adult world. Students are divided into "research teams" to work through activities cooperatively. Ideally, each research team should be composed of three to five students. (Fewer students per team makes monitoring more difficult; more students per team minimizes participation opportunities.) The best groupings combine students with different "gifts" (skills or abilities), complimentary personalities, etc. — the same kinds of combinations that make effective teams in the corporate or industrial world.

In addition, *A Reason For® Science* encourages collaboration between the different teams, again modeling the interactions found in the scientific community.

Individual Student Worktexts

Although students collaborate on activities and thought questions, the Student Worktexts provide opportunities for individual reaction and response. The importance of allowing students to write their own response to questions, keep their own notes, and journal about their individual experiences cannot be underestimated. (While collaboration is essential in the scientific community, no true scientist would neglect to keep his/her own personal notes and records!)

Individual Student Worktexts also provide teachers with an objective way to monitor student participation and learning throughout the school year.

Materials Kits

Quality materials are an integral part of any "hands-on" curriculum. *A Reason For® Science* offers complete, easy-to-use materials kits for every grade level. With some minor exceptions*, kits contain all the materials and supplies needed by one research team for an entire school year. Materials for each team come packaged in an attractive, durable storage container. You can choose to restock consumable portions of the kit from local materials, or purchase the convenient refill pack.

Personal Science Glossary

A glossary is a common component in many science textbooks, yet students rarely use traditional glossaries except when assigned to "look up" a word by the teacher. Since words and terms used in elementary science are not highly technical, this activity is better served by referring students to a standard dictionary.

A more effective approach to helping students learn science words at this level is to encourage them to develop and maintain a **personal science glossary**. This can be a plain spiral-bound notebook with one page (front and back) dedicated to each letter of the alphabet. Throughout the school year, students continually add new words and definitions — not only from their own reading and research, but from the findings of their team members as well. (For your convenience, a black-line master for a glossary cover is included in Appendix A.)

* To help minimize expenses, kits do not include common classroom supplies (pencils, paper, etc.) and a few large items (soft drink bottles, tin cans, etc.) that are easily obtained by the teacher. Kit and non-kit materials needed for each lesson are clearly marked in this Teacher Guidebook.

SAFETY ISSUES

When using hands-on science activities, teachers must be constantly aware of the potential for safety problems. Even the simplest activities using the most basic materials can be dangerous when used incorrectly. **Proper monitoring and supervision is required at all times!**

Although the publisher and authors have made every reasonable effort to ensure that all science activities in **A Reason For® Science** are safe when conducted as instructed, neither the publisher nor the authors assume any responsibility for damage or injury resulting from implementation.

It is the responsibility of the school to review available science safety resources and to develop science safety training for their teachers and students, as well as posting safety rules in every classroom.

An excellent source of science safety information is the Council of State Science Supervisors at: http://csss.enc.org/safety. The CSSS website offers a FREE, downloadable safety guide, "Science and Safety, Making the Connection." This booklet was created with support from the American Chemical Society, the Eisenhower National Clearinghouse for Mathematics and Science Education, the National Aeronautics and Space Administration, and the National Institutes of Health.

To support appropriate safety instruction, every **A Reason For® Science** Student Worktext includes a special section on safety. In addition to the safety precautions above, it is strongly recommended that every teacher verify all students clearly understand this information *before* beginning any science activities.

ASSESSMENT METHODS

Authentic assessment is an important part of any quality curriculum. **A Reason For® Science** offers a duel approach to assessment. First, participation, understanding, and higher-level thinking skills and can be assessed by periodically collecting and reading students' responses to the essay-style questions in the Student Worktext.

Second, this Teacher Guidebook provides black-line masters for a "weekly quiz" (see page 163). These quizzes offer a more traditional assessment based on fact acquisition. Questions are similar to the type that students might face on any standardized test.

In addition, you can use both these methods to create a customized quarterly or yearly assessment tool. Simply select a combination of true/false and multiple choice questions from the quizzes and essay-style questions from the Student Worktext.

SCRIPTURE CONNECTION

Integrating faith and learning is an essential part of a quality religious education. A unique component of **A Reason For® Science** is the incorporation of Scripture Object Lessons into every unit. As students discover basic science principles, they are encouraged to explore various spiritual connections through specific Scripture verses.

Since some school systems may prefer one Scripture translation to another, Scriptures are referenced by chapter and verse only, rather than direct quotations in the text.

CREATIONISM

Many people (including many notable scientists) believe that God created the universe and all the processes both physical and biological that resulted in our solar system and life on Earth.

However, advocates of "creation science" hold a variety of viewpoints. Some believe that Earth is relatively young, perhaps only 6,000 years old. Others believe that Earth may have existed for millions of years, but that various organisms (especially humans) could only be the result of divine intervention since they demonstrate "intelligent design."

Within the creation science community, there are dozens of variations on these themes, even within the specific denominational groups. Instead of promoting a specific view, the authors of this series have chosen to focus on the concept that "God created the Heavens and the Earth," and leave the specifics up to the individual school. Creationism is a faith-based issue.* As such, schools are strongly urged to have a clear position on this topic, and an understanding of how that belief is to be conveyed to their students.

For that matter, so is the theory of evolution.

---

[1] *National Science Education Standards*, 1999 Washington, D.C.: National Academy Press. (p. ix)
[2] *Ibid.* (p. 2)
[3] *Ibid.* (p. 20)
[4] *Ibid.* (p. 2)

HOW TO USE THIS GUIDE

This Teacher Guidebook . . .

is based on a simple, easy-to-understand format. Lessons throughout the series follow the same pattern, so once you're familiar with the format for one lesson, you can find information quickly for any other lesson. The samples on the following pages explain the purpose of each section.

- **Category**
  All lessons are divided into one of three primary categories — Life Science, Earth Science, or Physical Science. Physical Science is further divided into two parts — Forces or Energy/Matter.

- **Focus**
  "Focus" states the topic of the lesson.

- **Objective**
  "Objective" describes the purpose of the lesson.

- **National Standards**
  "National Standards" refers to content standards found in the **National Science Education Standards**. (For details on standards, see page 6.)

- **Materials Needed:**
  "Materials Needed" is a comprehensive list of materials used in the lesson. **Bold-faced** words indicate items provided in the Materials Kit.

- **Safety Concerns:**
  "Safety Concerns" provides details about potential safety hazards. (For more on Safety, see page 9.)

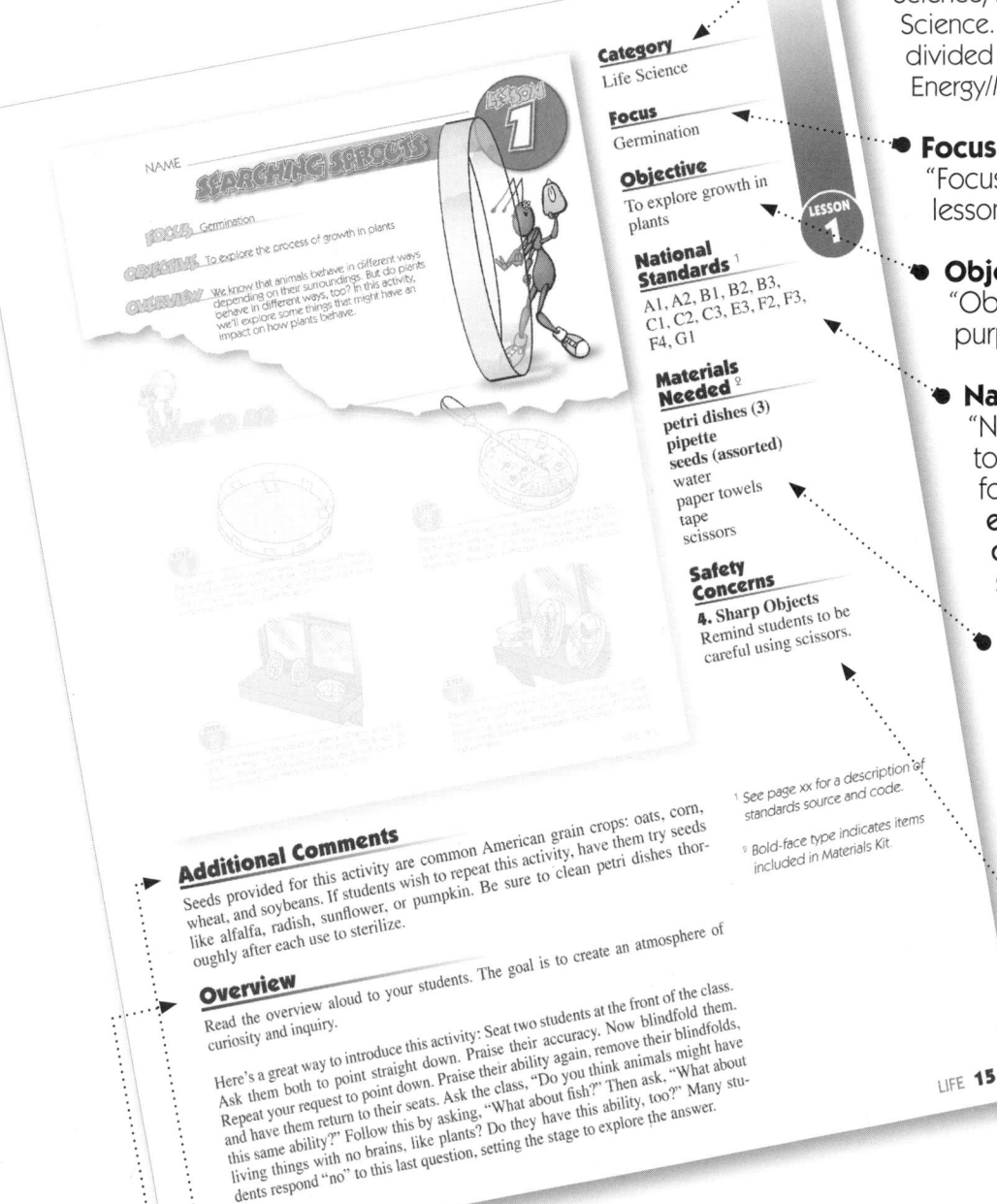

- **Additional Comments:** "Additional Comments" offers tips and techniques for making each lesson run more smoothly.

- **Overview:** The "Overview" provides lesson summaries, thoughts on introducing the lesson, ideas for dealing with materials, and other valuable lesson-specific tips.

HOW TO USE THIS GUIDE
Continued

What To Do
"What to Do" expands on the Steps found in the Student Workbook. It outlines potential problems, offers alternative procedures, and explains ways to enhance the lesson.

WHAT TO DO
Monitor student research teams as they complete each step.

Step 2
Grouping instructions are purposely ambiguous to allow several options. Depending on class size and materials available, 1) have each research team create their own set of three, 2) have each team create only one dish, then combine dishes to create groupings, 3) create a unique combination to meet your specific classroom needs. Regardless of the total number of dishes, at least one dish must lie flat, one must be on edge with seeds up, and one must be on edge with seeds down. These three environments are necessary for the primary comparisons.

Step 4
Emphasize the instruction, "*Don't change their position in any way!*" If dishes are moved, the results will be invalid.

Teacher To Teacher
"Teacher to Teacher" offers expanded science explanations designed to increase teacher understanding.

Another name for the energy stored in seeds is endosperm. Humans and animals use plant endosperm as a food source, too. For instance, flour is ground-up wheat endosperm!

Be sure students realize the two phases of a plant's life cycle that are involved: sprouting and growing. The sprouting process only requires warmth and water. A seed soaks up moisture, swells, splits, and a new plant emerges. But light is needed for the next stage. Light stimulates the new plant into producing the chemical chlorophyll (the green in plants). Without chlorophyll, plants have no way to make food once they've used up the energy in the endosperm. The process of using chlorophyll to direct more food is called photosynthesis.

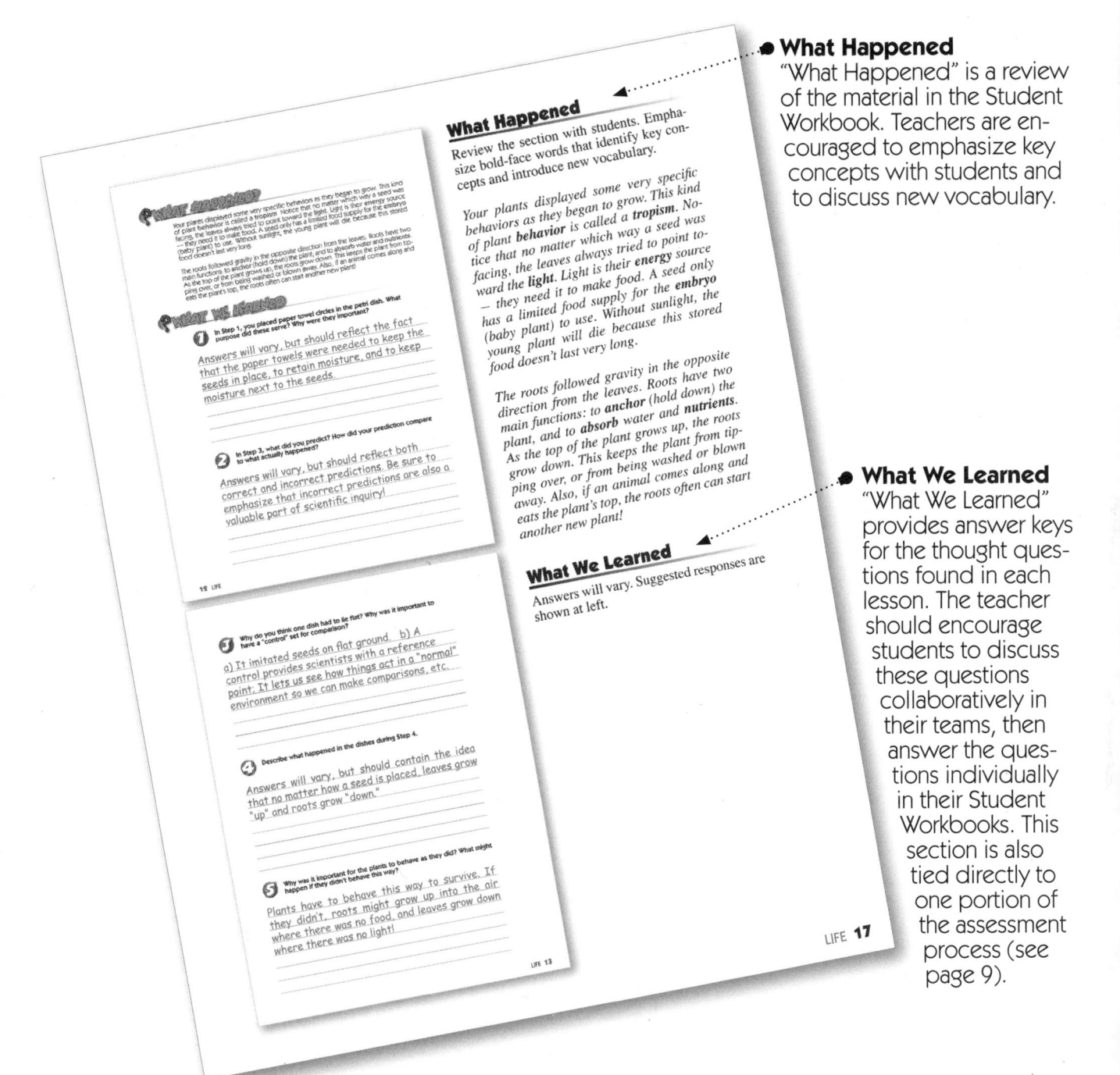

HOW TO USE THIS GUIDE
Continued

What Happened
"What Happened" is a review of the material in the Student Workbook. Teachers are encouraged to emphasize key concepts with students and to discuss new vocabulary.

What We Learned
"What We Learned" provides answer keys for the thought questions found in each lesson. The teacher should encourage students to discuss these questions collaboratively in their teams, then answer the questions individually in their Student Workbooks. This section is also tied directly to one portion of the assessment process (see page 9).

What Happened

Review the section with students. Emphasize bold-face words that identify key concepts and introduce new vocabulary.

Your plants displayed some very specific behaviors as they began to grow. This kind of plant **behavior** is called a **tropism**. Notice that no matter which way a seed was facing, the leaves always tried to point toward the **light**. Light is their **energy source** — they need it to make food. A seed only has a limited food supply for the **embryo** (baby plant) to use. Without sunlight, the young plant will die because this stored food doesn't last very long.

The roots followed gravity in the opposite direction from the leaves. Roots have two main functions: to **anchor** (hold down) the plant, and to **absorb** water and **nutrients**. As the top of the plant grows up, the roots grow down. This keeps the plant from tipping over, or from being washed or blown away. Also, if an animal comes along and eats the plant's top, the roots often can start another new plant!

What We Learned

Answers will vary. Suggested responses are shown at left.

What We Learned

1. In Step 1, you placed paper towel circles in the petri dish. What purpose did these serve? Why were they important?
   Answers will vary, but should reflect the fact that the paper towels were needed to keep seeds in place, to retain moisture, and to keep moisture next to the seeds.

2. In Step 3, what did you predict? How did your prediction compare to what actually happened?
   Answers will vary, but should reflect both correct and incorrect predictions. Be sure to emphasize that incorrect predictions are also a valuable part of scientific inquiry!

3. Why do you think one dish had to lie flat? Why was it important to have a "control" set for comparison?
   a) It imitated seeds on flat ground. b) A control provides scientists with a reference point; It lets us see how things act in a "normal" environment so we can make comparisons, etc.

4. Describe what happened in the dishes during Step 4.
   Answers will vary, but should contain the idea that no matter how a seed is placed, leaves grow "up" and roots grow "down".

5. Why was it important for the plants to behave as they did? What might happen if they didn't behave this way?
   Plants have to behave this way to survive. If they didn't, roots might grow up into the air where there was no food, and leaves grow down where there was no light!

13

HOW TO USE THIS GUIDE
Continued

Conclusion
The "Conclusion" is a summary of the key concepts presented in the lesson.

Food for Thought
"Food for Thought" suggests ways to enhance the Scripture Object Lesson. This section provides an important tool for integrating faith and learning.

Journal
"Journal" suggests ways to expand journaling opportunities related to the lesson. The teacher should encourage the students not only to take notes and keep records, but also to make sketches, draw diagrams, and create charts and lists as needed.

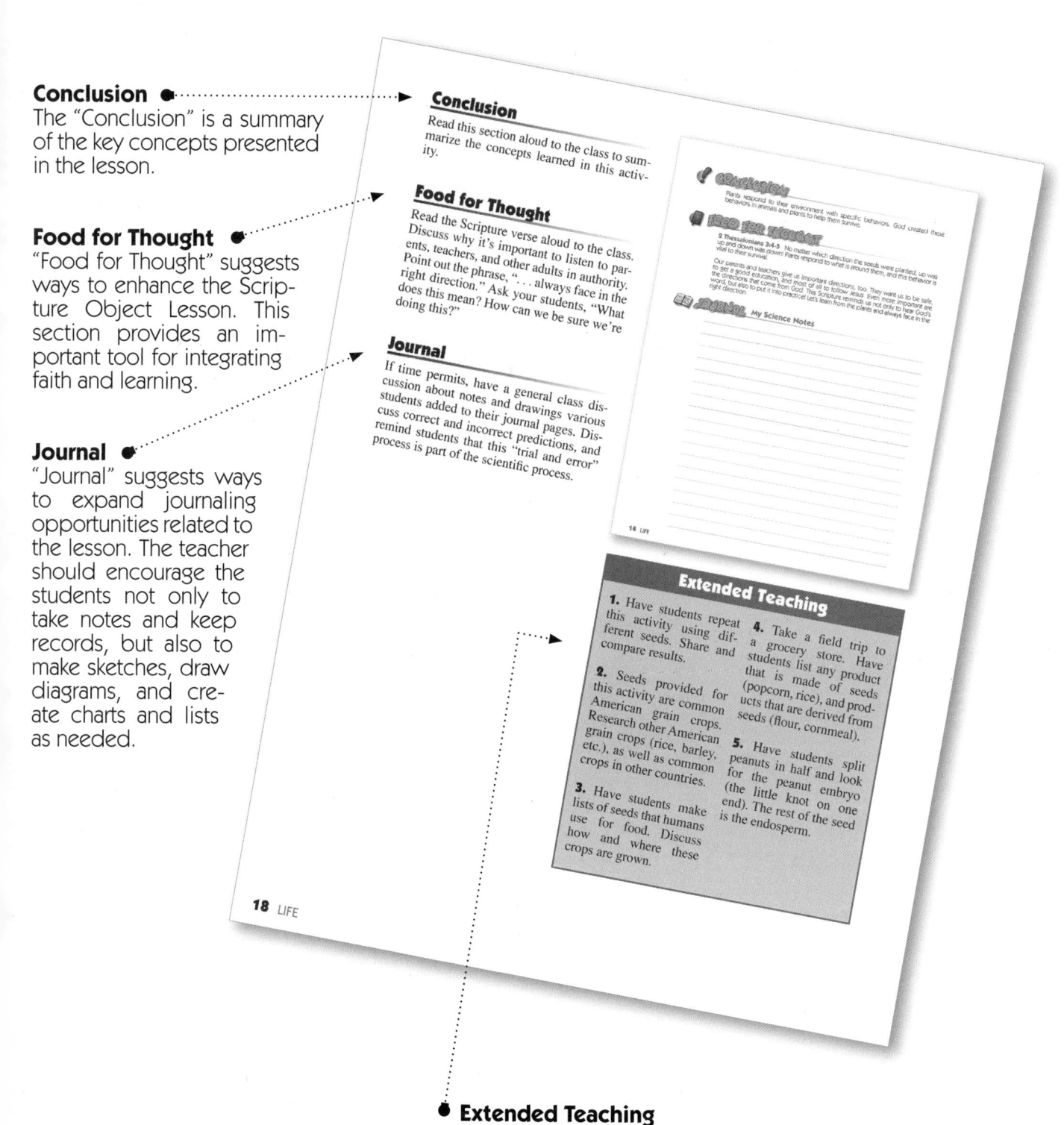

Extended Teaching
"Extended Teaching" presents a variety of extension ideas for those who wish to go further.

14

Lessons

SURVIVOR SEEDS

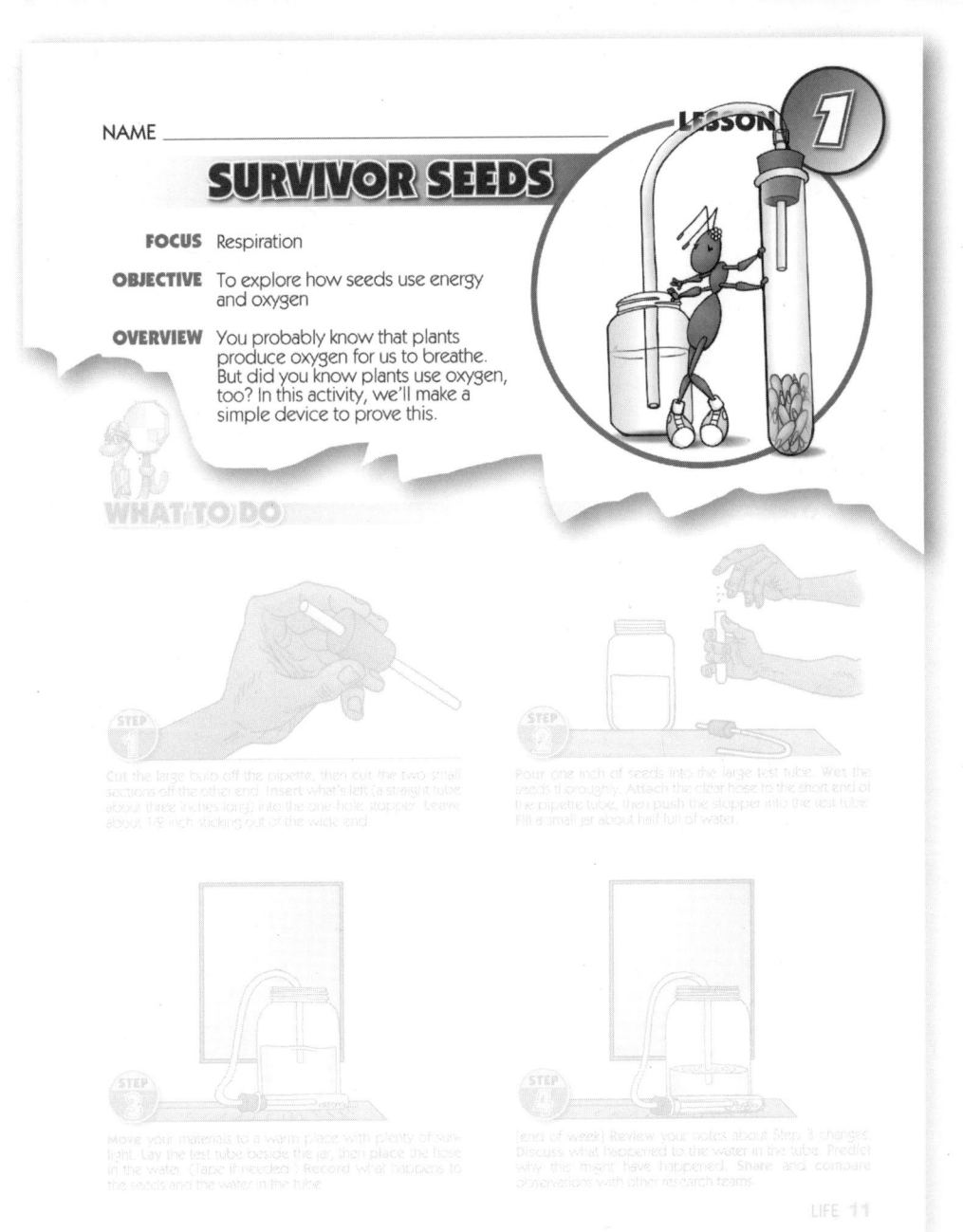

FOCUS Respiration

OBJECTIVE To explore how seeds use energy and oxygen

OVERVIEW You probably know that plants produce oxygen for us to breathe. But did you know plants use oxygen, too? In this activity, we'll make a simple device to prove this.

Category
Life Science

Focus
Respiration

Objective
To explore how seeds use energy and oxygen

National Standards [1]
A1, A2, B1, B3, C1, C2, C3, C4, C5, F1, F2, G1, G2

Materials Needed [2]
pipette
#2 stopper - 1 hole
large test tube
aquarium hose
plastic jar
seeds
scissors
water

Safety Concerns

4. Slipping
Clean up any spills immediately. Remind students to exercise caution when using fluids.

4. Sharp Objects
Remind students to be careful when using scissors.

Additional Comments

You can use any seeds for the activity. The seeds provided in the kit are milo, but other good choices are alfalfa, radish, sunflower, and pumpkin. The seeds should be discarded immediately after finishing this activity to avoid problems. Be sure to have students rinse and clean all materials thoroughly. Save the pipette stem for other projects.

Overview

Read the overview aloud to your students. The goal is to create an atmosphere of curiosity and inquiry.

[1] *See page 6 for a description of standards source and code.*

[2] *Bold-face type indicates items included in Materials Kit.*

Lesson 1 · 17

WHAT TO DO

Monitor student research teams as they complete each step.

Step 2
If you use a glass jar, talk to students about breakage concerns.

Step 4
After completing Step 4, ask students to carefully disassemble the device, dispose of the seeds and water, and carefully clean and dry all components. Remind them to wash their hands thoroughly when finished. Be sensitive to possible mold/fungal allergies.

NAME _____

SURVIVOR SEEDS

FOCUS Respiration

OBJECTIVE To explore how seeds use energy and oxygen

OVERVIEW You probably know that plants produce oxygen for us to breathe. But did you know plants use oxygen, too? In this activity, we'll make a simple device to prove this.

WHAT TO DO

STEP 1
Cut the large bulb off the pipette, then cut the two small sections off the other end. **Insert** what's left (a straight tube about three inches long) into the one-hole stopper. Leave about 1/2 inch sticking out of the wide end.

STEP 2
Pour one inch of seeds into the large test tube. **Wet** the seeds thoroughly. **Attach** the clear hose to the short end of the pipette tube, then **push** the stopper into the test tube. **Fill** a small jar about half full of water.

STEP 3
Move your materials to a warm place with plenty of sunlight. **Lay** the test tube beside the jar, then **place** the hose in the water. (Tape if needed.) **Record** what happens to the seeds and the water in the tube.

STEP 4
[end of week] **Review** your notes about Step 3 changes. **Discuss** what happened to the water in the tube. **Predict** why this might have happened. **Share** and **compare** observations with other research teams.

LIFE **11**

Teacher to Teacher

Although the chemical processes of photosynthesis is very complicated, it can be broken down into two primary parts: "light" and "dark." The light reaction requires light (usually the sun) and is powered by chlorophyll's absorbed energy. It splits water into oxygen (which is mostly released) and hydrogen. The dark reaction doesn't require light, and combines hydrogen with carbon dioxide to form a sugar called glucose. This sugar is the starting compound for everything a plant makes — from seeds to wood!

WHAT HAPPENED?

When conditions are right, seeds can **germinate** (sprout). That's what happened in this activity! Using the **food energy** stored in the main part of the seed, the **embryo** (baby plant) began to sprout.

But sprouting **seeds** need a lot of **oxygen** to grow. As the seeds used up the oxygen trapped in the test tube, there was less air, resulting in lower **air pressure**. This created a small **vacuum** that **pulled** water from the jar into the test tube.

As the seed begins to grow into a full-size plant, the chemical **chlorophyll** (which makes plants look green) starts the **photosynthesis** process. The plant begins converting **carbon dioxide** into oxygen, making much more oxygen than the plant needs. But as you can see from this activity, young seeds need a lot of oxygen in order to get to that point!

WHAT WE LEARNED

1. What was the only way anything could get into the test tube after Step 2? Why was this "closed system" important?

a) through the pipette stem and tubing.

b) without a good seal, air or water would have leaked out or in; a good seal was needed to make the water move; etc.

2. Why was it important to place the test tube in a warm place with plenty of light? What effect might it have had on the activity if you'd placed the test tube in a dark, cool closet?

a) to make the seeds grow or germinate

b) it would have been much slower or wouldn't have worked at all

3. Describe changes that occurred by the end of the week. How did the seeds look? What happened to water levels in the jar and test tube?

a) seeds grew roots/stems; water went up hose, etc.

b) they grew, they became fuzzy, they sprouted, etc.

c) more water in tube, less in jar

4. Compare a plant's needs during the germination stage with its needs at maturity. How are they similar? How are they different?

similar: both need water, both need light, both are growing

different: plant is small and needs oxygen during germination, plant is larger and gives off oxygen at maturity

5. Based on what you've learned, would it be easier to breathe in an airtight room full of sprouting seeds or mature plants? Explain your answer.

It would be easier to breathe in a room full of mature plants since they give off oxygen. By contrast, the sprouting seeds would be competing with us for oxygen.

What Happened

Review the section with students. Emphasize bold-face words that identify key concepts and introduce new vocabulary.

*When conditions are right, seeds can **germinate** (sprout). That's what happened in this activity! Using the **food energy** stored in the main part of the seed, the **embryo** (baby plant) began to sprout.*

*But sprouting **seeds** need a lot of **oxygen** to grow. As the seeds used up the oxygen trapped in the test tube, there was less air, resulting in lower **air pressure**. This created a small **vacuum** that **pulled** water from the jar into the test tube.*

*As the seed begins to grow into a full-size plant, the chemical **chlorophyll** (which makes plants look green) starts the **photosynthesis** process. The plant begins converting **carbon dioxide** into oxygen, making much more oxygen than the plant needs. But as you can see from this activity, young seeds need a lot of oxygen in order to get to that point!*

What We Learned

Answers will vary. Suggested responses are shown at left.

Conclusion

Read this section aloud to the class to summarize the concepts learned in this activity.

Food for Thought

Read the Scripture aloud to the class. Discuss ways that we benefit from the various plants God has made (food, shade, beauty, etc.). Talk about things students can do to help the ecology (not polluting, recycling, etc.).

Journal

If time permits, have a general class discussion about students' journal entries. Share and compare observations. Be sure to emphasize that "trial and error" is a valuable part of scientific inquiry!

CONCLUSION

Seeds are alive. As seeds germinate and begin to grow into plants, they require a lot of oxygen. When plants mature, they give off more oxygen than they use.

FOOD FOR THOUGHT

Genesis 1:29 Although hard, dry seeds look completely dead, they're really a storehouse full of life! Seeds are the primary source of food on Earth — for both humans and livestock. Take away seeds, and everyone starves.

This Scripture reminds us that seed-bearing plants are a gift from God. Our wondrous world is filled with an abundance of wonderful life-giving plants. Yet all too often, mankind abuses this gift, and large areas become barren and wasted. Maintaining a balanced ecology means developing good habits. Recycle, don't pollute, don't litter. Look for ways in your community to apply these ideas!

JOURNAL — My Science Notes

14 LIFE

Extended Teaching

1. Repeat this activity using different sizes and types of seeds. Try using different temperatures or light conditions. Be sure to change only one variable at a time.

2. Take a field trip to a grocery store. Have students list all the foods they can find that are forms of or based on seeds. When you return to class, sort these lists into logical categories.

3. Plants are great survivors! Many plants scatter their seeds to increase survival odds. Have students research seed dispersal methods. Make a bulletin board to share the results.

4. Have students plant various seeds. Monitor the seeds through an entire life cycle until they produce more seeds. Make drawings and record observations throughout the process.

5. Have students pick five favorite plants. Now have them write a story of how the world would be different if these were the only plants that existed!

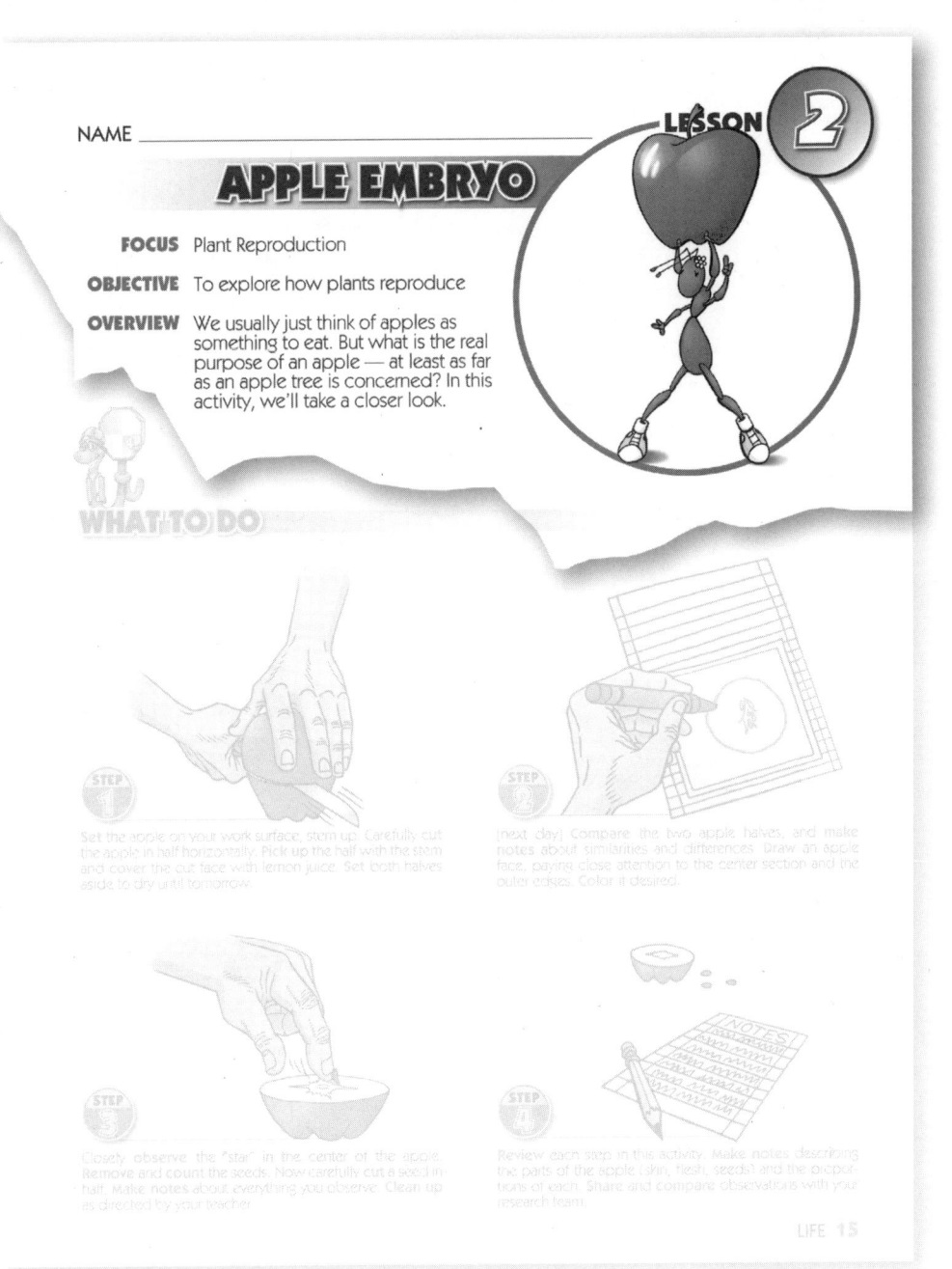

NAME _____

APPLE EMBRYO

FOCUS Plant Reproduction

OBJECTIVE To explore how plants reproduce

OVERVIEW We usually just think of apples as something to eat. But what is the real purpose of an apple — at least as far as an apple tree is concerned? In this activity, we'll take a closer look.

WHAT TO DO

STEP 1: Set the apple on your work surface, stem up. Carefully cut the apple in half horizontally. Pick up the half with the stem and cover the cut face with lemon juice. Set both halves aside to dry until tomorrow.

STEP 2: [next day] Compare the two apple halves, and make notes about similarities and differences. Draw an apple face, paying close attention to the center section and the outer edges. Color if desired.

STEP 3: Closely observe the "star" in the center of the apple. Remove and count the seeds. Now carefully cut a seed in half. Make notes about everything you observe. Clean up as directed by your teacher.

STEP 4: Review each step in this activity. Make notes describing the parts of the apple (skin, flesh, seeds) and the proportions of each. Share and compare observations with your research team.

LIFE 15

Category
Life Science

Focus
Plant Reproduction

Objective
To explore how plants reproduce

National Standards
A1, A2, B1, C1, C2, C5, F1, F2, G1, G2

Materials Needed
apples - 1 per team
sharp knife
lemon juice
crayons (if desired)

Safety Concerns
4. Sharp Objects
Remind students to be careful when using the knife.

Additional Comments

Remind students that good scientists don't EAT their experiments! Consuming a food item used for a science activity is never a good idea, unless that's the plan from the start, and proper hygiene precautions have been observed.

Overview

Read the overview aloud to your students. The goal is to create an atmosphere of curiosity and inquiry. Focus on the fact that we usually only view fruit as food. From the plant's perspective, it serves another purpose entirely.

WHAT TO DO

Monitor student research teams as they complete each step.

Step 1
Monitor students closely as they cut the apples. To avoid potential problems, collect the sharp knives immediately following this step.

Step 3
After completing Step 4, remind students to wash their hands thoroughly.

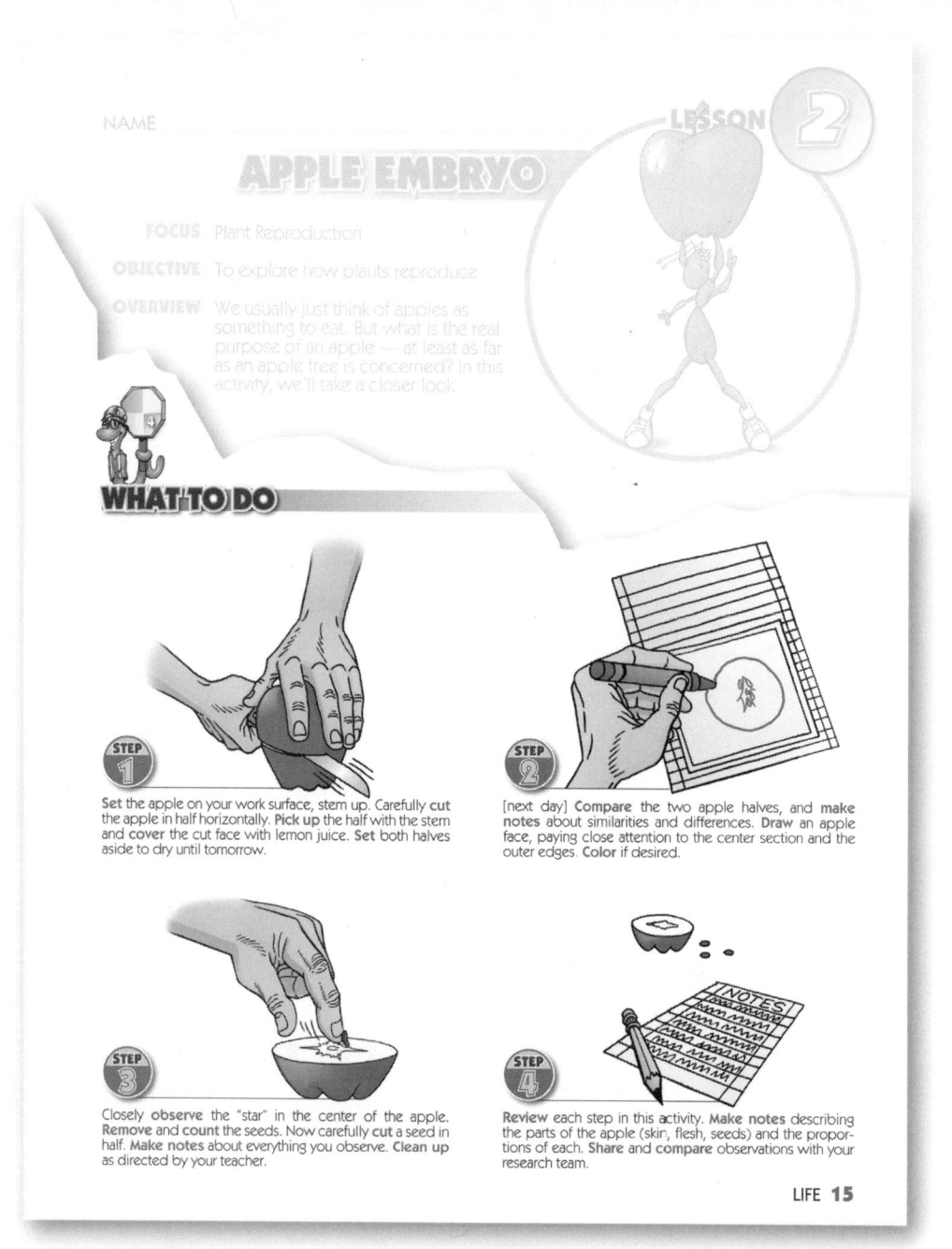

NAME

APPLE EMBRYO

LESSON 2

FOCUS Plant Reproduction

OBJECTIVE To explore how plants reproduce

OVERVIEW We usually just think of apples as something to eat. But what is the real purpose of an apple — at least as far as an apple tree is concerned? In this activity, we'll take a closer look.

WHAT TO DO

STEP 1
Set the apple on your work surface, stem up. Carefully **cut** the apple in half horizontally. **Pick up** the half with the stem and **cover** the cut face with lemon juice. **Set** both halves aside to dry until tomorrow.

STEP 2
[next day] **Compare** the two apple halves, and **make notes** about similarities and differences. **Draw** an apple face, paying close attention to the center section and the outer edges. **Color** if desired.

STEP 3
Closely **observe** the "star" in the center of the apple. **Remove** and count the seeds. Now carefully **cut** a seed in half. **Make notes** about everything you observe. **Clean up** as directed by your teacher.

STEP 4
Review each step in this activity. **Make notes** describing the parts of the apple (skin, flesh, seeds) and the proportions of each. **Share** and **compare** observations with your research team.

LIFE 15

Teacher to Teacher

Pollination means moving pollen from a male flower part (the stamen) to a female flower part (the pistil). Pollen is made in the anther. The pistil is shaped like a water pitcher, and has three parts: the stigma, style, and ovary. The stigma is the sticky top of the pistil where the pollen gets stuck. Nutrients on the stigma cause the pollen to germinate. The growing pollen forms a pollen tube that grows down the style (neck) of the pistil carrying two sperm cells. One sperm cell enters the ovary to fertilize a female cell (egg). The other combines with two polar nuclei to form endosperm — the "food" stored for the embryo's use.

WHAT HAPPENED?

An apple is really a storehouse for a baby apple tree (**embryo**)! The part we like to eat provides **food** for the **seeds** until they **sprout** and put out **roots** and **leaves**. When an apple falls to the ground, it soon begins to **decompose** (rot). You saw a glimpse of this in Step 1 when the untreated apple face began to turn brown. **Enzymes** were already beginning to break down the apple's **cells**. Lemon juice provided a coating of **acid** on the treated apple face to slow this process down.

Pollination is the first step in making an apple. **Pollen** from the **male** part of a **flower** has to get to the **female** part. If two flowers are involved, the process is called **cross-pollination**. Some flowers that have both male and female parts **self-pollinate**. Pollination requires some kind of assistance in order to occur. A light breeze provides one common method, and bees provide another.

WHAT WE LEARNED

1. Compare the treated and untreated apple faces from Step 2. How were they similar? How were they different?

a) similar: same size, same shape, same material, etc.

b) different: untreated face turning brown

2. What caused the color change on the untreated apple face? How is this process helpful in nature?

a) enzymes breaking down the apple's cells

b) decomposition (rotting) makes nutrients available for other life forms

3. What is the purpose of the white material (the main part of the apple)? How does it help seeds grow?

a) the endosperm stores food for use by the embryo

b) it provides food for seeds until they sprout and produce roots and leaves

4. Explain the difference between cross-pollination and self-pollination.

a) cross-pollination involves the male part of one flower and the female part of another

b) self-pollination uses male and female parts on the same flower

5. How does an apple edibility contribute to the propagation of apple trees? Over time, what might happen if apples weren't carried away?

a) since apples are tasty, animals (including humans) carry them away from the tree, causing the seeds to end up somewhere else.

b) not enough soil nutrients for multiple apple trees to grow in one spot; eventually the trees would all die

---

What Happened

Review the section with students. Emphasize bold-face words that identify key concepts and introduce new vocabulary.

An apple is really a storehouse for a baby apple tree *(embryo)*! The part we like to eat provides *food* for the *seeds* until they *sprout* and put out *roots* and *leaves*. When an apple falls to the ground, it soon begins to *decompose* (rot). You saw a glimpse of this in Step 1, when the untreated face began to turn brown. *Enzymes* were already beginning to break down the apple's *cells*. Lemon juice provided a coating of *acid* on the treated apple face to slow this process down.

Pollination is the first step in making an apple. *Pollen* from the *male* part of a *flower* has to get to the *female* part. If two flowers are involved, the process is called *cross-pollination*. Some flowers that have both male and female parts *self-pollinate*. Pollination requires some kind of assistance in order to occur. A light breeze provides one common method, and bees provide another.

What We Learned

Answers will vary. Suggested responses are shown at left.

Note: There are two different processes that can be used to answer question 3. One option is shown at left. The other option relates to how the fruit's edibility contributes to propagation (also covered in question 5). If a student uses this approach to question 3, then the correct answers would be:

3a) The endosperm stores food for animals that eat fruit.

3b) Animals carry the fruit away from the tree, thus dispersing the seeds.

You may wish to discuss these two variations with your class to show how science questions can have different answers depending on the researcher's focus.

Conclusion

Read this section aloud to the class to summarize the concepts learned in this activity.

Food for Thought

Read the Scripture aloud to the class. Talk about the kinds of "fruit" that Jesus' followers should produce. Discuss how a relationship with God helps us change from the inside out.

Journal

If time permits, have a general class discussion about students' journal entries. Share and compare observations. Be sure to emphasize that "trial and error" is a valuable part of scientific inquiry!

CONCLUSION

In some plants, pollination creates fruit. The fruit provides an energy source for the growing seeds. The edibility of fruit helps scatter seeds away from the parent plant.

FOOD FOR THOUGHT

Matthew 7:15-20 When you see apples growing on a tree, you can be sure it's an apple tree! Jesus used this idea to illustrate how we can tell what people are really like inside. If someone pretends to be beautiful, but doesn't treat others kindly, we know they aren't what they seem.

Whenever we try to pretend we're good but don't spend time getting to know God, our actions eventually give us away. The closer we get to God, the more we'll reflect his goodness and character. As God fills us with his love, we begin to bear "fruit" (see Galatians 5:22) that shows what we're really like inside.

JOURNAL My Science Notes

Extended Teaching

1. Have students research ways various kinds of plants reproduce. Compare peach trees with maple trees, corn with potatoes, cactus with kelp, etc. Encourage students to report their findings to the class.

2. Have students research grafting (a form of cloning). Have them illustrate how this process attaches one kind of plant to a totally different plant's roots. Make a bulletin board with the results.

3. Discuss preservation methods. Research other materials used to retard decomposition. Learn the history of preserving food.

4. Get permission to plant some fruit trees around your school, at a nursing home, or in someone's yard. Discuss the role trees play in improving an area (shade, fruit, beauty, etc.).

5. Research the historic character called "Johnny Appleseed." (He was a real person and loved apples!) Use his story as a starting point for discussing ways students might work to improve their community.

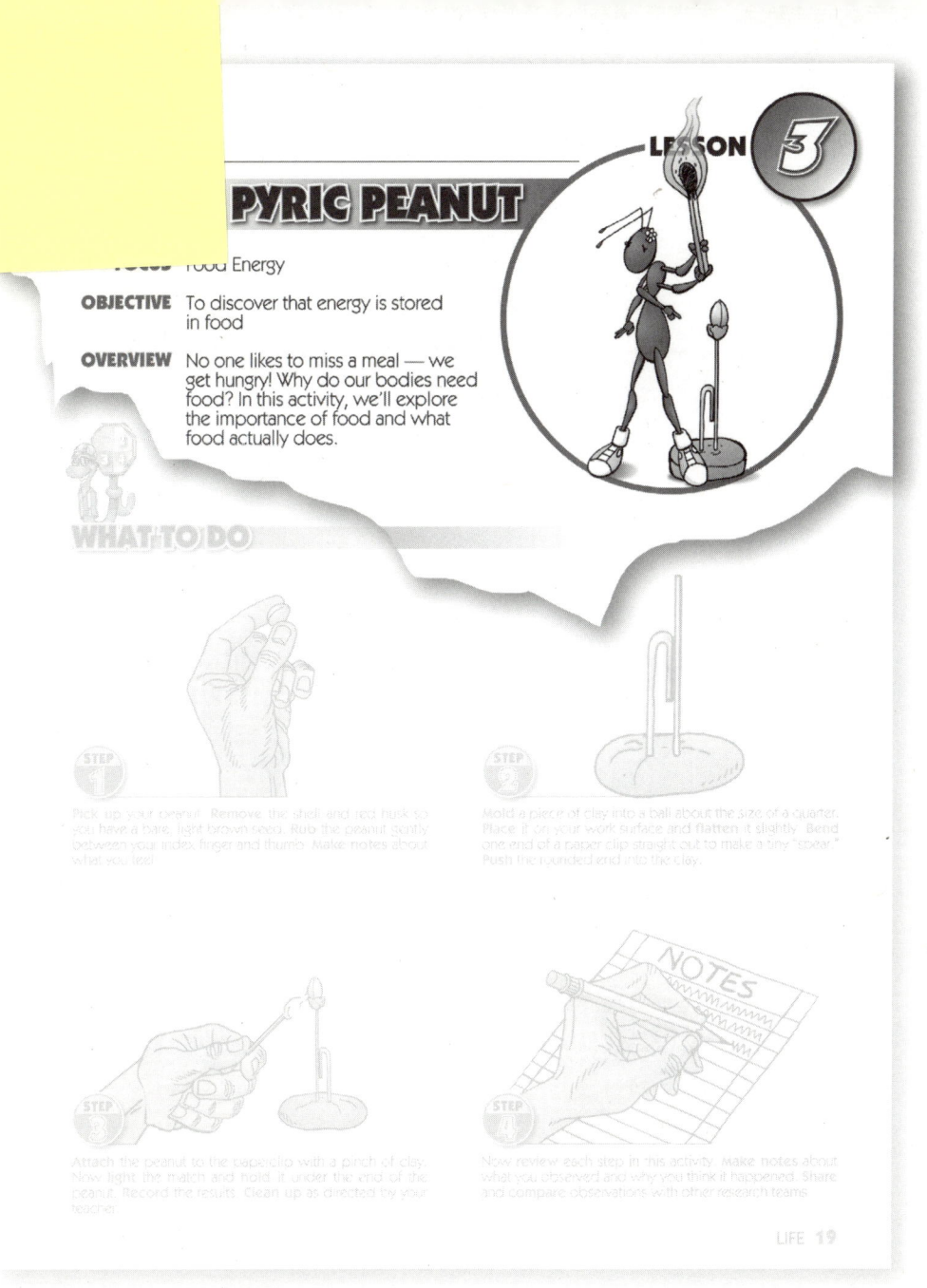

LESSON 3

PYRIC PEANUT

FOCUS Food Energy

OBJECTIVE To discover that energy is stored in food

OVERVIEW No one likes to miss a meal — we get hungry! Why do our bodies need food? In this activity, we'll explore the importance of food and what food actually does.

WHAT TO DO

STEP 1 Pick up your peanut. Remove the shell and red husk so you have a bare, light brown seed. Rub the peanut gently between your index finger and thumb. Make notes about what you feel.

STEP 2 Mold a piece of clay into a ball about the size of a quarter. Place it on your work surface and flatten it slightly. Bend one end of a paper clip straight out to make a tiny "spear." Push the rounded end into the clay.

STEP 3 Attach the peanut to the paperclip with a pinch of clay. Now light the match and hold it under the end of the peanut. Record the results. Clean up as directed by your teacher.

STEP 4 Now review each step in this activity. Make notes about what you observed and why you think it happened. Share and compare observations with other research teams.

LIFE 19

Category
Life Science

Focus
Food Energy

Objective
To discover that energy is stored in food

National Standards
A1, A2, B1, B3, C1, C3, C5, F1, F2, G1, G2

Materials Needed
peanut
clay
paperclip
match

Safety Concerns

2. Open Flame
Remind students to exercise caution around open flame (hair, loose clothing, etc.).

3. Hygiene
Remind students not to eat these peanuts. Ask them to wash their hands after handling the peanut.

4. Other
Some students may be allergic to nuts. If they disregard the previous warning, this can pose a serious health hazard.

Additional Comments

Depending on age and oil content, peanuts can really burn vigorously! Have a container of water or a fire extinguisher handy in case of emergencies. Occasionally you'll have the opposite problem. For stubborn peanuts, hold the arrangement horizontally (peanut over match) to get things started. If you're not comfortable letting students handle matches, do this activity as a demonstration. You may need to repeat it two or three times so everyone gets a close look.

Overview

Read the overview aloud to your students. The goal is to create an atmosphere of curiosity and inquiry. Focus on the concept of food as an energy source.

Lesson 3 · 25

WHAT TO DO

Monitor student research teams as they complete each step.

Step 2

Make sure every team has created a stand similar to the illustration before moving on to Step 3.

Step 3

Monitor students closely during this step (see warnings above). To avoid problems, collect used matches immediately after peanuts are lit.

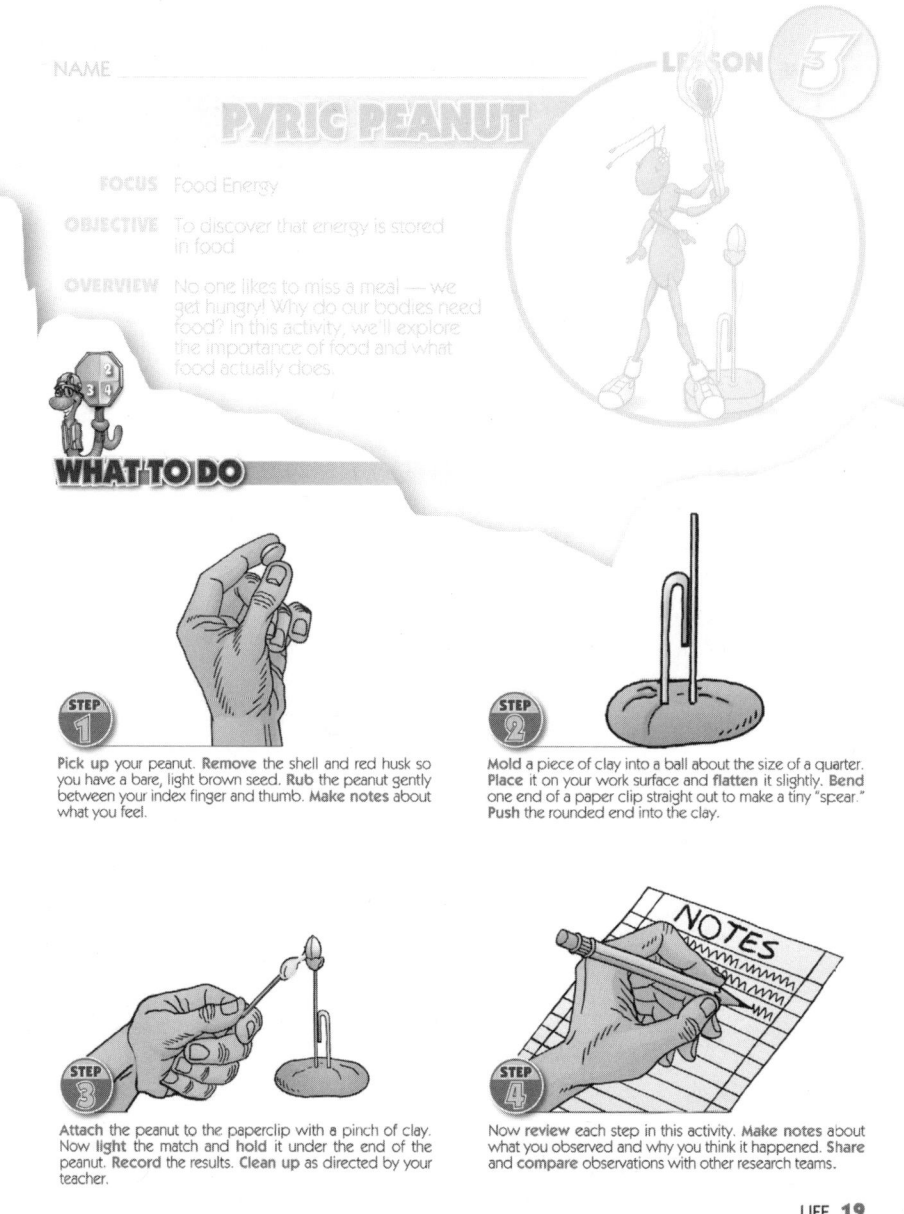

PYRIC PEANUT

FOCUS Food Energy

OBJECTIVE To discover that energy is stored in food.

OVERVIEW No one likes to miss a meal — we get hungry! Why do our bodies need food? In this activity, we'll explore the importance of food and what food actually does.

WHAT TO DO

Step 1 Pick up your peanut. Remove the shell and red husk so you have a bare, light brown seed. Rub the peanut gently between your index finger and thumb. Make notes about what you feel.

Step 2 Mold a piece of clay into a ball about the size of a quarter. Place it on your work surface and flatten it slightly. Bend one end of a paper clip straight out to make a tiny "spear." Push the rounded end into the clay.

Step 3 Attach the peanut to the paperclip with a pinch of clay. Now light the match and hold it under the end of the peanut. Record the results. Clean up as directed by your teacher.

Step 4 Now review each step in this activity. Make notes about what you observed and why you think it happened. Share and compare observations with other research teams.

LIFE 19

Teacher to Teacher

The process of changing food into energy is called respiration. There are two types of respiration: aerobic and anaerobic. Aerobic respiration (with air) is slow and complicated, taking oxygen directly from the air and combining it with food to produce energy. Anaerobic respiration (without air) is much faster, but not nearly as efficient. Our bodies rely on anaerobic respiration when we need energy quickly.

A by-product of anaerobic respiration is lactic acid, the chemical that makes your muscles sore after you've been working or playing hard. The energy produced by respiration runs two basic chemical reactions: catabolism and anabolism. Catabolism is a chemical reaction that breaks things down. Anabolism is a chemical reaction that repairs or builds things up.

WHAT HAPPENED?

Peanuts have a lot of **oil** (fat) stored inside. When you set the oil on fire (**combustion**), it resulted in **light** and **heat**. This is a great example of the **transfer of energy**. The process of combustion converted the energy from **potential energy** to heat — a form of **kinetic** (moving) **energy**.

Your body does a great job of changing food energy (**calories**) into an energy form you can use. Within your body, calories are converted into all kinds of energy: the warmth of your body (**heat** energy); your brain signaling your muscles (**electrical** energy); your muscles moving to perform work (**mechanical** energy).

Remember, your body can only process what you put into it. For optimum efficiency, you should avoid foods with "empty" calories (like junk food), and feed your body the right kinds of foods.

WHAT WE LEARNED

1. Describe the feel of the seed in Step 1. What material causes this slippery feeling?

a) hard, smooth, slick, slippery, etc.

b) the oil in the peanut

2. Explain the combustion process that took place in Step 3. Why did the peanut burn? How did this demonstrate energy conversion?

a, b) the match provided heat to start combustion, resulting in light and more heat; the peanut's oil provided the fuel

c) potential energy in the oil became kinetic or heat energy

3. Compare burning a peanut to eating a peanut. In terms of energy production, how are they similar? How are they different?

a) similar: both use peanut oil as a fuel source

b) different: burning a peanut converts it to flame (fast energy conversion); eating a peanut converts it to food energy (slow conversion)

4. What would happen if your body quit converting food energy? How can diet affect how well your body processes food?

a) you would eventually die

b) your body processes healthy food more effectively than junk food

5. Do all foods contain the same amount of energy? Give some examples and explain your answer.

a) no

b) peanut has lots of oil and energy; by contrast, a lettuce leaf is mostly water junk foods can give you a burst of energy, but in the long run they only provide empty calories

---

What Happened

Review the section with students. Emphasize bold-face words that identify key concepts and introduce new vocabulary.

*Peanuts have a lot of **oil** (fat) stored inside. When you set the oil on fire (**combustion**), it resulted in **light** and **heat**. This is a great example of the **transfer of energy**. The process of combustion converted the energy from **potential energy** to heat — a form of **kinetic** (moving) **energy**.*

*Your body does a great job of changing food energy (**calories**) into an energy form you can use. Within your body, calories are converted into all kinds of energy: the warmth of your body (**heat** energy); your brain signaling your muscles (**electrical** energy); your muscles moving to perform work (**mechanical** energy).*

Remember, your body can only process what you put into it. For optimum efficiency, you should avoid foods with "empty" calories (like junk food), and feed your body the right kinds of foods.

What We Learned

Answers will vary. Suggested responses are shown at left.

Conclusion

Read this section aloud to the class to summarize the concepts learned in this activity.

Food for Thought

Read the Scripture aloud to the class. Discuss ways we can keep our "lamps" filled, and talk about the importance of a daily devotional life.

Journal

If time permits, have a general class discussion about students' journal entries. Share and compare observations. Be sure to emphasize that "trial and error" is a valuable part of scientific inquiry!

CONCLUSION
Food contains energy. Your body converts food into the energy forms we need for life. Some foods work better for this process than others.

FOOD FOR THOUGHT
Matthew 25; 1-13 Peanuts are full of tasty calories that come in the form of oil. This oil is what made the peanut burn so well. Proper food is essential. It's never a good idea to run out of fuel — whether it's calories for your body, gas for your car, or spiritual food for your soul!

This Scripture talks about some foolish girls who didn't prepare and ran out of fuel. Instead of filling their lamps that day, they tried to rely on leftover oil. How about your "fuel" supply? Are you relying on leftovers, or are you "filling your lamp" with the love of Jesus every day?

JOURNAL: My Science Notes

Extended Teaching

1. Have students research recommendations on the amount of daily food energy (calories) required for males and females of various ages. Have them create a chart showing comparisons.

2. Collect dozens of food labels. Include beverages and junk food. Have students calculate how many servings of various foods would be needed for an average adult female's daily calorie intact.

3. Hold a class discussion comparing 2,000 calories of candy and soda pop to 2,000 calories of rice and beans. How are they similar? How are they different?

4. Have students keep a food diary for one week, writing down everything they eat. The following week, have them analyze the data as a nutritionist, and write a report making recommendations for an improved diet.

5. Have students research careers in nutrition, finding out what types of jobs are available. Arrange to have a dietician or other nutrition professional visit your classroom.

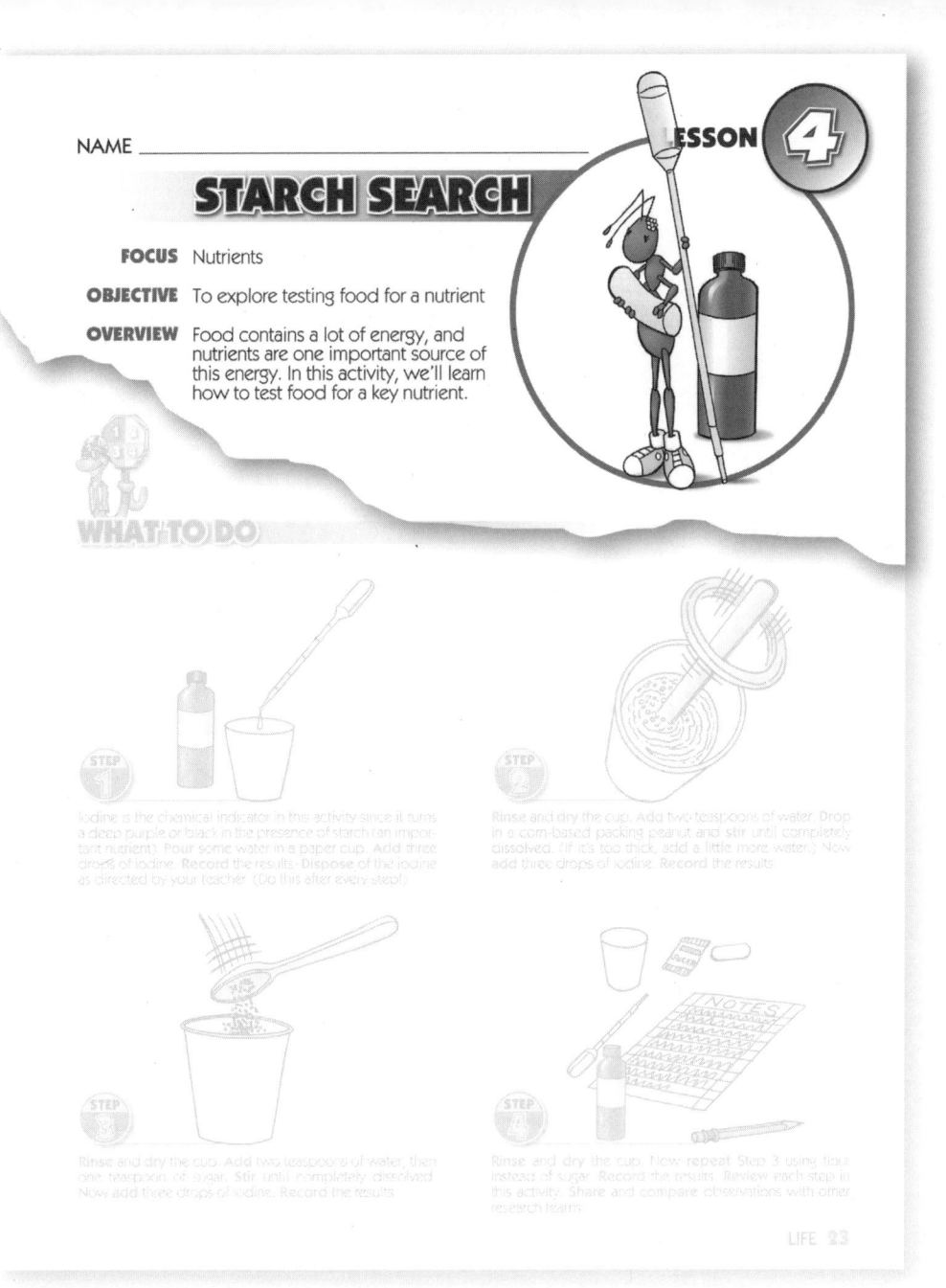

NAME _____

STARCH SEARCH

FOCUS Nutrients

OBJECTIVE To explore testing food for a nutrient

OVERVIEW Food contains a lot of energy, and nutrients are one important source of this energy. In this activity, we'll learn how to test food for a key nutrient.

WHAT TO DO

STEP 1
Iodine is the chemical indicator in this activity, since it turns a deep purple or black in the presence of starch (an important nutrient). Pour some water in a paper cup. Add three drops of iodine. Record the results. Dispose of the iodine as directed by your teacher. (Do this after every step!)

STEP 2
Rinse and dry the cup. Add two teaspoons of water. Drop in a corn-based packing peanut and stir until completely dissolved. (If it's too thick, add a little more water.) Now add three drops of iodine. Record the results.

STEP 3
Rinse and dry the cup. Add two teaspoons of water, then one teaspoon of sugar. Stir until completely dissolved. Now add three drops of iodine. Record the results.

STEP 4
Rinse and dry the cup. Now repeat Step 3 using flour instead of sugar. Record the results. Review each step in this activity. Share and compare observations with other research teams.

LIFE 23

Additional Comments

Iodine can stain skin, clothing, or anything else it touches. Carefully dispose of the iodine-contaminated solution after each step, by pouring it down the drain and flushing with plenty of water. Remind students that good scientists don't eat their experiments. This includes packing peanuts!

Overview

Read the overview aloud to your students. The goal is to create an atmosphere of curiosity and inquiry.

Category
Life Science

Focus
Nutrients

Objective
To explore testing food for a nutrient

National Standards
A1, A2, B1, C1, C3, C5, F1, F2, G1, G2

Materials Needed
pipette
iodine
paper cup
packing pellets
flour
sugar
spoon
water
goggles
gloves

Safety Concerns

1. Goggles/Gloves
Goggles and gloves are recommended whenever students are using chemicals.

2. Open Flame
Iodine fumes can be flammable. Avoid any open flame.

3. Skin Contact
Iodine in this form can be toxic. Avoid contact with skin.

4. Slipping
Clean up any spills immediately. Remind students to exercise caution when using fluids.

Lesson 4 • 29

WHAT TO DO

Monitor student research teams as they complete each step.

Step 1
Repeat cautions about iodine (Safety Issues) just before allowing students to begin this activity.

Step 4
Results from every team should be the same, although there may be some slight variations if cups were not rinsed thoroughly between steps.

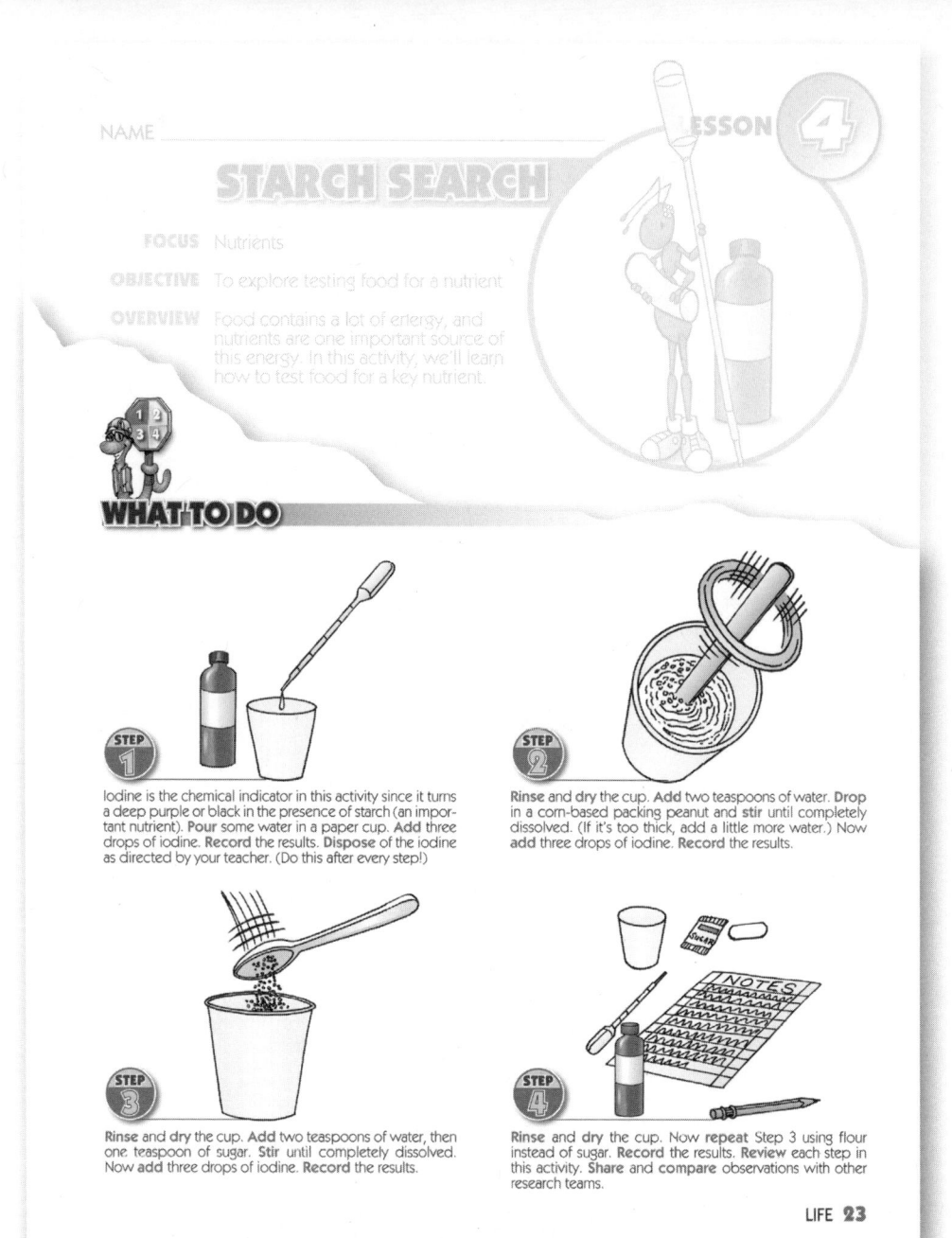

NAME _____

STARCH SEARCH

FOCUS Nutrients

OBJECTIVE To explore testing food for a nutrient

OVERVIEW Food contains a lot of energy, and nutrients are one important source of this energy. In this activity, we'll learn how to test food for a key nutrient.

WHAT TO DO

STEP 1
Iodine is the chemical indicator in this activity since it turns a deep purple or black in the presence of starch (an important nutrient). **Pour** some water in a paper cup. **Add** three drops of iodine. **Record** the results. **Dispose** of the iodine as directed by your teacher. (Do this after every step!)

STEP 2
Rinse and **dry** the cup. **Add** two teaspoons of water. **Drop** in a corn-based packing peanut and **stir** until completely dissolved. (If it's too thick, add a little more water.) Now **add** three drops of iodine. **Record** the results.

STEP 3
Rinse and **dry** the cup. **Add** two teaspoons of water, then one teaspoon of sugar. **Stir** until completely dissolved. Now **add** three drops of iodine. **Record** the results.

STEP 4
Rinse and **dry** the cup. Now **repeat** Step 3 using flour instead of sugar. **Record** the results. **Review** each step in this activity. **Share** and **compare** observations with other research teams.

LIFE **23**

Teacher to Teacher

Nutrients must be ingested (eaten), digested (broken into usable sizes), absorbed (taken into the blood or the cell), and assimilated (incorporated into the structure of the living thing). Primary nutrients include carbohydrates, lipids, proteins, vitamins, minerals, and water. Carbohydrates (simple sugars) are the primary fuel source. Lipids (fats, etc.) work as food storage and body padding. Proteins are composed of links called amino acids. Complete proteins contain all the amino acids needed; incomplete proteins don't. Vitamins are organic (carbon-based) compounds not made in the body, so they must be ingested. Minerals (calcium, potassium, magnesium, iron, etc.) help produce healthy bones, teeth, etc. The last and most plentiful nutrient, water, is often the most deficient. Many studies show we simply don't drink enough water!

WHAT HAPPENED?

Food contains **energy**. **Nutrients** are one form of this energy. Key nutrients include **proteins, vitamins, minerals, fats, sugars,** and **starches**. Sugars and starches are a group of nutrients called **carbohydrates**. The name describes a combination of the **elements** carbon (carbo) and water (hydrate).

The packing peanuts we used are made from corn starch. Since iodine changes colors in the presence of starch, the corn starch solution turned deep purple.

Although you may have seen **petroleum**-based packing pellets made from materials like Styrofoam®, many companies are switching to the starch-based material. Unlike petroleum oil, corn (the source of this material) is a **renewable resource** — one that can be grown and even **recycled**.

WHAT WE LEARNED

1. Describe what happened when you added the iodine to the solution in Step 2.

Iodine was added to a starch solution, then stirred. The starch solution turned dark blue (or purple, or black).

2. Describe what happened when you added the iodine to the solution in Step 3.

Iodine was added to a sugar solution, then stirred. There was little or no change in the color of the solution.

24 LIFE

3. Describe what happened when you added the iodine to the solution in Step 4.

Iodine was added to a flour solution, then stirred. The solution turned dark blue (or purple, or black).

4. Name at least three nutrients. What is the group of nutrients containing sugar and starch called?

a) any three of the following: proteins, vitamins, minerals, fats, sugars, starches

b) carbohydrates

5. Explain the difference between the packing peanuts we used and Styrofoam® peanuts. Which is more environmentally friendly? Why?

a) Styrofoam® packing pellets are petroleum based; the packing pellets we used were made from corn starch
b) Styrofoam® pellets are made from a non-renewable resource and are not biodegradable; corn starch pellets are made from a renewable resource and are biodegradable

LIFE 25

What Happened

Review the section with students. Emphasize bold-face words that identify key concepts and introduce new vocabulary.

*Food contains **energy**. **Nutrients** are one form of this energy. Key nutrients include **proteins**, **vitamins**, **minerals**, **fats**, **sugars**, and **starches**. Sugars and starches are a group of nutrients called **carbohydrates**. The name describes a combination of the **elements** carbon (carbo) and water (hydrate).*

The packing pellets we used are made from corn starch. Since iodine changes colors in the presence of starch, the corn starch solution turned deep purple.

*Although you may have seen **petroleum-based** packing pellets made from materials like Styrofoam®, many companies are switching to the starch-based material. Unlike petroleum oil, corn (the source of this material) is a **renewable resource** — one that can be grown and even **recycled**.*

What We Learned

Answers will vary. Suggested responses are shown at left.

Note: In Step 3, a few students may detect a slight color change from the iodine itself. This will affect the answer they produce for question 2.

Lesson 4 · 31

Conclusion

Read this section aloud to the class to summarize the concepts learned in this activity.

Food for Thought

Read the Scripture aloud to the class. Discuss ways to replace the bad things of sin with the good things that come from Jesus.

Journal

If time permits, have a general class discussion about students' journal entries. Share and compare observations. Be sure to emphasize that "trial and error" is a valuable part of scientific inquiry!

Extended Teaching

1. Have students research whether sugar or starch supplies more energy. Ask them to describe how calories figure into this. Encourage them to report their findings to the class.

2. The "Standard American Diet" (also known as SAD) is rarely balanced. Have students research nutrition, then make a list of foods that should be included in a balanced diet.

3. Invite a nutritionist to visit your class. Discuss typical student diets and their long-term effects. (Many students don't realize that habits formed now will impact them for life!)

4. Challenge students to research ways corn, wheat, and soybeans are used. Make a bulletin board of common and unusual products made from these crops.

5. Have students research careers in agriculture. Invite an agricultural professional to visit your classroom. (County agricultural agents or local 4-H clubs often offer programs designed for this purpose.)

SEALED CELL

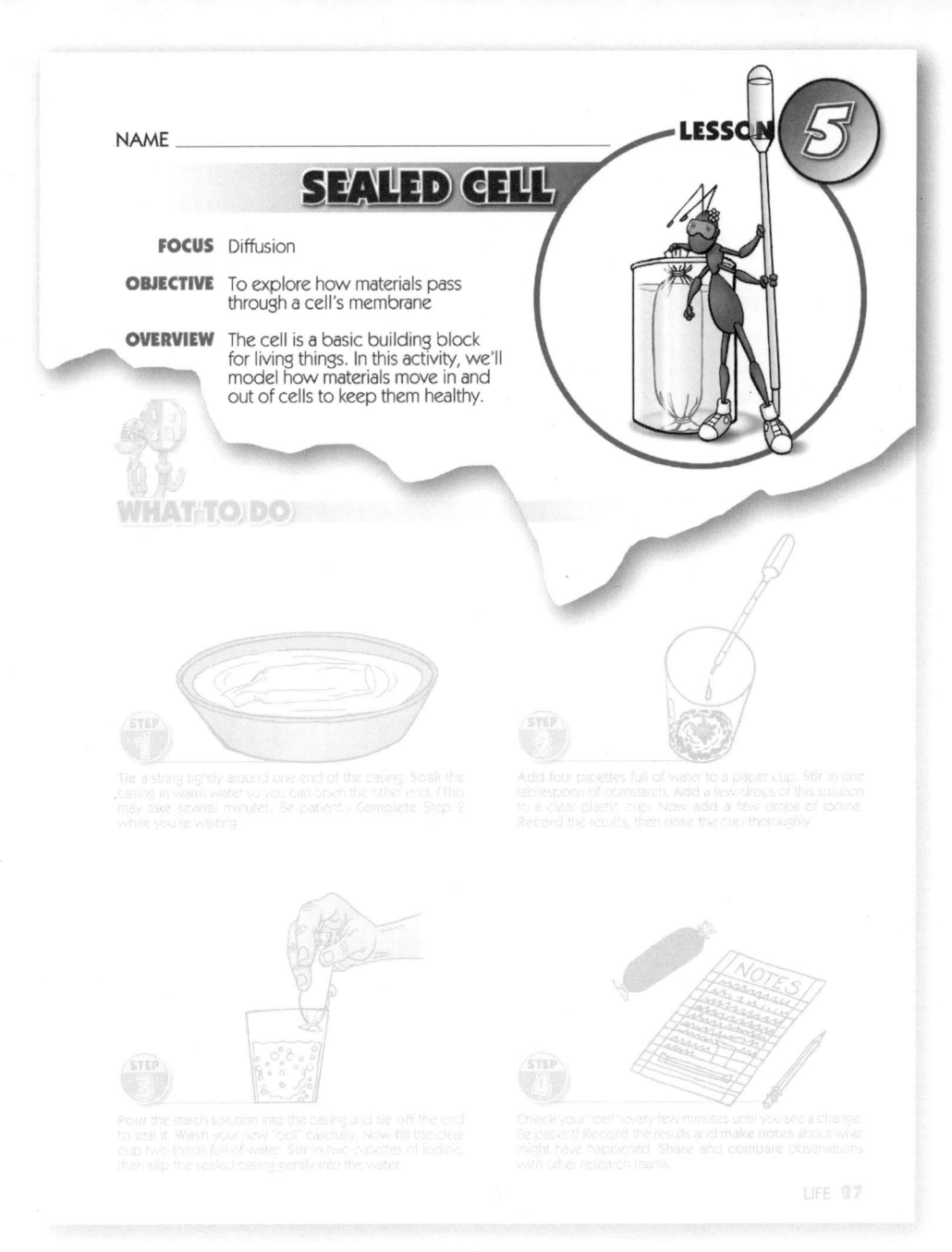

LESSON 5

FOCUS Diffusion

OBJECTIVE To explore how materials pass through a cell's membrane

OVERVIEW The cell is a basic building block for living things. In this activity, we'll model how materials move in and out of cells to keep them healthy.

WHAT TO DO

STEP 1
Tie a string tightly around one end of the casing. Soak the casing in warm water so you can open the other end. (This may take several minutes. Be patient.) Complete Step 2 while you're waiting.

STEP 2
Add four pipettes full of water to a paper cup. Stir in one tablespoon of cornstarch. Add a few drops of this solution to a clear plastic cup. Now add a few drops of iodine. Record the results, then rinse the cup thoroughly.

STEP 3
Pour the starch solution into the casing and tie off the end to seal it. Wash your new "cell" carefully. Now fill the clear cup two-thirds full of water. Stir in two pipettes of iodine, then slip the sealed casing gently into the water.

STEP 4
Check your "cell" every few minutes until you see a change. Be patient. Record the results and make notes about what might have happened. Share and compare observations with other research teams.

Category
Life Science

Focus
Diffusion

Objective
To explore how materials pass through a cell's membrane

National Standards
A1, A2, B1, B2, C1, C3, C5, F1, F2, G1, G2

Materials Needed
pipette
iodine
casing material
string
paper cup
craft stick
cornstarch
water
bowl

Safety Concerns

3. Goggles/Gloves
Goggles and gloves are recommended whenever students are using chemicals.

2. Open Flame
Iodine fumes can be flammable. Avoid any open flame.

3. Skin Contact
Iodine in this form can be toxic. Avoid contact with skin.

4. Slipping
Clean up any spills immediately. Remind students to exercise caution when using fluids.

Additional Comments

Encourage students to gently stir the starch solution just before pouring it from the paper cup into the casing. As we mentioned in the last lesson, iodine can stain skin, clothing, or anything else it touches. Carefully dispose of the iodine-contaminated materials by pouring them down the drain and flushing with plenty of water.

Overview

Read the overview aloud to your students. The goal is to create an atmosphere of curiosity and inquiry.

Lesson 5 · 33

WHAT TO DO

Monitor student research teams as they complete each step.

Step 1
Make sure the string is tied tightly! The casing usually needs to soak a few minutes before it's soft enough to open easily.

Step 2
Repeat cautions about iodine (Safety Issues) before students begin this step. Make sure they transfer a few drops of starch solution from the paper cup to the clear plastic cup before adding iodine. Adding iodine to the contents of the paper cup will invalidate the experiment!

Step 4
Changes inside the casing may take up to an hour to become noticeable. Students may work on other projects while the change is taking place.

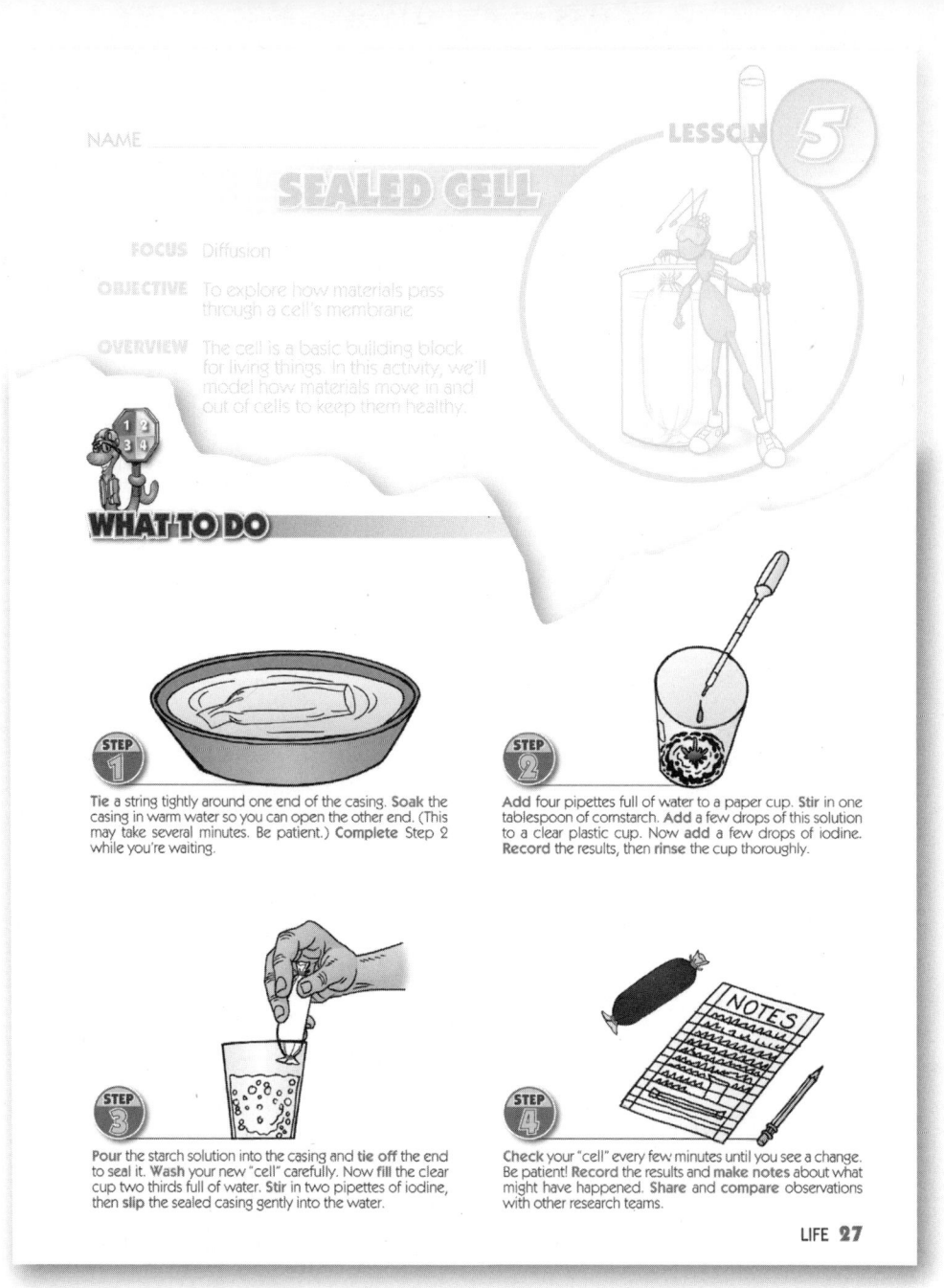

NAME _____

SEALED CELL

LESSON 5

FOCUS Diffusion

OBJECTIVE To explore how materials pass through a cell's membrane

OVERVIEW The cell is a basic building block for living things. In this activity, we'll model how materials move in and out of cells to keep them healthy.

WHAT TO DO

STEP 1
Tie a string tightly around one end of the casing. Soak the casing in warm water so you can open the other end. (This may take several minutes. Be patient.) Complete Step 2 while you're waiting.

STEP 2
Add four pipettes full of water to a paper cup. Stir in one tablespoon of cornstarch. Add a few drops of this solution to a clear plastic cup. Now add a few drops of iodine. Record the results, then rinse the cup thoroughly.

STEP 3
Pour the starch solution into the casing and tie off the end to seal it. Wash your new "cell" carefully. Now fill the clear cup two thirds full of water. Stir in two pipettes of iodine, then slip the sealed casing gently into the water.

STEP 4
Check your "cell" every few minutes until you see a change. Be patient! Record the results and make notes about what might have happened. Share and compare observations with other research teams.

LIFE 27

Teacher to Teacher

In addition to diffusion, materials may move through the cell's membrane in three ways: osmosis, active transport, and phagocytosis. Diffusion is a balancing act: when substances are equal on both sides of the membrane, diffusion stops. Osmosis is a special name applied to the diffusion of water. When plants wilt from water loss (or straighten back up after watering), osmosis is taking place. Active transport uses special carrier molecules to "escort in" larger molecules that can't easily pass through the membrane. Phagocytosis is when a cell flows around a large particle and takes it in. A good example is white blood cells swallowing invading microbes.

WHAT HAPPENED?

As you discovered in Lesson 4, this color change is the result of a **chemical reaction** between **starch** and **iodine**. But how did the two get together? The starch was inside the casing, but the iodine was outside!

The secret lies in the material that the casing is made from. Although it looks like water-tight plastic, it actually behaves much like a living cell's **membrane**, letting tiny particles pass in and out in a process called **diffusion**. Diffusion keeps cells healthy by letting **oxygen** and **nutrients** in, and letting **waste** products out.

Why didn't the starch diffuse out as the iodine diffused in? It's because starch particles are much larger, made from hundreds of **sugar molecules** hooked together end to end. The starch particles were much too big to pass through the **Sealed Cell's** membrane like the tiny iodine particles did.

WHAT WE LEARNED

1) What happened in the clear cup in Step 2? Why did this occur?

a) the solution turned dark blue (or purple, or black)

b) the iodine reacted with the starch

2) What living thing was modeled by the filled and tied casing in Step 3? How was the model similar? How was it different?

a) a cell
b) similar: it allowed for diffusion, was filled with a substance, was surrounded by another substance, etc.
c) different: it wasn't alive, it was larger, different substances inside and out, etc.

3) Describe what happened in Step 4. Explain why this occurred.

a) iodine turned water yellow, then later the contents of the bag became dark

b) the iodine got through the casing's walls and reacted with the starch solution inside

4) What is the name of the process by which materials pass through the cell membrane? How did this process differ between the iodine and the starch in Step 4? Why?

a) diffusion

b) the iodine got into the casing, but the starch didn't get out

c) the iodine molecules were much smaller

5) Based on what you've learned, do all substances have equal access to a cell's interior? Why or why not?

a) no

b) the size of the molecules involved can affect diffusion

What Happened

Review the section with students. Emphasize bold-face words that identify key concepts and introduce new vocabulary.

*As you discovered in Lesson 4, this color change is the result of a **chemical reaction** between **starch** and **iodine**. But how did the two get together? The starch was inside the casing, but the iodine was outside!*

*The secret lies in the material that the casing is made from. Although it looks like water-tight plastic, it actually behaves much like a living cell's **membrane**, letting tiny particles pass in and out in a process called **diffusion**. Diffusion keeps cells healthy by letting **oxygen** and **nutrients** in, and letting **waste** products out.*

*Why didn't the starch diffuse out as the iodine diffused in? It's because starch particles are much larger, made from hundreds of **sugar molecules** hooked together end to end. The starch particles were much too big to pass through the Sealed Cell's membrane like the tiny iodine particles did.*

What We Learned

Answers will vary. Suggested responses are shown at left.

Lesson 5 · 35

Conclusion

Read this section aloud to the class to summarize the concepts learned in this activity.

Food for Thought

Read the Scripture aloud to the class. Talk about the importance of keeping a constant channel open to God. Discuss ways to develop or enhance personal, daily devotions.

Journal

If time permits, have a general class discussion about students' journal entries. Share and compare observations. Be sure to emphasize that "trial and error" is a valuable part of scientific inquiry!

CONCLUSION
Materials pass though the cell membrane in a process called diffusion. Diffusion may vary depending on the substance. Diffusion helps keep cells healthy and alive.

FOOD FOR THOUGHT
Genesis 28:12 The purpose of the membrane is to keep a cell alive. The membrane lets the cell exchange materials back and forth across its boundary, keeping the cell alive and healthy. If this exchange ceases, the cell will die.

This Scripture tells of Jacob's dream about a ladder between Earth and Heaven. Angels constantly went up and down the ladder — perhaps an illustration of taking prayers up to God and bringing God's blessings down to his people. Regardless of the symbolism, the exchange between God and man is vital. God's love is what keeps us alive, and whether we recognize it or not, we are dependent on God's constant care to survive.

JOURNAL — My Science Notes

Extended Teaching

1. Invite a nurse to visit your classroom. Discuss how drinking pure water helps keep our bodies healthy. Talk about long-term health problems associated with low water consumption.

2. Ask students to research the difference between fresh water and salt water. Have them find out how our bodies react to the two differently. Discuss why someone in a life raft couldn't just drink sea water.

3. Have students keep a water diary for one week, recording every time they drink a glass of water. Have them compare the results to the amount of water consumption recommended by experts.

4. When plants are short of water, they wilt. If water is added soon enough, they stand back up! Have students research this phenomenon and make a bulletin board based on their findings.

5. Invite a skilled gardener to visit your classroom. Discuss how water helps keep plants healthy. Talk about plant problems associated with reduced water supplies.

BEADS OF BLOOD

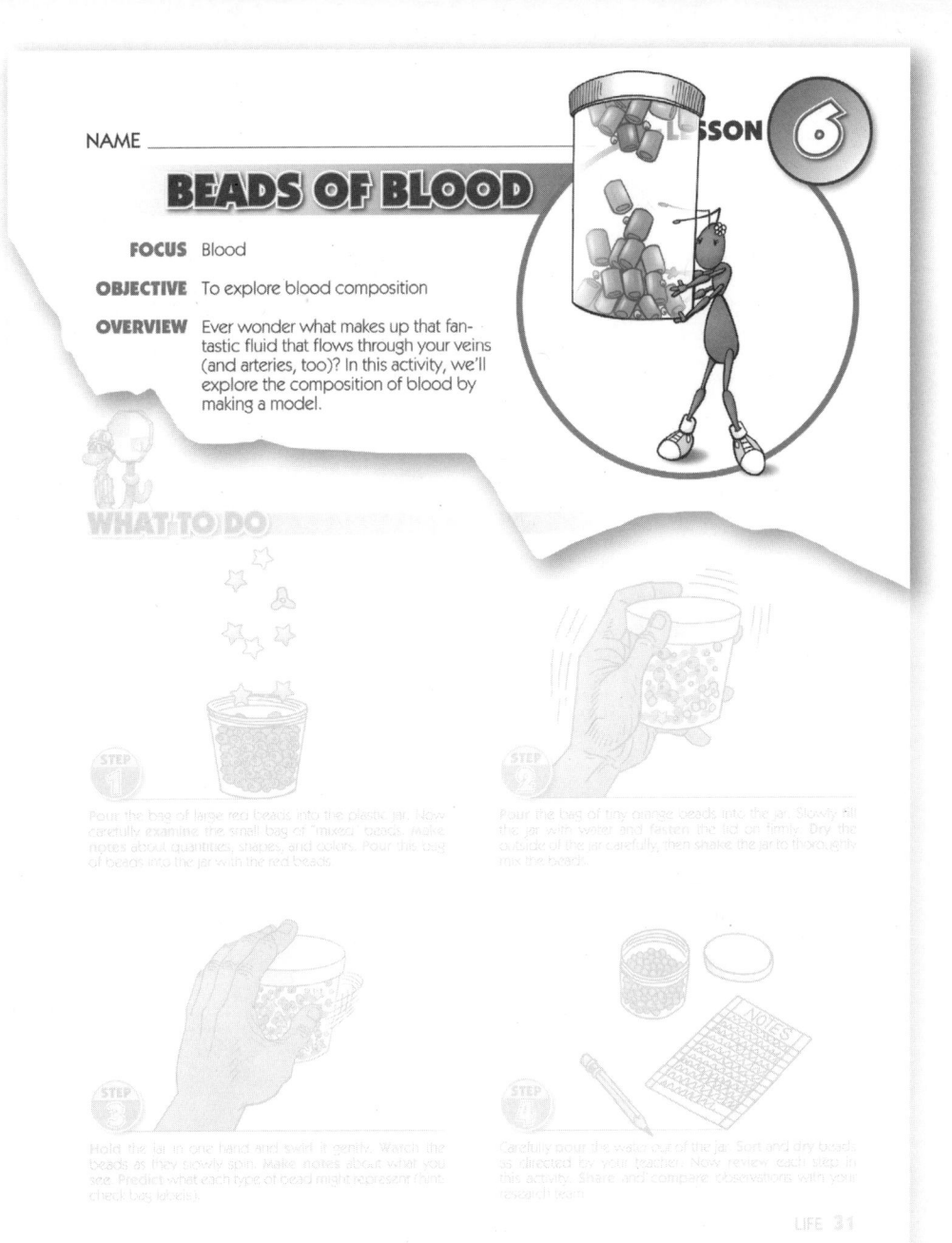

FOCUS Blood

OBJECTIVE To explore blood composition

OVERVIEW Ever wonder what makes up that fantastic fluid that flows through your veins (and arteries, too)? In this activity, we'll explore the composition of blood by making a model.

WHAT TO DO

STEP 1
Pour the bag of large red beads into the plastic jar. Now carefully examine the small bag of "mixed" beads. Make notes about quantities, shapes, and colors. Pour this bag of beads into the jar with the red beads.

STEP 2
Pour the bag of tiny orange beads into the jar. Slowly fill the jar with water and fasten the lid on firmly. Dry the outside of the jar carefully, then shake the jar to thoroughly mix the beads.

STEP 3
Hold the jar in one hand and swirl it gently. Watch the beads as they slowly spin. Make notes about what you see. Predict what each type of bead might represent (hint: check bag labels).

STEP 4
Carefully pour the water out of the jar. Sort and dry beads as directed by your teacher. Now review each step in this activity. Share and compare observations with your research team.

LIFE 31

Category
Life Science

Focus
Blood

Objective
To explore blood composition

National Standards
A1, A2, B1, C1, C3, C5, F1, G1, G2

Materials Needed
plastic jar
red blood cell beads
white blood cell beads
platelet beads
water

Safety Concerns

4. Slipping
Both the water and the beads can pose a slipping hazard! Clean up any spills immediately. Remind students to exercise caution with both beads and fluids.

Additional Comments

For added effect, you can require students to use medical-style latex gloves (perhaps donated by a local medical center). This models the correct procedure for handling human fluids like blood. By changing the number of beads, students can model various blood disorders: fewer platelets = hemophilia; red beads cut in half = sickle cell anemia; extra white blood cells = leukemia or a bacterial infection. After the activity is completed, have students carefully dry and sort the beads for use next year.

Overview

Read the overview aloud to your students. The goal is to create an atmosphere of curiosity and inquiry.

WHAT TO DO

Monitor student research teams as they complete each step.

Step 1
Repeat cautions about handling beads and water (Safety Issues) just before students begin this activity.

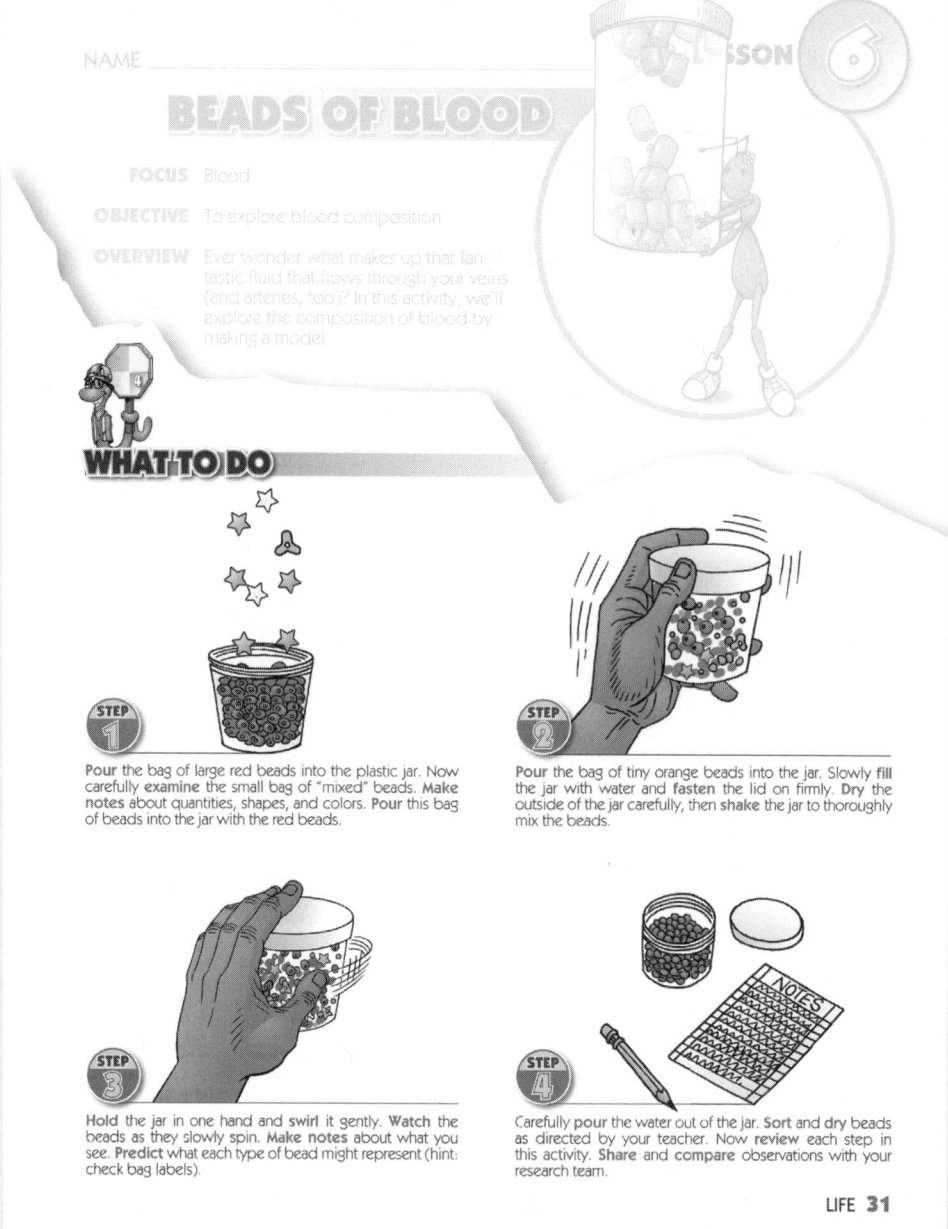

NAME _____

BEADS OF BLOOD

FOCUS Blood

OBJECTIVE To explore blood composition

OVERVIEW Ever wonder what makes up that fantastic fluid that flows through your veins (and arteries, too)? In this activity, we'll explore the composition of blood by making a model.

WHAT TO DO

STEP 1
Pour the bag of large red beads into the plastic jar. Now carefully **examine** the small bag of "mixed" beads. **Make notes** about quantities, shapes, and colors. **Pour** this bag of beads into the jar with the red beads.

STEP 2
Pour the bag of tiny orange beads into the jar. Slowly **fill** the jar with water and **fasten** the lid on firmly. **Dry** the outside of the jar carefully, then **shake** the jar to thoroughly mix the beads.

STEP 3
Hold the jar in one hand and **swirl** it gently. **Watch** the beads as they slowly spin. **Make notes** about what you see. **Predict** what each type of bead might represent (hint: check bag labels).

STEP 4
Carefully pour the water out of the jar. **Sort** and **dry** beads as directed by your teacher. Now **review** each step in this activity. **Share** and **compare** observations with your research team.

LIFE 31

Teacher to Teacher

Your blood type reflects the genes you inherited from your parents. The major blood types are A, B, and O. In addition, blood has an Rh factor (named for the Rhesus monkeys where it was first detected). If you have the Rh antigen, you are Rh positive (Rh+). If you don't, you're Rh negative (Rh-). Roughly 38% of people have type O+ and about 34% have A+. The other six combinations each account for less than 10% of the population. In an emergency, anyone can receive type O red blood cells. Type AB individuals can receive red blood cells of any blood type. Therefore, people with type O- are known as "universal donors," and people with type AB+ are known as "universal recipients."

WHAT HAPPENED?

Here's what the parts of your **model** represent: First, human **blood** is primarily a water-based **liquid** called **plasma** (represented by water). Plasma contains dissolved **nutrients**, **waste products**, **gasses** like carbon dioxide and oxygen, disease-fighting chemicals called **antibodies**, chemical messengers called **hormones**, and many other substances. Plasma also moves **heat** to warm up or cool down the body.

Second are the **red blood cells** (represented by the red beads) called **erythrocytes**. They get their color from the **hemoglobin** they contain. This iron-rich chemical helps carry oxygen. Next are the **white blood cells** (represented by the other colored beads) called **leukocytes**. It's their job to fight **disease**! There are five different types of leukocytes. Finally come small, specialized cells (represented by the tiny beads) called **platelets**. These important cells cause blood to **clot** during an injury, preventing the loss of life-sustaining fluid!

WHAT WE LEARNED

1. What does the water in your model represent? Describe the purpose of this blood part.

a) plasma

b) plasma moves heat around to warm or cool the body; it also transports nutrients, waste products, gasses, antibodies, hormones, and other substances

2. What do the red beads in your model represent? Describe the purpose of this blood part.

a) red blood cells

b) red blood cells carry oxygen

3. What do the other colored beads in your model represent? Describe the purpose of this blood part.

a) white blood cells

b) white blood cells help fight disease

4. What do the tiny beads in your model represent? Describe the purpose of this blood part.

a) platelets

b) platelets cause blood to clot during an injury

5. Name at least three of the substances that plasma contains.

Any three of the following: nutrients, waste products, gasses, antibodies, or hormones.

What Happened

Review the section with students. Emphasize bold-face words that identify key concepts and introduce new vocabulary.

*Here's what the parts of your **model** represent: First, human **blood** is primarily a water-based **liquid** called **plasma** (represented by water). Plasma contains dissolved **nutrients**, **waste products**, **gasses** like carbon dioxide and oxygen, disease-fighting chemicals called **antibodies**, chemical messengers called **hormones**, and many other substances. Plasma also moves **heat** to warm up or cool down the body.*

*Second, are the **red blood cells** (represented by the red beads) called **erythrocytes**. They get their color from the **hemoglobin** they contain. This iron-rich chemical helps carry oxygen. Next are the **white blood cells** (represented by the other colored beads) called **leukocytes**. It's their job to fight **disease**! There are five different types of leukocytes. Finally, come small, specialized cells (represented by the tiny beads) called **platelets**. These important cells cause blood to **clot** during an injury, preventing the loss of life-sustaining fluid!*

What We Learned

Answers will vary. Suggested responses are shown at left.

Conclusion

Read this section aloud to the class to summarize the concepts learned in this activity.

Food for Thought

Read the Scripture aloud to the class. Discuss blood as a symbol of cleansing and salvation.

Journal

If time permits, have a general class discussion about students' journal entries. Share and compare observations. Be sure to emphasize that "trial and error" is a valuable part of scientific inquiry!

CONCLUSION

Human blood is a complex mixture of cells and liquids whose individual parts perform important functions in our bodies.

FOOD FOR THOUGHT

Mark 14:24 Human blood is a fantastic fluid that is tremendously complicated. When you are ill, it's one of the first places doctors check because it tells so much about what's going on inside your body. The importance of healthy blood to a human survival cannot be overemphasized.

The most important blood in the Universe is the blood of Jesus. God's innocent son shed his blood in a violent, brutal crucifixion to ensure our salvation. Because of Jesus' sacrifice, we are offered the chance to live forever. What a marvelous symbol of God's enduring love!

JOURNAL — My Science Notes

Extended Teaching

1. Invite an American Red Cross representative to visit your classroom. Discuss the need for blood donations, and the different ways blood is processed and used.

2. Have students research HIV (the virus that causes AIDS), Hepatitis B, and similar blood-borne pathogens. Discuss the safety precautions that health workers take and why they are needed.

3. Arrange a visit to a hospital or medical laboratory. Talk with technicians about how and why blood testing is done.

4. Have students research human blood types. If possible, have each student discover his/her own blood type. Compare the blood types of students with blood types in the general population.

5. Invite a EMT or similar medical professional to visit your classroom. Talk about first aid and ways of stopping blood flow in an emergency.

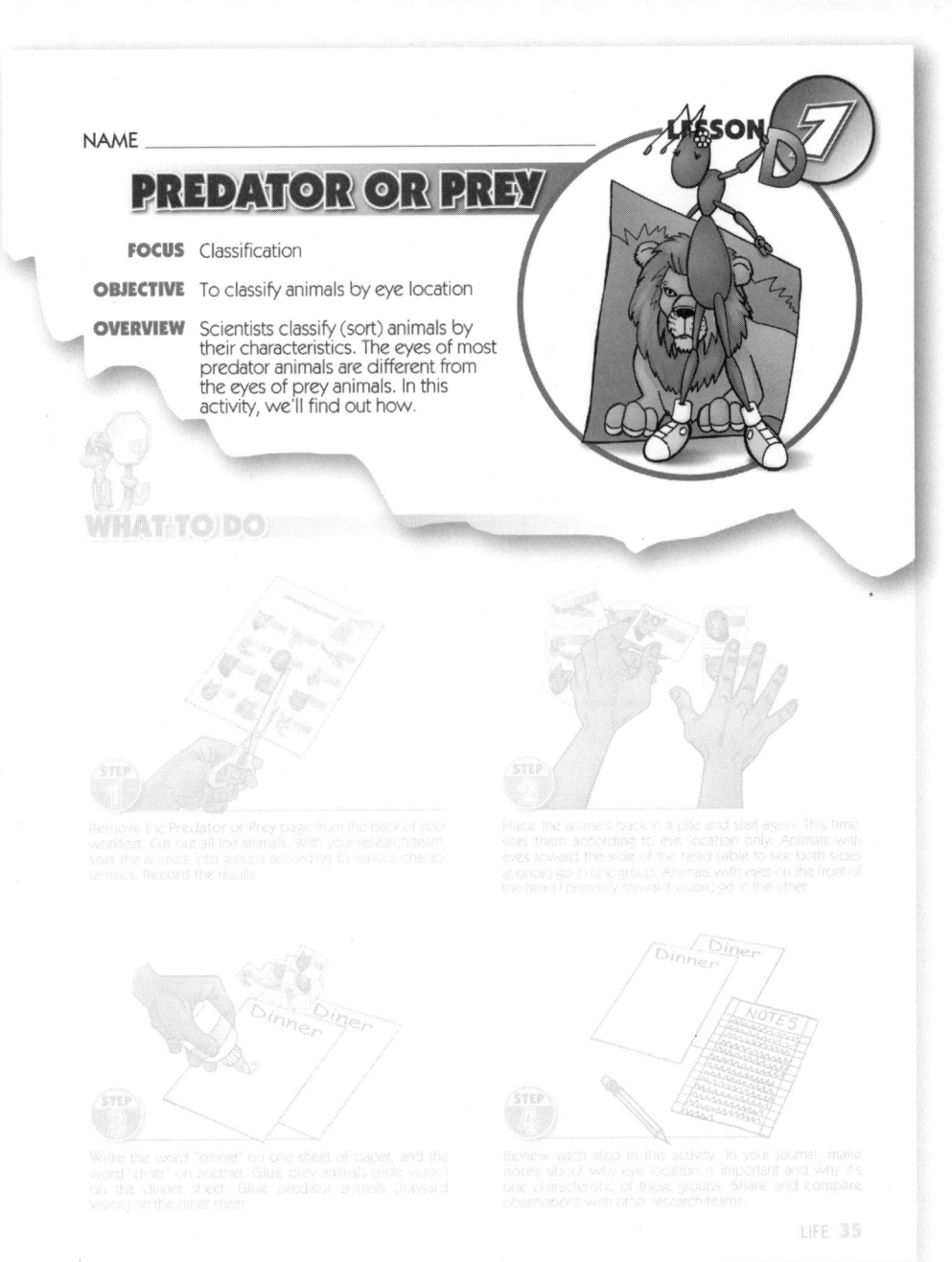

Category

Life Science

Focus

Classification

Objective

To classify animals by eye location

National Standards

A1, A2, B1, C1, C4, C5, F2, G1, G2

Materials Needed

Predator or Prey worksheet *(student worktext, p. 163)*
paper - 2 sheets
glue or glue stick
scissors

Safety Concerns

4. Sharp Objects
Remind students to be careful when using scissors.

Additional Comments

This activity's focus is to help students discover that creatures have different characteristics, and those characteristics can help scientists sort (classify) them into groups for study. If students are confused about sorting, here's a helpful hint: Because of their eye placement, predators usually turn their heads completely to see behind themselves; prey animals usually don't. Remember to remind students that "predator" and "prey" are relative terms. A predator animal can occasionally become prey to a larger predator!

Overview

Read the overview aloud to your students. The goal is to create an atmosphere of curiosity and inquiry.

Lesson 7 · **41**

WHAT TO DO

Monitor student research teams as they complete each step.

Step 1
Check each team's results after Step 1. (There is no incorrect answer as long as the grouping is logical.) With the class, discuss the various ways teams grouped animals according to characteristics.

Step 3
Liquid glue works just fine, but glue sticks provide neater and quicker results for this step.

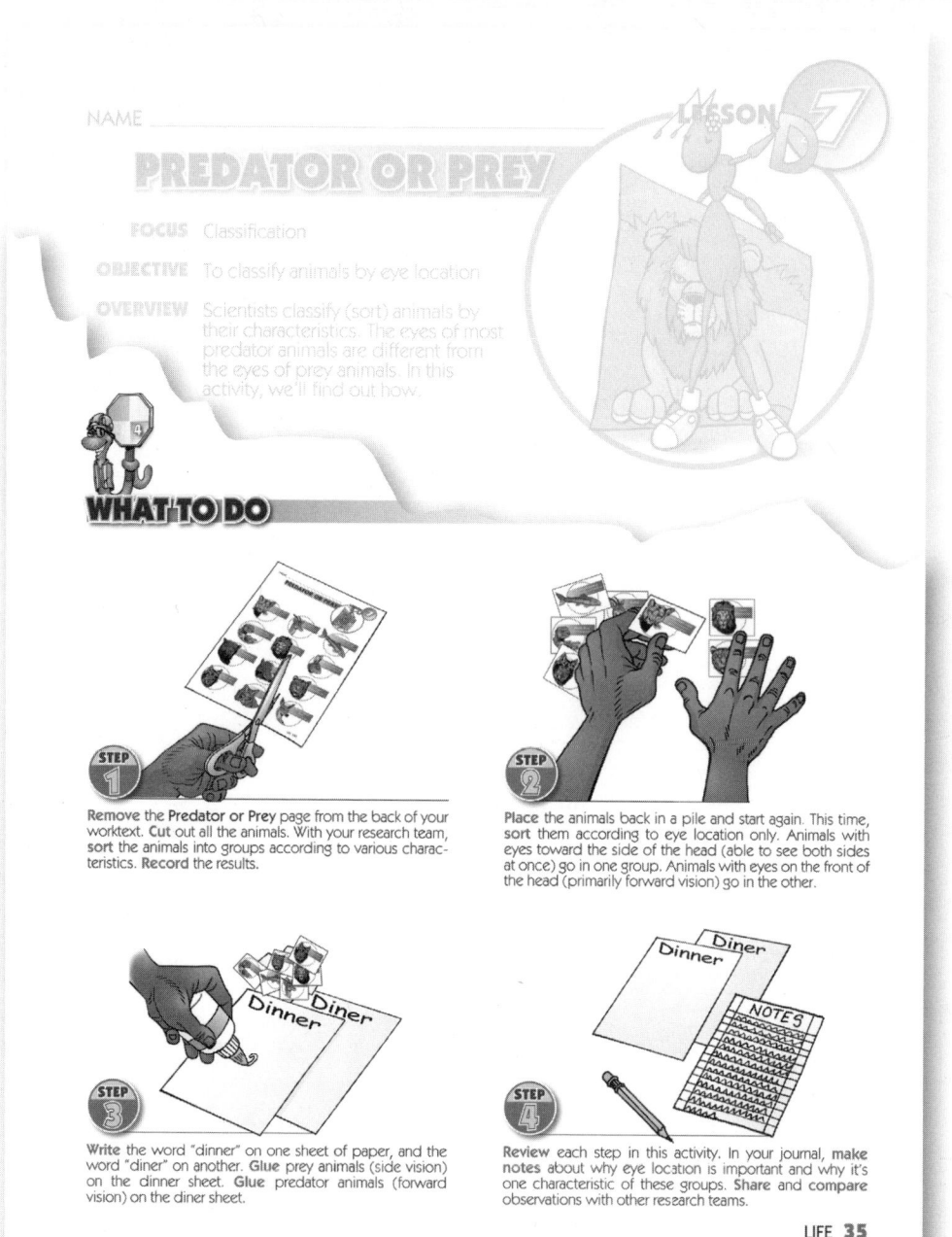

Teacher to Teacher

It's helpful to understand the role of predator and prey in the "balance of nature." A loss of predators initially results in benefits for prey, but without predators, the prey's normal reproduction numbers quickly overwhelm local habitat. Carrying capacity (the number of animals a habitat can sustain) is one of the most basic and important ecology concepts. It's also a complex mix. For example, the plant life in an area affects the rabbit population. With an abundance of rabbits comes an increase in the fox population. Thus, removing vegetation indirectly results in fewer foxes. That's why seemingly minor actions by humans often have major effects on local wildlife populations.

WHAT HAPPENED?

Just like a scientist, you sorted the animals into groups based on a specific **characteristic**. This process is called **classification**. Animals in the dinner group are often eaten by other animals. We call these animals **prey**. Animals in the diner group eat other animals. This kind of animal is called a **predator**. Such classifications make it easier for scientists to study different creatures.

Eyes located in front make it easier for predators to spot and follow a potential meal. Eyes on the side allow prey animals to watch a much wider area around them without turning their heads. This helps them spot potential danger much sooner, giving them a chance to avoid becoming someone's lunch!

WHAT WE LEARNED

1. What classification system did you use in Step 1? How was this similar to Step 2? How was it different?

a) answers will vary; accept any logical grouping

b) answers will vary

2. Describe the eye location of most predators. How does this contribute to their survival?

a) most predators have eyes that look forward

b) forward-looking eyes help them spot and follow a potential meal

3. Describe the eye location of most prey animals. How does this contribute to their survival?

a) most prey animals have eyes on the sides of their heads

b) this helps them watch a much wider area without turning their heads, helping them spot potential danger sooner

4. What is another name for "scientific sorting"? How does such organization help scientists?

a) classification

b) it allows scientists to group creatures according to similar characteristics for easier study

5. Based on what you've learned, classify the following animals: a horse, a dog, a rabbit, a cat. Explain your answers.

a) horse = prey, dog = predator, rabbit = prey, cat = predator

b) the horse and rabbit have eyes on the side of the head; the dog and cat have forward-looking eyes

---

What Happened

Review the section with students. Emphasize bold-face words that identify key concepts and introduce new vocabulary.

*Just like a scientist, you sorted the animals into groups based on a specific **characteristic**. This process is called **classification**. Animals in the dinner group are often eaten by other animals. We call these animals **prey**. Animals in the diner group eat other animals. This kind of animal is called a **predator**. Such classifications make it easier for scientists to study different creatures.*

Eyes located in front make it easier for predators to spot and follow a potential meal. Eyes on the side allow prey animals to watch a much wider area around them without turning their heads. This helps them spot potential danger much sooner, giving them a chance to avoid becoming someone's lunch!

What We Learned

Answers will vary. Suggested responses are shown at left.

Conclusion

Read this section aloud to the class to summarize the concepts learned in this activity.

Food for Thought

Read the Scripture aloud to the class. Discuss ways believers can stay safe from spiritual predators. Talk about the role a daily devotional life plays in this process.

Journal

If time permits, have a general class discussion about students' journal entries. Share and compare observations. Be sure to emphasize that "trial and error" is a valuable part of scientific inquiry!

CONCLUSION
Sorting animals into groups based on specific characteristics is called classification. Such organization makes it easier for scientists to study different kinds of creatures.

FOOD FOR THOUGHT
1 Peter 5:8 In this activity, we learned about predators and prey. Prey animals must remain constantly alert and pay close attention to their surroundings if they want to survive. Eye location can help them do this.

Scripture warns us of another kind of predator. Peter reminds us that Satan is constantly prowling around like a hungry lion, looking for some victim to tear apart. Staying close to Jesus helps us develop the spiritual eyes we need to keep us alert to danger. By trusting in God's power, we can stay safe from harm.

JOURNAL — My Science Notes

38 LIFE

Extended Teaching

1. Invite an optometrist to visit your classroom. Talk about how the eye works and different kinds of vision. Ask her/him to explain "depth of field."

2. Discuss the "balance of nature" and how it relates to the predator/prey relationship. Talk about what might happen to the deer population if all the predators in an area were eliminated.

3. Have students research ways scientists classify creatures. What are some major groups? What creatures are in these groups? Using these classification systems, compile lists of creatures.

4. Have students research conservation groups and how they protect large habitats. Find examples of successful and unsuccessful conservation efforts. Discuss reasons for success or failure.

5. Invite a biologist to visit your classroom. Talk about classification and its importance to his/her work.

44 · Lesson 7

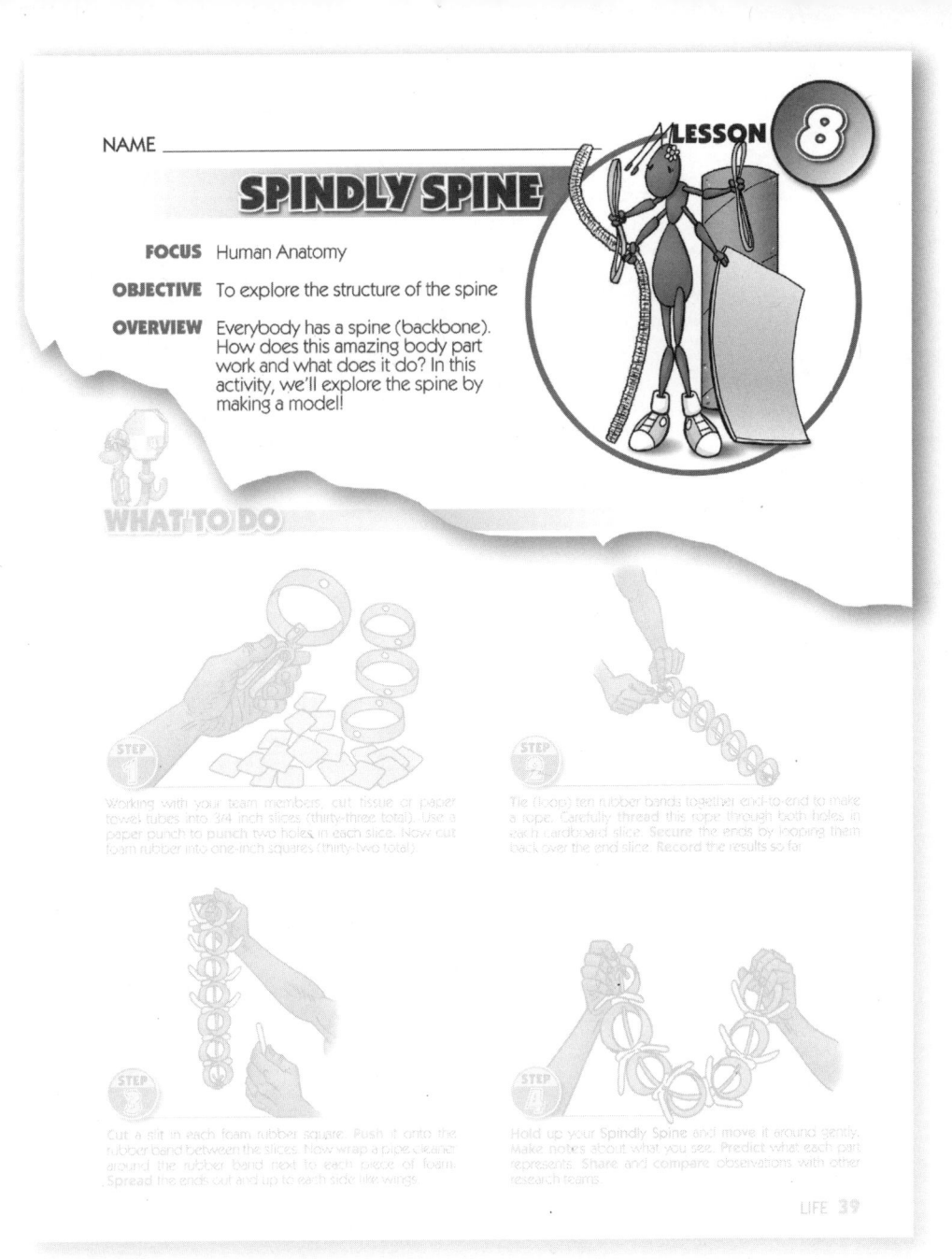

SPINDLY SPINE

FOCUS Human Anatomy

OBJECTIVE To explore the structure of the spine

OVERVIEW Everybody has a spine (backbone). How does this amazing body part work and what does it do? In this activity, we'll explore the spine by making a model!

WHAT TO DO

STEP 1: Working with your team members, cut tissue or paper towel tubes into 3/4 inch slices (thirty-three total). Use a paper punch to punch two holes in each slice. Now cut foam rubber into one-inch squares (thirty-two total).

STEP 2: Tie (loop) ten rubber bands together end-to-end to make a rope. Carefully thread this rope through both holes in each cardboard slice. Secure the ends by looping them back over the end slice. Record the results so far.

STEP 3: Cut a slit in each foam rubber square. Push it onto the rubber band between the slices. Now wrap a pipe cleaner around the rubber band next to each piece of foam. Spread the ends out and up to each side like wings.

STEP 4: Hold up your Spindly Spine and move it around gently. Make notes about what you see. Predict what each part represents. Share and compare observations with other research teams.

Category
Life Science

Focus
Human Anatomy

Objective
To explore the structure of the spine

National Standards
A1, A2, B1, C1, C5, F1, G1, G2

Materials Needed
foam rubber
rubber bands
pipe cleaners
scissors
ruler
cardboard tube
hole punch

Safety Concerns
1. Sharp Objects
Remind students to be careful when using scissors.

Additional Comments

The model is much easier to assemble if it's lying on a work surface. Practice creating one ahead of time so you thoroughly understand how it goes together. This way you can monitor teams for correct assembly and assist where needed. Although one hole punch can circulate around the room, it makes things smoother to have a punch available for each team. (You may be able to borrow extras for a few hours from other teachers.)

Overview

Read the overview aloud to your students. The goal is to create an atmosphere of curiosity and inquiry.

WHAT TO DO

Monitor student research teams as they complete each step.

Step 1
Note that there are 33 loops and 32 squares. This is because the squares go between each set of loops, but none go on the ends. Using 10 rubber bands to make the "rope" allows the spine to be stretched several feet for examination purposes.

Step 2
The slit in the foam rubber square should be centered on one side and cut about halfway through.

Step 4
To enhance this step, have one team member hold the top of the "spine" while another team member holds the bottom (lightly). A third team member can then gently move the center back and forth in various ways while the entire team watches the interaction between the parts.

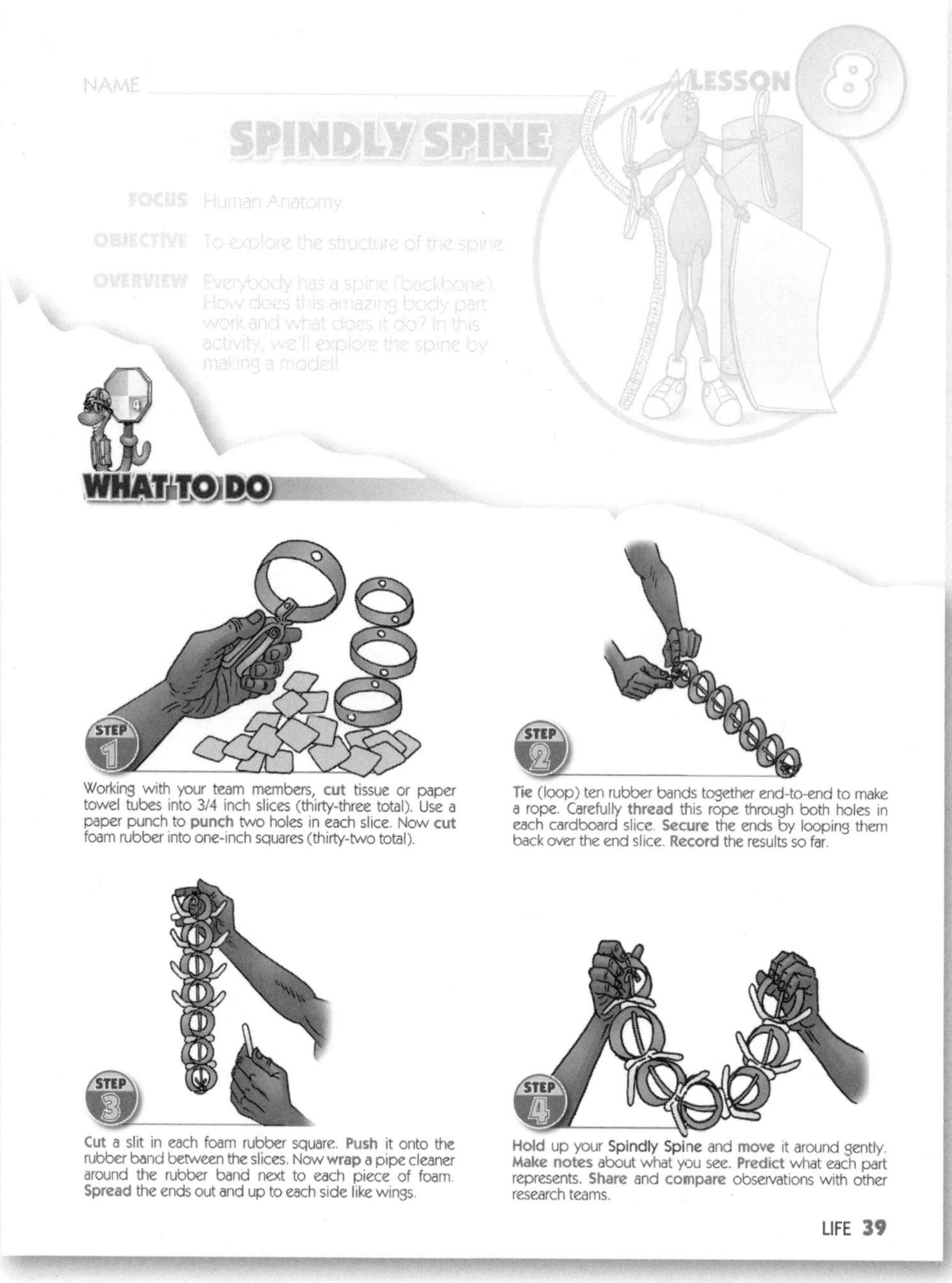

NAME _____

SPINDLY SPINE

FOCUS Human Anatomy

OBJECTIVE To explore the structure of the spine

OVERVIEW Everybody has a spine (backbone). How does this amazing body part work and what does it do? In this activity, we'll explore the spine by making a model!

WHAT TO DO

STEP 1 Working with your team members, **cut** tissue or paper towel tubes into 3/4 inch slices (thirty-three total). Use a paper punch to **punch** two holes in each slice. Now **cut** foam rubber into one-inch squares (thirty-two total).

STEP 2 **Tie** (loop) ten rubber bands together end-to-end to make a rope. Carefully **thread** this rope through both holes in each cardboard slice. **Secure** the ends by looping them back over the end slice. **Record** the results so far.

STEP 3 **Cut** a slit in each foam rubber square. **Push** it onto the rubber band between the slices. Now **wrap** a pipe cleaner around the rubber band next to each piece of foam. **Spread** the ends out and up to each side like wings.

STEP 4 **Hold** up your **Spindly Spine** and move it around gently. **Make notes** about what you see. **Predict** what each part represents. **Share** and **compare** observations with other research teams.

LIFE 39

Teacher to Teacher

Of the 33 vertebrae in the human backbone, seven are cervical (neck), 12 are thoracic (chest), five are lumbar (lower back), five are in the sacrum (part of the pelvic girdle), and four are in the coccyx (tailbone). These bones interlock, yet allow flexible movement for the entire upper body. The primary function of these bones is to protect the spinal cord and related nerves. The adult spinal cord is about as thick as a finger and roughly 18 inches long. Together with the brain, it forms the central nervous system. Because of its core role, an injury or disease involving the spine can result in paralysis.

WHAT HAPPENED?

You just made a **model** of your **spine**! Although it's sometimes called the **backbone**, the spine is not one bone but 33 individual bones called **vertebrae** (represented by the cardboard tubes). A large, thick **nerve** called the **spinal cord** (represented by the rubber band) runs from your **brain** down through the middle of these vertebrae. There are also areas of protective padding called **cartilage** (represented by the foam rubber). This is the same material that forms your nose and ears. Small **spinal nerves** (represented by the pipe cleaners) branch off the spinal cord. They help send information back and forth to your brain.

Even though it's a very complex system, your spine is amazingly strong. It not only supports your entire body, but it's also flexible enough to let your body move in many different ways.

WHAT WE LEARNED

1. Describe the body structure represented by the cardboard tubes. What does this structure do?

a) the cardboard tubes represent the vertebrae

b) they form the framework for the spine; they protect the spinal cord from injury, etc.

2. Describe the body structure represented by the rubber band. What does this structure do?

a) the rubber bands represent the spinal cord

b) the spinal cord is a large, thick nerve that passes information from your body to your brain

3. Describe the body structure represented by the foam rubber pieces. What do these structures do?

a) the foam rubber pieces represent the cartilage

b) cartilage provides protective padding

4. Describe the body structure represented by the pipe cleaners. What do these structures do?

a) the pipe cleaners represent small spinal nerves

b) they branch off from the spinal cord, and send information through the spinal cord to the brain

5. If your spinal cord was damaged, interrupting the flow of information from the spinal nerves to the brain, what might happen to the body structures below the damaged area?

They would be impaired, they would not function at all, they might be paralyzed, etc.

What Happened

Review the section with students. Emphasize bold-face words that identify key concepts and introduce new vocabulary.

*You just made a **model** of your **spine**! Although it's sometimes called the **backbone**, the spine is not one bone but 33 individual bones called **vertebrae** (represented by the cardboard tubes). A large, thick **nerve** called the **spinal cord** (represented by the rubber band) runs from your **brain** down through the middle of these vertebrae. There are also areas of protective padding called **cartilage** (represented by the foam rubber). This is the same material that forms your nose and ears. Small **spinal nerves** (represented by the pipe cleaners) branch off the spinal cord. They help send information back and forth to your brain.*

Even though it's a very complex system, your spine is amazingly strong. It not only supports your entire body, but it's also flexible enough to let your body move in many different ways.

What We Learned

Answers will vary. Suggested responses are shown at left.

Conclusion

Read this section aloud to the class to summarize the concepts learned in this activity.

Food for Thought

Read the Scripture aloud to the class. Discuss the incredible complexity of the human body and what this tells us about our creator. Encourage students to take time to thank God for the things he has made.

Journal

If time permits, have a general class discussion about students' journal entries. Share and compare observations. Be sure to emphasize that "trial and error" is a valuable part of scientific inquiry!

CONCLUSION
Your spine (backbone) protects your spinal cord, supports your body, and provides channels for information to flow between your brain and the rest of your body.

FOOD FOR THOUGHT
Genesis 1:20-30 Making this model helped you see the incredible complexity of the human spine. Yet this model represents only one part of a human body. Imagine making models of all the human body parts — or modeling all the parts of all the animals that ever lived! Now that's complex!

It's mind-boggling to think about the incredible complexity God dealt with during creation. The first chapter of Genesis talks about the fantastic forms of life God created. Can you imagine what went into designing and making even one species of animal? What a marvelous God we serve! Take time this week to thank God for all the wonderful things he has made.

JOURNAL — My Science Notes

Extended Teaching

1. Challenge students to research the best ways to prevent spinal cord injuries. Have them present team reports to the class on their findings.

2. Invite a chiropractor to visit your classroom (and bring a model). Discuss the spine and its importance to good health.

3. Have students research involuntary reflexes. Invite a nurse to visit your classroom and show how reflexes are tested.

4. Compare the human spine with the backbone of other mammals. Using pictures of skeletons from snakes, frogs, birds, and other animals, discuss how they are similar and different.

5. Have students research spinal cord injuries and how they impact people's lives. Discuss mechanical devices that are used to help them regain some degree of mobility.

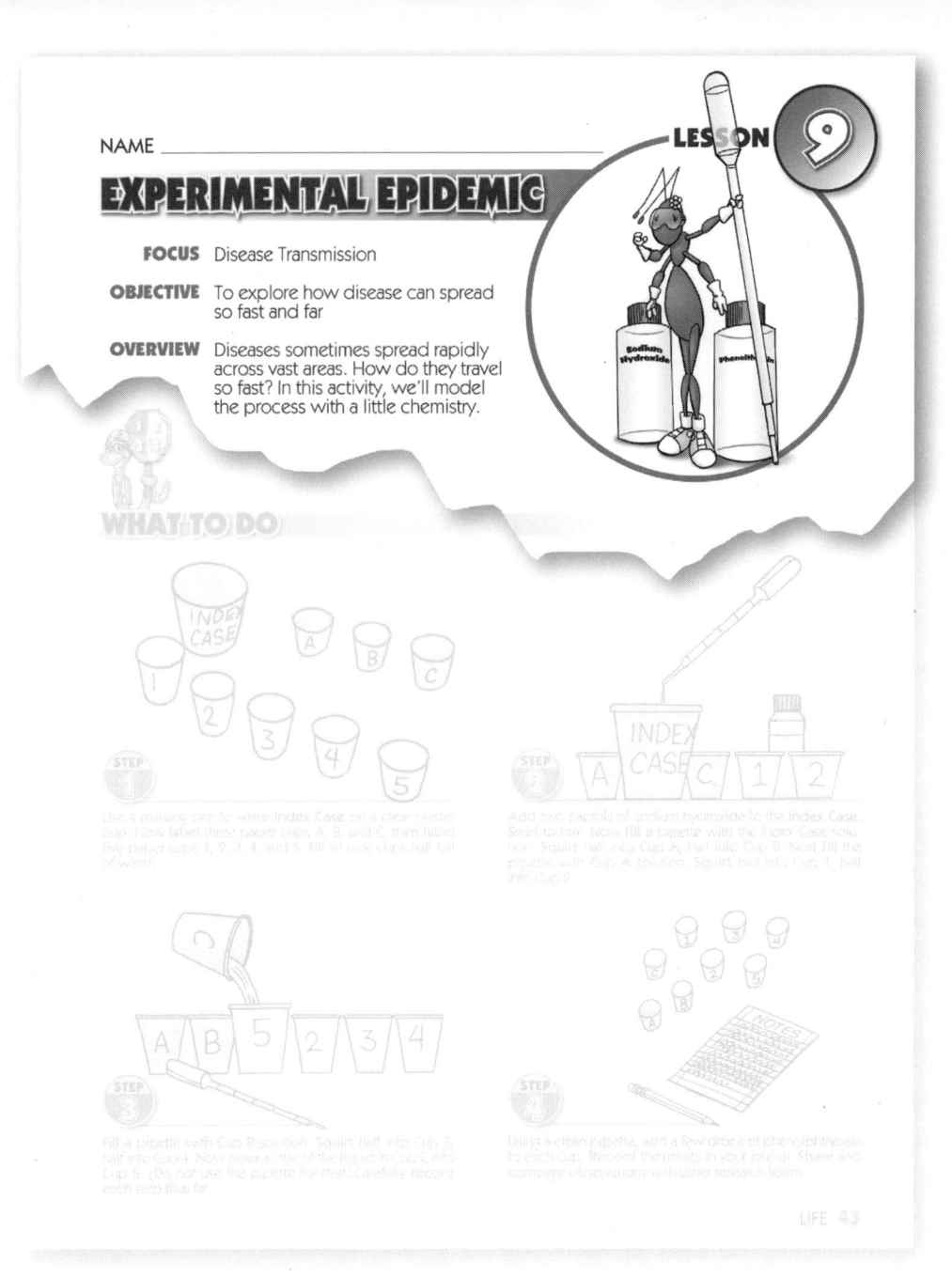

Category
Life Science

Focus
Disease Transmission

Objective
To explore how disease can spread so fast and far

National Standards
A1, A2, B1, C1, C3, C4, C5, E1, E2, F1, F2, F3, F4, F5, G1, G2

Materials Needed
pipette - 2
sodium hydroxide
phenolphthalein
paper cups - 8
plastic cup - clear
marking pen
water

Safety Concerns

1. Goggles/Gloves
Goggles and gloves are recommended whenever students are using chemicals.

2. Corrosion
Sodium hydroxide can burn skin or clothing.

3. Skin Contact
Avoid contact between phenolphthalein or sodium hydroxide and skin.

4. Slipping
Clean up any spills immediately. Remind students to exercise caution when using fluids.

Additional Comments

Many students will immediately see a parallel between this activity and the rapid spread of the HIV (the virus responsible for the condition known as AIDS). Be prepared for this important discussion! Also, remind students to exercise extra caution when using sodium hydroxide. Improper use can cause burns, especially in students with sensitive skin.

Overview

Read the overview aloud to your students. The goal is to create an atmosphere of curiosity and inquiry.

Lesson 9 · **49**

WHAT TO DO

Monitor student research teams as they complete each step. Make sure students follow instructions exactly, otherwise results will be incorrect. If a team accidently contaminates additional cups, use this as a further illustration of how disease spreads.

NAME _____

EXPERIMENTAL EPIDEMIC

FOCUS Disease Transmission

OBJECTIVE To explore how disease can spread so fast and far

OVERVIEW Diseases sometimes spread rapidly across vast areas. How do they travel so fast? In this activity, we'll model the process with a little chemistry.

WHAT TO DO

STEP 1
Use a marking pen to **write Index Case** on a clear plastic cup. Now **label** three paper cups A, B, and C, then **label** five paper cups 1, 2, 3, 4, and 5. **Fill** all nine cups half full of water.

STEP 2
Add two capfuls of sodium hydroxide to the **Index Case**. **Swirl** to mix. Now **fill** a pipette with the Index Case solution. **Squirt** half into Cup A; half into Cup B. Next **fill** the pipette with Cup A solution. **Squirt** half into Cup 1; half into Cup 2.

STEP 3
Fill a pipette with Cup B solution. **Squirt** half into Cup 3; half into Cup 4. Now **pour** a little of the liquid in Cup C into Cup 5. (Do not use the pipette for this!) Carefully **record** each step thus far.

STEP 4
Using a clean pipette, **add** a few drops of phenolphthalein to each cup. **Record** the results in your journal. **Share** and **compare** observations with other research teams.

LIFE 43

Teacher to Teacher

Infectious disease spreads through a variety of methods. This activity modeled the spread of disease through direct contact, but some diseases (like Hepatitis B) pass through food, water, or blood. Disease can be transmitted by insects (fleas, mosquitos, etc.) or carried as an air-borne infection. Disease can also pass through the placenta to the unborn, or be transmitted by sexual contact. Until recent history, mass diseases (bubonic plague, spanish flu, tuberculosis, etc.) were the primary cause of death in our world — sometimes even changing the course of history! A pandemic is an epidemic which essentially has gone global.

WHAT HAPPENED?

You just **modeled** how **disease** can spread rapidly beginning with just one person! Scientists call the rapid spread of a disease an **epidemic**. In this activity, the sodium hydroxide represented a disease. The **index case** cup represented the first person in an area to **contract** the disease. Notice this person only came into contact with two people (Cup A and Cup B). Then those two people came into contact with other groups (represented by Cups 1 though 4). The result? Several people got the disease very rapidly!

The **phenolphthalein** we used is a **chemical indicator** which changes color when it contacts a **base** (like sodium hydroxide). In this activity, it represents a medical testing procedure given to a person suspected of having a disease. Diseases that spread rapidly may be referred to as **contagious**, **infectious**, or **communicable**.

WHAT WE LEARNED

1. What do the cups in this activity represent? Explain what the term "index case" means.

a) individual people

b) the index case was the first person with the disease

2. What does the sodium hydroxide represent? Define the term "epidemic."

a) the disease

b) an epidemic is the rapid spread of a disease

3. In Step 4, why did some cups show color and others didn't? What did this represent?

a) some had a trace of sodium hydroxide, others didn't

b) some caught the disease, others didn't

4. What does the phenolphthalein represent? Why are medical tests important in an epidemic?

a) medical testing for a disease

b) to help identify people who need treatment, and to prevent them from spreading the disease further

5. Based on what you've learned, how do contagious diseases spread? What steps might health authorities take to stop an epidemic?

a) from one person to another through direct contact

b) anything needed to isolate the disease (quarantine, etc.)

What Happened

Review the section with students. Emphasize bold-face words that identify key concepts and introduce new vocabulary.

*You just **modeled** how **disease** can spread rapidly beginning with just one person! Scientists call the rapid spread of a disease an **epidemic**. In this activity, the sodium hydroxide represented a disease. The **index case** cup represented the first person in an area to **contract** the disease. Notice this person only came into contact with two people (Cup A and Cup B). Then those two people came into contact with other groups (represented by Cups 1 through 4). The result? Several people got the disease very rapidly!*

*The **phenolphthalein** we used is a **chemical indicator** which changes color when it contacts a **base** (like sodium hydroxide). In this activity, it represents a medical testing procedure given to a person suspected of having a disease. Diseases that spread rapidly may be referred to as **contagious**, **infectious**, or **communicable**.*

What We Learned

Answers will vary. Suggested responses are shown at left.

Conclusion

Read this section aloud to the class to summarize the concepts learned in this activity.

Food for Thought

Read the Scripture aloud to the class. Discuss how sin can be like a contagious disease. Ask students to come up with some ways we can get closer to God.

Journal

If time permits, have a general class discussion about students' journal entries. Share and compare observations. Be sure to emphasize that "trial and error" is a valuable part of scientific inquiry!

CONCLUSION

Certain kinds of diseases can spread rapidly. The rapid spread of a contagious disease is called an epidemic. Such diseases are often spread through human contact.

FOOD FOR THOUGHT

2 Corinthians 7:1 Disease has been one of mankind's greatest enemies since earliest recorded history. Scripture contains many stories of how Jesus healed people who were very sick. Struggling to survive a disease is not a pleasant experience!

In this Scripture, Paul reminds us that our bodies are not the only thing that can experience sickness. Like a contagious disease, bad habits, wicked companions, or poor attitudes can infect our souls with the poison of sin. But staying close to Jesus can help us keep our hearts and minds disease free!

JOURNAL — My Science Notes

Extended Teaching

1. Have students research the "black death" (bubonic plague) — a pandemic that devasted Europe in the 1300s. Find out what affect this had on history. (The resulting labor shortage changed the balance of power, etc.)

2. Another pandemic was the Spanish Flu during World War I. Have students research this disease. Compare the disease death toll to the number of combat deaths during this time.

3. Most people think an antibiotic can fight a virus. Invite a doctor or nurse to visit your classroom and explain why this is not true. Discuss the differences between bacterial and viral infections.

4. Have students research famous men and women who fought disease. Make bulletin boards showing the results. (Some good names to start with are Edward Jenner, Louis Pasteur, Marie Curie, and Baruch Blumberg.)

5. Have students research different diseases caused by viruses. Have them make a list of those for which there are vaccinations, and create a bulletin board to show their findings.

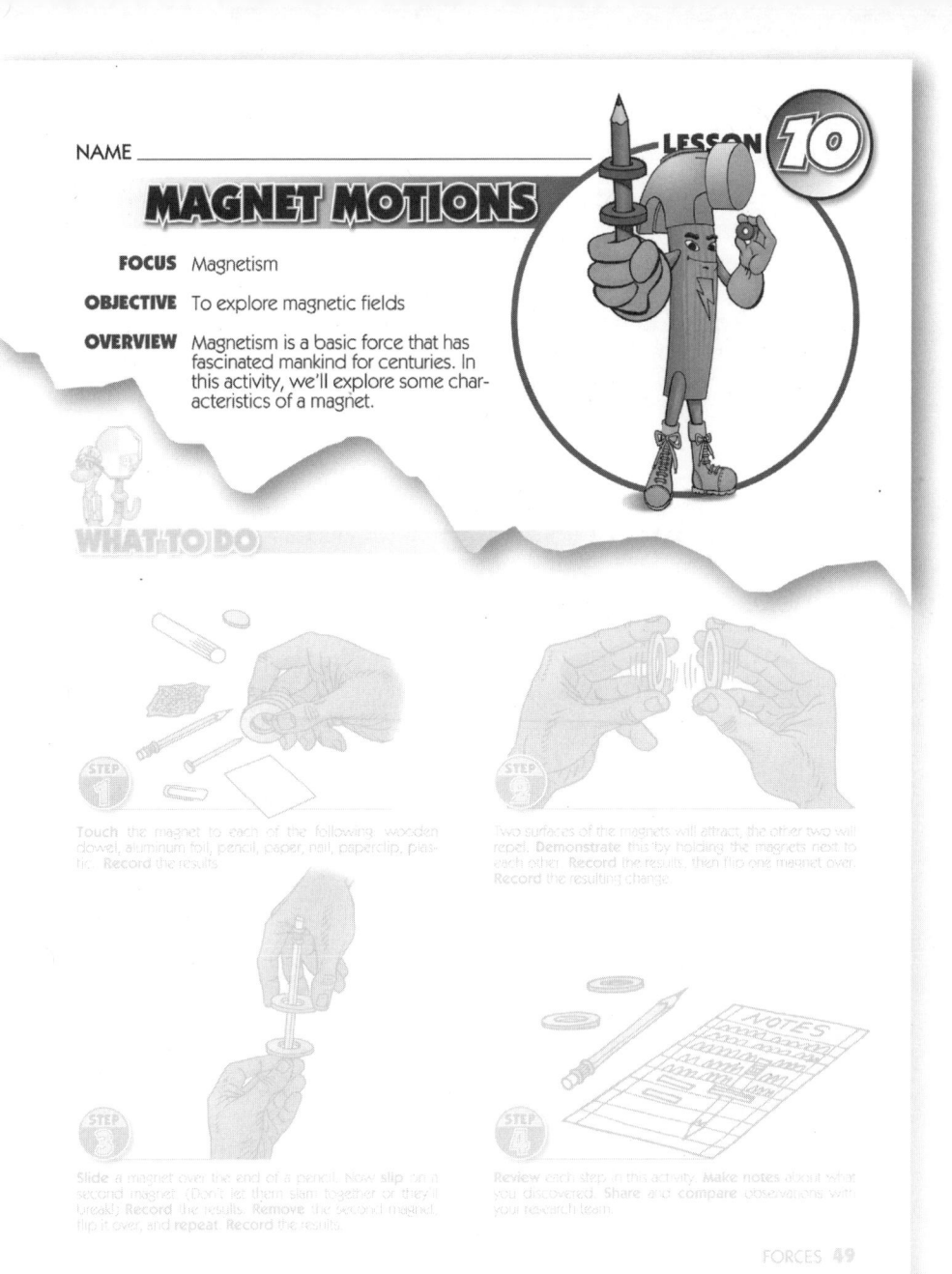

NAME _____

MAGNET MOTIONS

LESSON 10

FOCUS Magnetism

OBJECTIVE To explore magnetic fields

OVERVIEW Magnetism is a basic force that has fascinated mankind for centuries. In this activity, we'll explore some characteristics of a magnet.

WHAT TO DO

STEP 1 Touch the magnet to each of the following: wooden dowel, aluminum foil, pencil, paper, nail, paperclip, plastic. Record the results.

STEP 2 Two surfaces of the magnets will attract, the other two will repel. Demonstrate this by holding the magnets next to each other. Record the results, then flip one magnet over. Record the resulting change.

STEP 3 Slide a magnet over the end of a pencil. Now slip on a second magnet. (Don't let them slam together or they'll break.) Record the results. Remove the second magnet, flip it over, and repeat. Record the results.

STEP 4 Review each step in this activity. Make notes about what you discovered. Share and compare observations with your research team.

FORCES **49**

Category
Physical Science
Forces

Focus
Magnetism

Objective
To explore magnetic fields

National Standards
A1, A2, B1, B2, B3, E1, E2, F5, G1, G2

Materials Needed
magnets - 2
wooden dowel
nail
paperclip
aluminum foil
pencil
paper
plastic

Safety Concerns
4. Sharp Objects
Remind students to be careful using the nail.

Additional Comments

Remind students that magnets will break if they slam together. Keep magnets away from computers, and put away loose discs and videotapes before beginning this activity.

Overview

Read the overview aloud to your students. The goal is to create an atmosphere of curiosity and inquiry.

Lesson 10 · **53**

WHAT TO DO

Monitor student research teams as they complete each step.

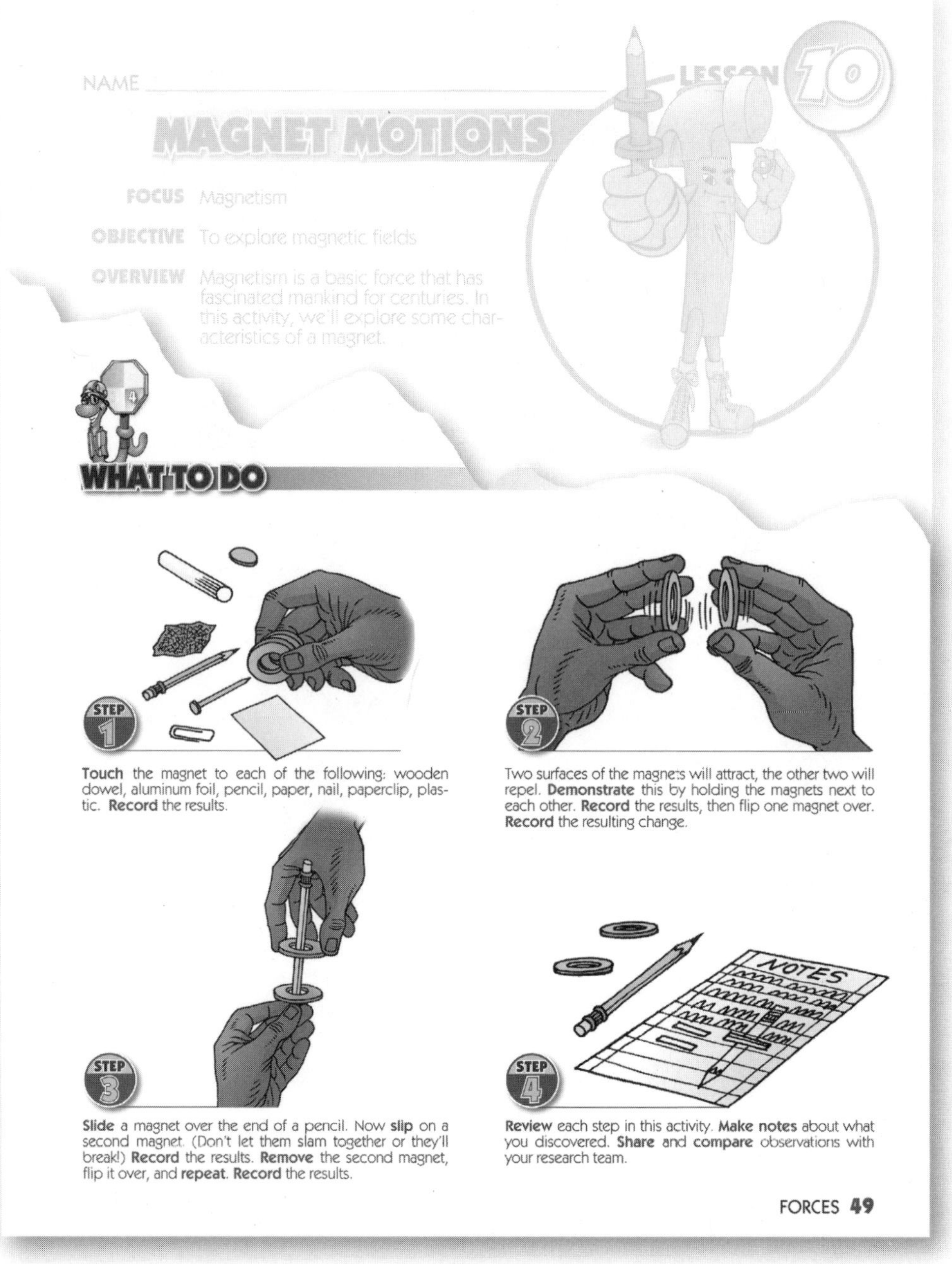

NAME _____

MAGNET MOTIONS

LESSON 10

FOCUS Magnetism

OBJECTIVE To explore magnetic fields

OVERVIEW Magnetism is a basic force that has fascinated mankind for centuries. In this activity, we'll explore some characteristics of a magnet.

WHAT TO DO

STEP 1
Touch the magnet to each of the following: wooden dowel, aluminum foil, pencil, paper, nail, paperclip, plastic. **Record** the results.

STEP 2
Two surfaces of the magnets will attract, the other two will repel. **Demonstrate** this by holding the magnets next to each other. **Record** the results, then flip one magnet over. **Record** the resulting change.

STEP 3
Slide a magnet over the end of a pencil. Now **slip** on a second magnet. (Don't let them slam together or they'll break!) **Record** the results. **Remove** the second magnet, flip it over, and **repeat**. **Record** the results.

STEP 4
Review each step in this activity. **Make notes** about what you discovered. **Share** and **compare** observations with your research team.

FORCES **49**

Teacher to Teacher

Although we don't completely understand magnetism, we still rely on its forces to run our world. Electricity is generated by spinning a coil of wire inside a powerful magnetic field. Electric motors run because internal magnets repel and attract each other. Magnetic force is even used in advanced medical procedures (like Magnetic Resonance Imagery).

WHAT HAPPENED?

Some materials (like nails) attract **magnets**. Other materials (like aluminum foil) do not. **Metals** that attract magnets are called **ferrous** or **ferromagnetic**. They usually contain iron, nickel, or cobalt. Magnets can be **permanent** (like the ones we used), or **temporary**. Temporary magnets are made by wrapping **insulated** wire around ferromagnetic metal, then passing **direct current (DC) electricity** through the wire. When the current turns off, so does the magnet!

Magnets have opposite **poles** or ends called north and south. If you bring *unlike* poles (one north, one south) together, they **attract** each other. If you bring *like* poles (both north or both south) together, they **repel** each other. **Magnetic forces** help create **electricity**, drive electric motors, store data — or even perform simple tasks like holding messages on your refrigerator!

WHAT WE LEARNED

1. Which materials in Step 1 were ferromagnetic? Which materials were not? What are some common ingredients of ferromagnetic metals?

a) nail, paperclip

b) wooden dowel, aluminum foil, pencil, paper, plastic

c) iron, nickel, cobalt

2. Compare Step 2 and Step 3. How were they similar? How were they different? What characteristics of magnets did you discover?

Answers will vary, but should reflect the second paragraph of "What Happened."

3. Explain the difference between "like" and "unlike" poles. Describe their behavior.

Like poles (both north or both south) repel each other; unlike poles (one north, one south) attract each other.

4. Describe how temporary magnets are made. Why might a magnet like this be useful?

a) a wire is wrapped around metal, then current is passed through it

b) it can be turned on or off

5. Based on what you've learned, why wouldn't you stick notes to your computer with a refrigerator magnet?

The magnetic field could rearrange the magnetic particles on a disc or videotape, erasing the data.

What Happened

Review the section with students. Emphasize bold-face words that identify key concepts and introduce new vocabulary.

*Some materials (like nails) attract **magnets**. Other materials (like aluminum foil) do not. **Metals** that attract magnets are called **ferrous** or **ferromagnetic**. They usually contain iron, nickel, or cobalt. Magnets can be **permanent** (like the ones we used), or **temporary**. Temporary magnets are made by wrapping **insulated** wire around ferromagnetic metal, then passing **direct current (DC) electricity** through the wire. When the current turns off, so does the magnet!*

*Magnets have opposite **poles** or ends called north and south. If you bring unlike poles (one north, one south) together, they **attract** each other. If you bring like poles (both north or both south) together, they **repel** each other. **Magnetic forces** help create **electricity**, drive electric motors, store data — or even perform simple tasks like holding messages on your refrigerator!*

What We Learned

Answers will vary. Suggested responses are shown at left.

Conclusion

Read this section aloud to the class to summarize the concepts learned in this activity.

Food for Thought

Read the Scripture aloud to the class. Discuss how people are sometimes persecuted for their religious beliefs. Talk about why it's important for Christians to support one another.

Journal

If time permits, have a general class discussion about notes and drawings various students added to their journal pages. Discuss correct and incorrect predictions, and remind students that this "trial and error" process is part of the scientific process.

CONCLUSION

Some materials attract magnets, other materials do not. Magnets can be permanent or temporary. Like poles on a magnet repel each other, unlike poles attract.

FOOD FOR THOUGHT

John 15:17-19 Magnets repel or attract each other depending on how they're aligned. When magnets are not in the correct alignment, they won't stick together — no matter how hard you push them together!

This Scripture reminds us that God's children must stick together. Unbelievers often cause trouble for those who love God. In some countries, believers are persecuted or even killed. Yet Christians often create their own troubles by fighting among themselves! Why not ask God to align your heart so you're repelled by evil and attracted to good?

JOURNAL — My Science Notes

52 FORCES

Extended Teaching

1. Using the Internet, search for information about Japan's famous "magnetic train." Challenge each team to create a poster about this amazing form of transportation and how it works.

2. Find a local dealer that carries hybrid or electric cars. Invite a technician to visit your classroom. Ask him/her to explain how these cars work. Have students write a paragraph about one thing they learn.

3. Visit a local doctor's office. Have him/her explain how MRI's are performed and what this procedure allows them to see. Have students write a paragraph about one thing they learn.

4. Challenge each team to compile a list of things that use electric motors, especially at home or school. Have students write a short story about what their lives would be like without these devices.

5. Have students research ancient magnets called "lodestones." Find out how they helped ancient explorers and how they got their name. Challenge each team to make a poster showing what they learn.

56 · Lesson 10

PEANUT PASTE — LESSON 11

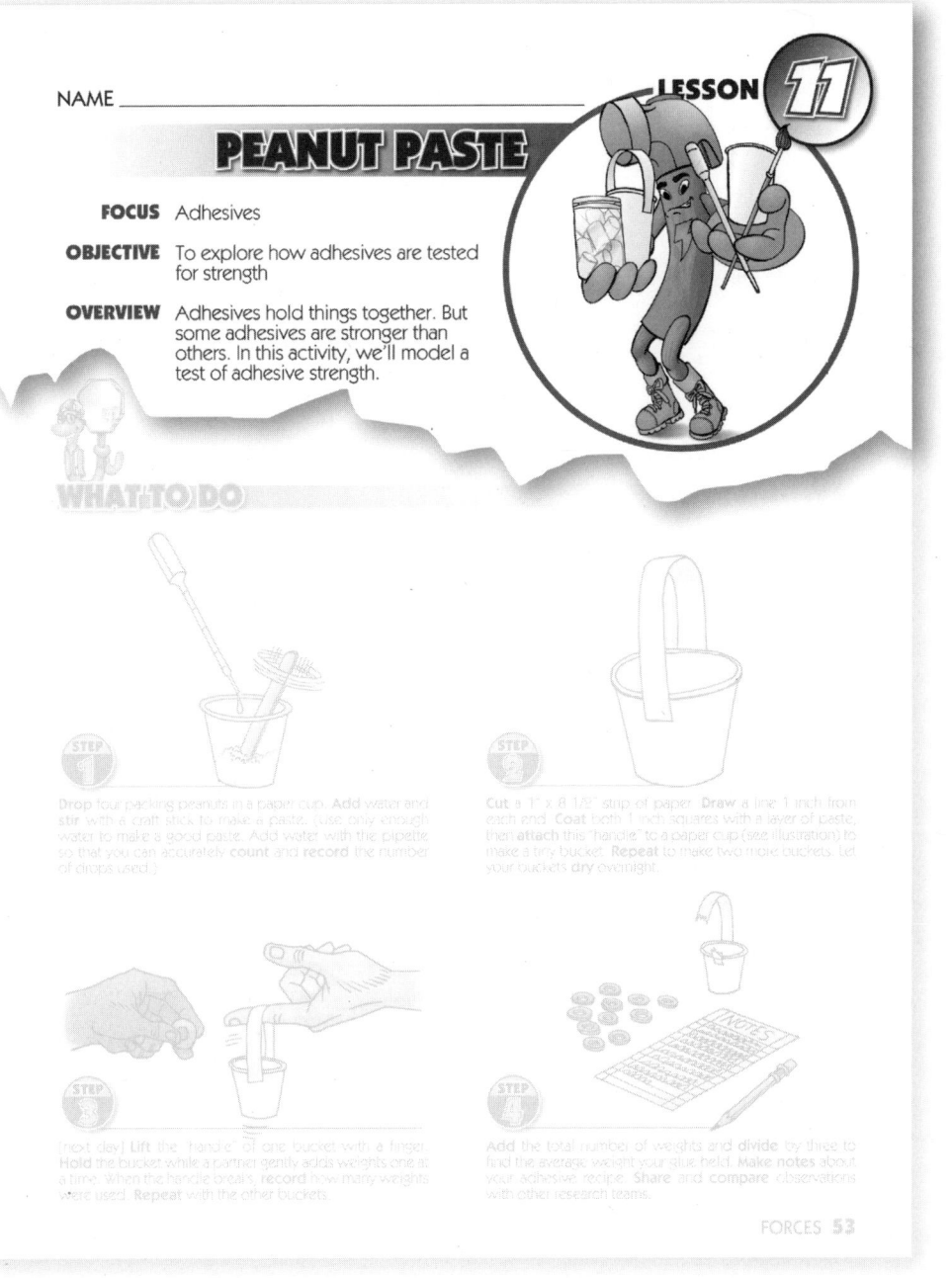

NAME _____

FOCUS Adhesives

OBJECTIVE To explore how adhesives are tested for strength

OVERVIEW Adhesives hold things together. But some adhesives are stronger than others. In this activity, we'll model a test of adhesive strength.

WHAT TO DO

STEP 1: Drop four packing peanuts in a paper cup. Add water and stir with a craft stick to make a paste. (Use only enough water to make a good paste. Add water with the pipette so that you can accurately **count** and **record** the number of drops used.)

STEP 2: Cut a 1" x 8 1/2" strip of paper. Draw a line 1 inch from each end. Coat both 1 inch squares with a layer of paste, then **attach** this "handle" to a paper cup (see illustration) to make a tiny bucket. **Repeat** to make two more buckets. Let your buckets **dry** overnight.

STEP 3: [next day] **Lift** the "handle" of one bucket with a finger. Hold the bucket while a partner gently adds weights one at a time. When the handle breaks, **record** how many weights were used. **Repeat** with the other buckets.

STEP 4: Add the total number of weights and **divide** by three to find the average weight your glue held. Make notes about your adhesive recipe. **Share** and **compare** observations with other research teams.

FORCES 53

Additional Comments

Use only the starch-based packing pellets supplied in your kit. Water won't dissolve petroleum-based pellets. Don't allow students to place these pellets in their mouth.

Overview

Read the overview aloud to your students. The goal is to create an atmosphere of curiosity and inquiry.

Category
Physical Science
Forces

Focus
Adhesives

Objective
To explore how adhesives are tested for strength

National Standards
A1, A2, B1, B2, B3, E1, E2, F5, G1, G2

Materials Needed
packing pellets - 4
paper cup - 4
washers - 10
craft stick
pipette
water
scissors
paper
ruler

Safety Concerns

4. Sharp Objects
Remind students to be careful using scissors.

4. Slipping
There is a potential for spills with this activity. Remind students to exercise caution.

4. Other
Monitor to make sure students are not eating the packing pellets!

Lesson 11 · 57

WHAT TO DO

Monitor student research teams as they complete each step.

Step 3
This can be a bit tricky. The strength of the adhesive is based on the formula each group creates (water to starch) in Step 1. Encourage groups to compare notes to find out which formula works best.

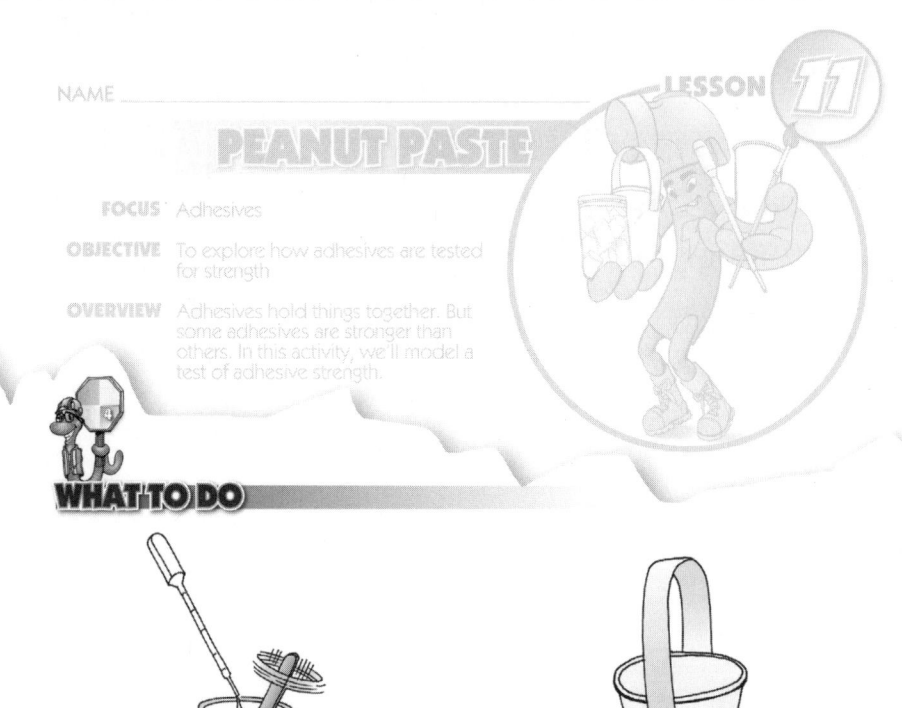

PEANUT PASTE

FOCUS Adhesives

OBJECTIVE To explore how adhesives are tested for strength

OVERVIEW Adhesives hold things together. But some adhesives are stronger than others. In this activity, we'll model a test of adhesive strength.

WHAT TO DO

STEP 1
Drop four packing peanuts in a paper cup. **Add** water and **stir** with a craft stick to make a paste. (Use only enough water to make a good paste. Add water with the pipette so that you can accurately **count** and **record** the number of drops used.)

STEP 2
Cut a 1" x 8 1/2" strip of paper. **Draw** a line 1 inch from each end. **Coat** both 1 inch squares with a layer of paste, then **attach** this "handle" to a paper cup (see illustration) to make a tiny bucket. **Repeat** to make two more buckets. Let your buckets **dry** overnight.

STEP 3
[next day] **Lift** the "handle" of one bucket with a finger. **Hold** the bucket while a partner gently adds weights one at a time. When the handle breaks, **record** how many weights were used. **Repeat** with the other buckets.

STEP 4
Add the total number of weights and **divide** by three to find the average weight your glue held. **Make notes** about your adhesive recipe. **Share** and **compare** observations with other research teams.

FORCES 53

Teacher to Teacher

Accurate records are vital to good science. The "peer review" process allows a scientist to repeat the original work of another scientist. It also offers a way to check specific variables (such as the effect of humidity). Accurate records help insure that reported results are correct before the work is carried further.

58 · Lesson 11

WHAT HAPPENED?

You began this activity by making an **adhesive**. There are many kinds of adhesives designed for specific applications. But all adhesives have one thing in common: they hold things together! The simple adhesive you created was a thick **starch solution**, or paste, designed to hold two pieces of paper together.

The careful **measuring** and **recording** that you did **models** how scientists conduct **experiments**. Everything tested is the same except one thing (called the **variable**). You used the same number of packing peanuts, the same kind of paper, the same amount of paste. The only variable was the amount of water each team used. By comparing notes with other teams, you were able to determine the ideal (**optimum**) water content needed in the recipe to create the strongest paste.

WHAT WE LEARNED

1. Name at least three kinds of adhesives. What do all adhesives have in common? Why are there different kinds of adhesives?

a) wood glue, liquid nails, tapes, etc.

b) they hold things together

c) different materials require different bonding agents

2. Describe the paste you created in step 2. Why was it important to let this paste dry overnight?

a) answers will vary

b) it doesn't form a bond until it's dry

3. Why were multiple "buckets" used in this activity? How did this add to the accuracy of the results? Why not just use one bucket for testing?

a) answers should reflect the need for consistancy

b) multiples allowed for "average" strength

4. How much water did your team use in Step 1? How did this compare to other teams? Based on other teams' results, what is the optimum water content for this particular formula?

Answers will vary, but should reflect logical conclusions.

5. Describe the use of a variable in scientific testing. How does changing only one variable each time make testing more accurate?

If two variables were used at the same time, you wouldn't know which one caused a change.

What Happened

Review the section with students. Emphasize bold-face words that identify key concepts and introduce new vocabulary.

*You began this activity by making an **adhesive**. There are many kinds of adhesives designed for specific applications. But all adhesives have one thing in common: they hold things together! The simple adhesive you created was a thick **starch solution**, or paste, designed to hold two pieces of paper together.*

*The careful **measuring** and **recording** that you did **models** how scientists conduct **experiments**. Everything tested is the same except one thing (called the **variable**). You used the same number of packing pellets, the same kind of paper, the same amount of paste. The only variable was the amount of water each team used. By comparing notes with other teams, you were able to determine the ideal (**optimum**) water content needed in the recipe to create the strongest paste.*

What We Learned

Answers will vary. Suggested responses are shown at left.

Lesson 11 · 59

Conclusion

Read this section aloud to the class to summarize the concepts learned in this activity.

Food for Thought

Read the Scripture aloud to the class. Talk about what it takes to be a "true" friend. Discuss how developing a relationship with Jesus gives us the ultimate best friend, who will always be there for us.

Journal

If time permits, have a general class discussion about notes and drawings various students added to their journal pages. Discuss correct and incorrect predictions, and remind students that this "trial and error" process is part of the scientific process.

CONCLUSION

Scientists conduct experiments to find answers. Scientific experiments must be carefully controlled, observed, and recorded to yield accurate results. Only one variable should be changed for each experiment.

FOOD FOR THOUGHT

Proverbs 18:24 The strength of a good adhesive can be surprising. If you have the right recipe, the bond can be even stronger than the surrounding materials! A good adhesive has the ability to hold things together no matter what happens.

Scripture reminds us the world is full of people who pretend to be friends until times get tough. Suddenly when you need them most, they're gone! But true friends are like an excellent adhesive. They'll stick with you even on those bad days. Remember, Jesus is the truest friend of all. No matter what happens, he'll always be there!

JOURNAL — My Science Notes

Extended Teaching

1. Challenge teams to conduct a "peer review", by repeating this activity using another team's formula. Have them compare the results to their original work. How were they similar? How were they different?

2. Using the Internet, have teams research adhesives. Find out about different kinds, how strong they are, and any special handling required. Challenge each team to create a poster about a specific adhesive.

3. Invite a carpenter and a plumber to your classroom. Ask both of them to demonstrate the kind of adhesives they use in their work. Have students write a few paragraphs comparing these different adhesives.

4. Take a field trip to a box factory. Find out how cardboard boxes are made and what adhesives are used. Have students write a paragraph about one thing they learn. (Another option: visit a plywood factory.)

5. Have teams research Martin Fleischmann, Stanley Pons, and cold fusion. Find out how peer review damaged their careers and why. Have students write about the importance of accurate, reproducible results.

Worksheet

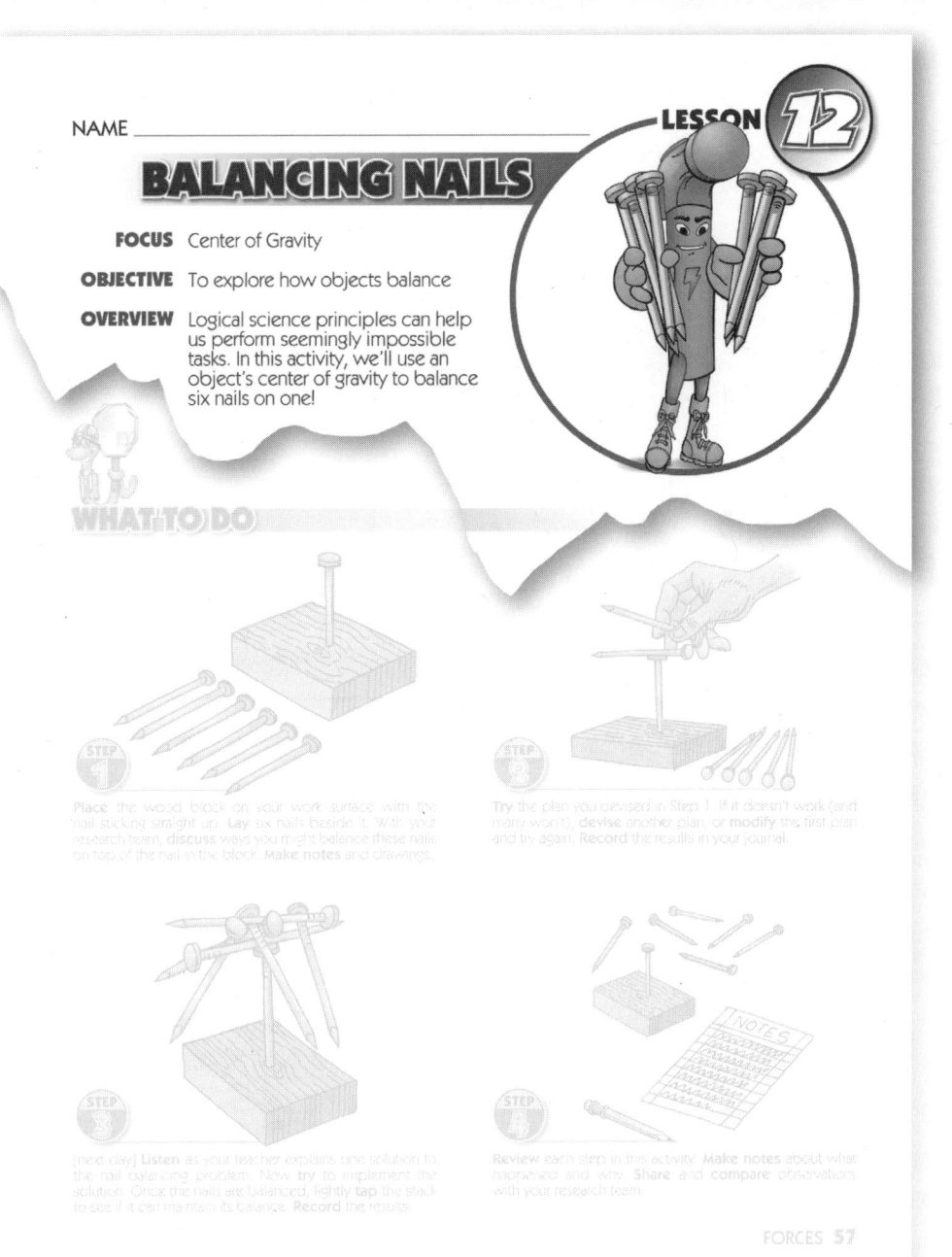

NAME _____

LESSON 12
BALANCING NAILS

FOCUS Center of Gravity

OBJECTIVE To explore how objects balance

OVERVIEW Logical science principles can help us perform seemingly impossible tasks. In this activity, we'll use an object's center of gravity to balance six nails on one!

WHAT TO DO

STEP 1 Place the wood block on your work surface with the nail sticking straight up. Lay six nails beside it. With your research team, discuss ways you might balance these nails on top of the nail in the block. Make notes and drawings.

STEP 2 Try the plan you devised in Step 1. If it doesn't work (and many won't), devise another plan, or modify the first plan and try again. Record the results in your journal.

STEP 3 [next day] Listen as your teacher explains one solution to the nail balancing problem. Now try to implement the solution. Once the nails are balanced, lightly tap the stack to see if it can maintain its balance. Record the results.

STEP 4 Review each step in this activity. Make notes about what happened and why. Share and compare observations with your research team.

FORCES 57

Category
Physical Science
Forces

Focus
Center of Gravity

Objective
To explore how objects balance

National Standards
A1, A2, B1, B2, B3, G1, G2

Materials Needed
block (wood or Styrofoam®)
nails - 7
hammer

Safety Concerns
4. Sharp Objects
Remind students to exercise caution when working with nails.

Additional Comments
In newer kits, Styrofoam® has been substituted for the wood block. This makes it easier to insert the upright nail, eliminating the need for a hammer. Be sure to allow teams plenty of time to come up with solutions in Step 2.

Overview
Read the overview aloud to your students. The goal is to create an atmosphere of curiosity and inquiry.

Lesson 12 · **61**

WHAT TO DO

Monitor student research teams as they complete each step.

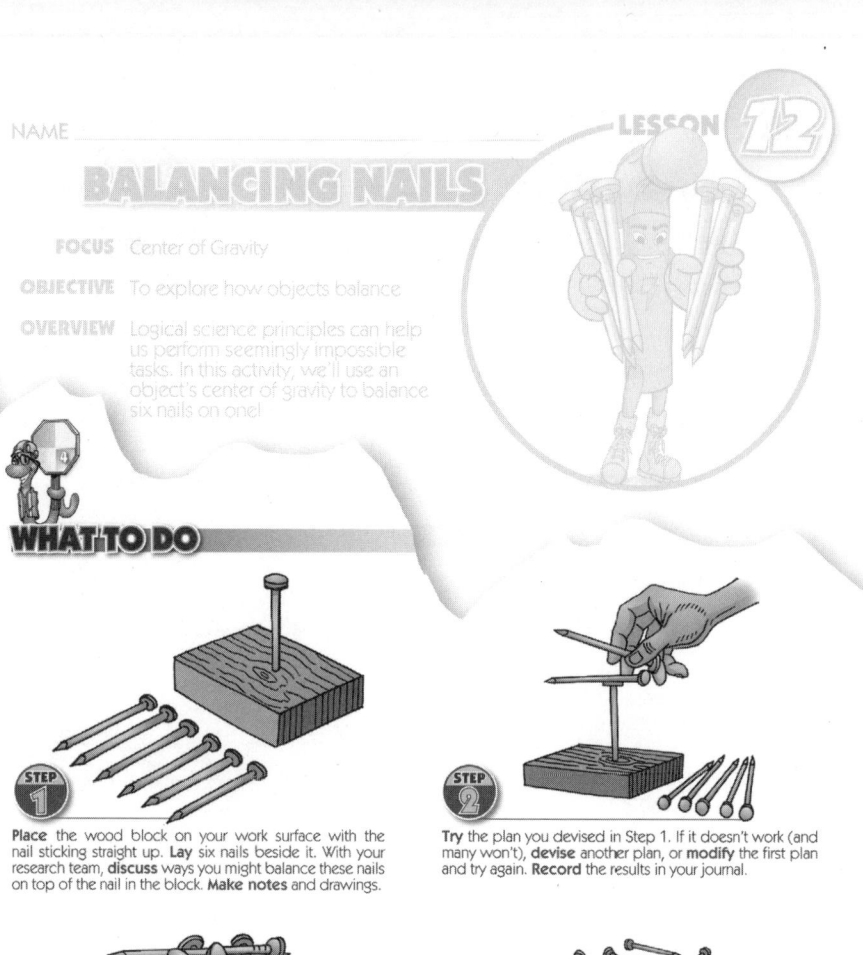

NAME _____

BALANCING NAILS

FOCUS Center of Gravity

OBJECTIVE To explore how objects balance

OVERVIEW Logical science principles can help us perform seemingly impossible tasks. In this activity, we'll use an object's center of gravity to balance six nails on one!

WHAT TO DO

STEP 1
Place the wood block on your work surface with the nail sticking straight up. **Lay** six nails beside it. With your research team, **discuss** ways you might balance these nails on top of the nail in the block. **Make notes** and drawings.

STEP 2
Try the plan you devised in Step 1. If it doesn't work (and many won't), **devise** another plan, or **modify** the first plan and try again. **Record** the results in your journal.

STEP 3
[next day] **Listen** as your teacher explains one solution to the nail balancing problem. Now **try** to implement the solution. Once the nails are balanced, lightly **tap** the stack to see if it can maintain its balance. **Record** the results.

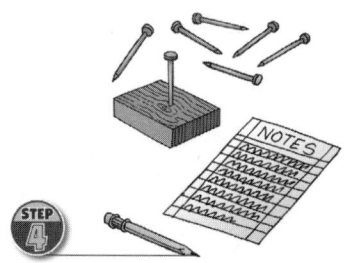

STEP 4
Review each step in this activity. **Make notes** about what happened and why. **Share** and **compare** observations with your research team.

FORCES **57**

Teacher to Teacher

In addition to balance, this activity also offers an example of torque. Any twisting force (from swinging a bat to turning a doorknob to a gymnast's flip) involves torque.

As students tried to balance the nails in Step 2, torque tried to constantly twist them around the center of gravity. That made balancing the nails even trickier!

62 · Lesson 12

WHAT HAPPENED?

To balance all those nails, you had to find the **balance point** (also called the **center of gravity**). The nails had to be arranged around this point so that there was an even **force** going in every direction. This balancing of forces is called **equilibrium**.

The center of gravity on a ruler is exactly in the middle. This is because its shape and **weight** are uniform. But don't be fooled! An object's center of gravity is based on the mid-point of its **mass**, not its shape.

Objects with odd shapes (like baseball bats), or objects with uniform shapes but unevenly distributed weight (like pencils with heavy erasers), have centers of gravity that are . . . off center! You'll find the mid-point of their mass toward the heavier end rather than at the center.

WHAT WE LEARNED

1. Describe your team's first attempt to balance the nails in Step 2. What was the result? Describe modifications to your first plan. What were the results?

answers will vary

2. What is the scientific name for an object's "balance point"? What is a balancing of forces called?

a) *center of gravity*

b) *equilibrium*

3. Describe the solution to the nail-balancing problem. Why did this solution work?

Answers should reflect the need for evenness or symmetry to the stack.

4. This activity is difficult, even when you know the solution! Explain how your "failures" helped you move toward a solution. How does this relate to the work scientists do?

a) *answers will vary*

b) *trial and error*

5. Based on what you've learned, would the balance point of a hammer be near the handle end or the head? Explain your answer.

a) *the head*

b) *the midpoint of mass is always toward the heavier end*

What Happened

Review the section with students. Emphasize bold-face words that identify key concepts and introduce new vocabulary.

*To balance all those nails, you had to find the **balance point** (also called the **center of gravity**). The nails had to be arranged around this point so that there was an even **force** going in every direction. This balancing of forces is called **equilibrium**.*

*The center of gravity on a ruler is exactly in the middle. This is because its shape and **weight** are uniform. But don't be fooled! An object's center of gravity is based on the mid-point of its **mass**, not its shape.*

Objects with odd shapes (like baseball bats), or objects with uniform shapes but unevenly distributed weight (like pencils with heavy erasers), have centers of gravity that are . . . off center! You'll find the mid-point of their mass toward the heavier end rather than at the center.

What We Learned

Answers will vary. Suggested responses are shown at left.

Conclusion

Read this section aloud to the class to summarize the concepts learned in this activity.

Food for Thought

Read the Scripture aloud to the class. Talk about the importance of building on a solid foundation. Discuss how basing our lives on a relationship with Jesus is "building for eternity."

Journal

If time permits, have a general class discussion about notes and drawings various students added to their journal pages. Discuss correct and incorrect predictions, and remind students that this "trial and error" process is part of the scientific process.

CONCLUSION
All objects have a center of gravity. This "balance point" is based on the distribution of an object's mass, not just its shape.

FOOD FOR THOUGHT
1 Corinthians 3:10-12 This activity was tough to do, even when you knew the solution. Imagine how much harder it would have been if the support nail were loose! No matter how good you were at balancing, without a good foundation, your work would have collapsed.

In this Scripture, Paul reminds us that faith is much the same. Regardless of your ability, your education, or your wealth, if you don't build on a solid foundation, your work will be meaningless. But when you base your life on a relationship with Jesus and learn to trust in God's plans, you're building for eternity!

JOURNAL — My Science Notes

60 FORCES

Extended Teaching

1. Have teams repeat this activity, this time using large landscaping nails. (The upright nail needs to be driven into a 2x4 scrap.) Compare the results with the original activity. How were they similar? How were they different?

2. Challenge teams to discuss torque, then compile a list of examples. Share each team's list with the class, and talk about how torque impacts our lives.

3. Invite a football coach to visit your classroom. Have him/her demonstrate how center of gravity and torque affect football players. Have students write a paragraph about one thing they learn.

4. Take a field trip to a local tire shop. Have a technician demonstrate how the lead weights on rims work to balance tires. Have students write a paragraph about one thing they learn.

5. Challenge teams to collect pictures of "torque in action." Have each team contribute materials (including written descriptions) for a classroom bulletin board on this

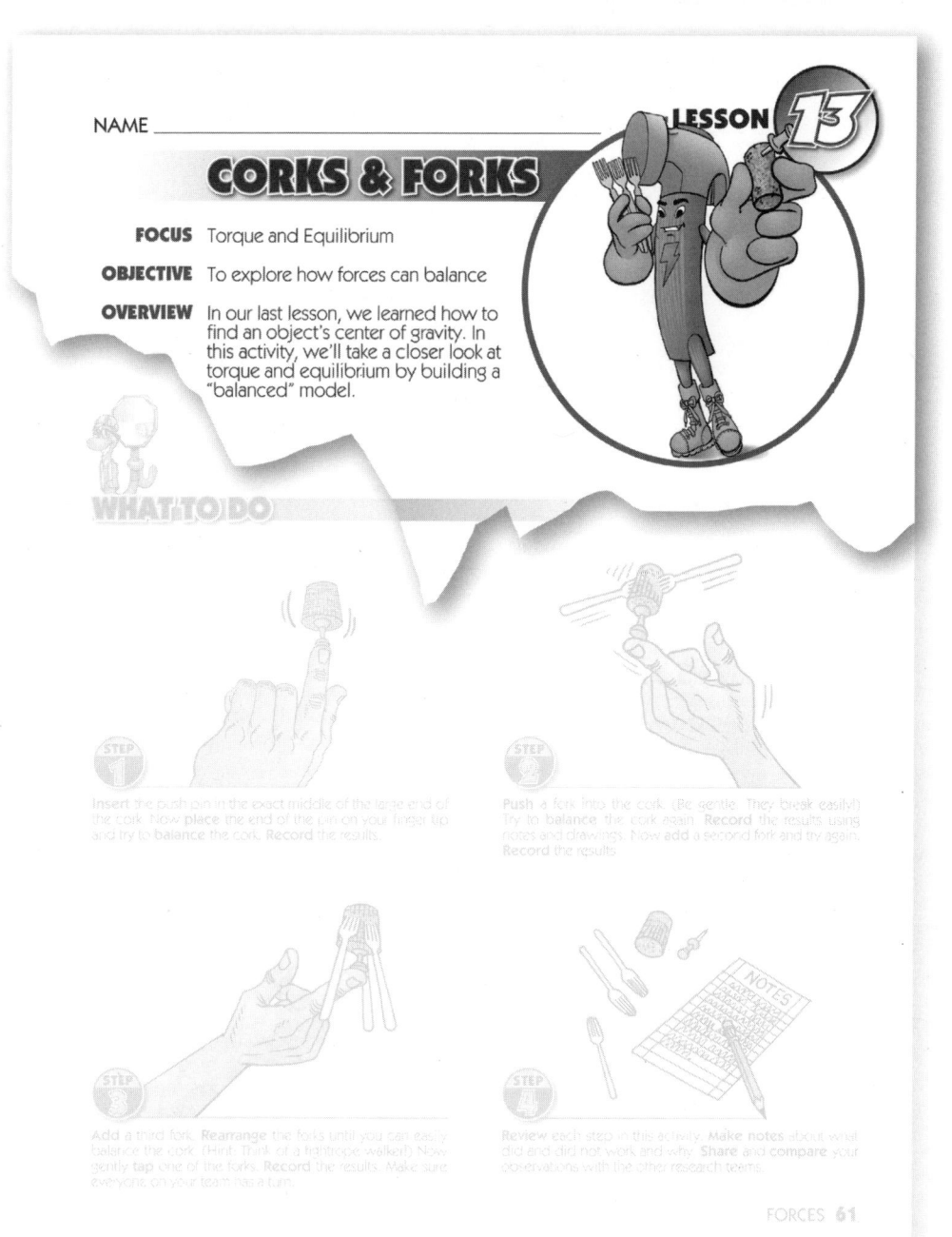

NAME _____

CORKS & FORKS

LESSON 13

FOCUS Torque and Equilibrium

OBJECTIVE To explore how forces can balance

OVERVIEW In our last lesson, we learned how to find an object's center of gravity. In this activity, we'll take a closer look at torque and equilibrium by building a "balanced" model.

WHAT TO DO

STEP 1
Insert the push pin in the exact middle of the large end of the cork. Now place the end of the pin on your finger tip and try to balance the cork. Record the results.

STEP 2
Push a fork into the cork. (Be gentle. They break easily!) Try to balance the cork again. Record the results using notes and drawings. Now add a second fork and try again. Record the results.

STEP 3
Add a third fork. Rearrange the forks until you can easily balance the cork. (Hint: Think of a tightrope walker!) Now gently tap one of the forks. Record the results. Make sure everyone on your team has a turn.

STEP 4
Review each step in this activity. Make notes about what did and did not work and why. Share and compare your observations with the other research teams.

FORCES 61

Category
Physical Science
Forces

Focus
Torque and Equilibrium

Objective
To explore how forces can balance

National Standards
A1, A2, B1, B2, E1, E2, F5, G1, G2

Materials Needed
push pin
cork
forks - 3

Safety Concerns
4. Sharp Objects
Remind students to exercise caution when pushing the pin into the cork.

Additional Comments

A great way to introduce this activity is to have students place the forks, push pin, and cork on their work surface. Challenge teams to balance these items on an index finger. After a few minutes of trying, open the worktext and begin with Step 1. Keep extra forks on hand in case of broken tines.

Overview

Read the overview aloud to your students. The goal is to create an atmosphere of curiosity and inquiry.

WHAT TO DO

Monitor student research teams as they complete each step.

CORKS & FORKS

FOCUS Torque and Equilibrium

OBJECTIVE To explore how forces can balance

OVERVIEW In our last lesson, we learned how to find an object's center of gravity. In this activity, we'll take a closer look at torque and equilibrium by building a "balanced" model.

WHAT TO DO

STEP 1
Insert the push pin in the exact middle of the large end of the cork. Now place the end of the pin on your finger tip and try to balance the cork. Record the results.

STEP 2
Push a fork into the cork. (Be gentle. They break easily!) Try to balance the cork again. Record the results using notes and drawings. Now add a second fork and try again. Record the results.

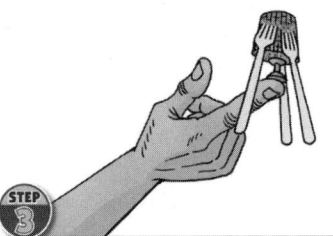

STEP 3
Add a third fork. Rearrange the forks until you can easily balance the cork. (Hint: Think of a tightrope walker!) Now gently tap one of the forks. Record the results. Make sure everyone on your team has a turn.

STEP 4
Review each step in this activity. Make notes about what did and did not work and why. Share and compare your observations with the other research teams.

FORCES **61**

Teacher to Teacher

Scientists refer to the balance point as the "center of gravity." Forces tend to move toward or away from the center of gravity. Students could feel this in action when they tapped the fork in Step 3.

66 · Lesson 13

WHAT HAPPENED?

As we learned in our last lesson, balancing **forces** is called **equilibrium**. Like children playing on a teeter-totter, the **weight** must be shifted until the forces are equal around the **center of gravity**.

There was another force involved in Step 4. When you tapped on one fork, the balanced arrangement tried to twist. This twisting movement is called **torque**.

You use torque every time you swing a bat, use a hammer, or perform any action that requires a circular or semi-circular motion. The arrangement handled the torque force well since movement of one fork was offset by the other fork. In other words, the cork's forks torque was balanced. (Try to say that one fast!)

WHAT WE LEARNED

1. Describe your attempts to balance the cork in Step 1. Why was it difficult?

a) answers will vary

b) weight was not equal on all sides

2. Describe how adding the forks in Step 2 helped or hurt your balancing efforts. Explain why this occurred.

a) answers will vary, but probably harder to balance

b) weight still not equal on all sides

3. What difference did rearranging the forks (Step 3) make? What is this balancing of forces called?

a) balanced the weight on all sides

b) equilibrium

4. What additional force was introduced in Step 4? What kind of force is this? What effect did it have on the balanced arrangement? Why?

a) torque

b) a twisting force

c) made it try to twis.

5. Based on what you've learned, why do tight-rope walkers use long poles? Explain the forces involved and how the pole helps.

The pole extends the sides, making the center easier to find and balance.

What Happened

Review the section with students. Emphasize bold-face words that identify key concepts and introduce new vocabulary.

As we learned in our last lesson, balancing forces is called equilibrium. Like children playing on a teeter-totter, the weight must be shifted until the forces are equal around the center of gravity.

There was another force involved in Step 4. When you tapped on one fork, the balanced arrangement tried to twist. This twisting movement is called torque.

You use torque every time you swing a bat, use a hammer, or perform any action that requires a circular or semi-circular motion. The arrangement handled the torque force well since movement of one fork was offset by the other fork. In other words, the cork's forks torque was balanced. (Try to say that one fast!)

What We Learned

Answers will vary. Suggested responses are shown at left.

Conclusion

Read this section aloud to the class to summarize the concepts learned in this activity.

Food for Thought

Read the Scripture aloud to the class. Talk about God's knowledge, wisdom, and power. Discuss how developing a relationship with God gives us access to his power in our lives.

Journal

If time permits, have a general class discussion about notes and drawings various students added to their journal pages. Discuss correct and incorrect predictions, and remind students that this "trial and error" process is part of the scientific process.

CONCLUSION

Forces can be balanced. Balanced forces are called equilibrium. Equilibrium can be achieved with many kinds of forces including torque (a twisting force).

FOOD FOR THOUGHT

Job 38:4-11 The purpose of science is to discover answers about the world around us. Deciding how to achieve equilibrium was a little tough, but with some time you figured it out. Scientists have figured out many useful things, leading to the inventions of new tools, new medicines, and new ways of doing things.

Sometimes people act like they have all the answers. But good scientists know that the more we learn, the more we discover new areas we know nothing about! This Scripture reminds us that God's knowledge, wisdom, and power are infinitely beyond our comprehension. Always remember that we serve an awesome God who created all the marvels of the Universe!

JOURNAL My Science Notes

Extended Teaching

1. Repeat this activity using an apple, orange, or even a banana as the central balance point. Compare the results with the original activity. How were they similar? How were they different?

2. Have teams go on a "torque hunt" around the school. Challenge each team to collect examples of torque, including drawings and descriptions. Make a classroom bulletin board from the results.

3. Have teams list all the hand tools they can think of, then circle the ones that involve torque. Challenge each team to create a poster depicting one of these tools and how it works.

4. Visit a large playground. Give students 15 minutes to experiment with torque-related equipment (teeter-totter, swings, etc.). Now have a group discussion describing how torque was used and how it felt.

5. Take a field trip to a factory. Have teams watch for examples of torque in action, and take notes about their discoveries. Hold a class discussion, then have students write a paragraph about one thing they've learned.

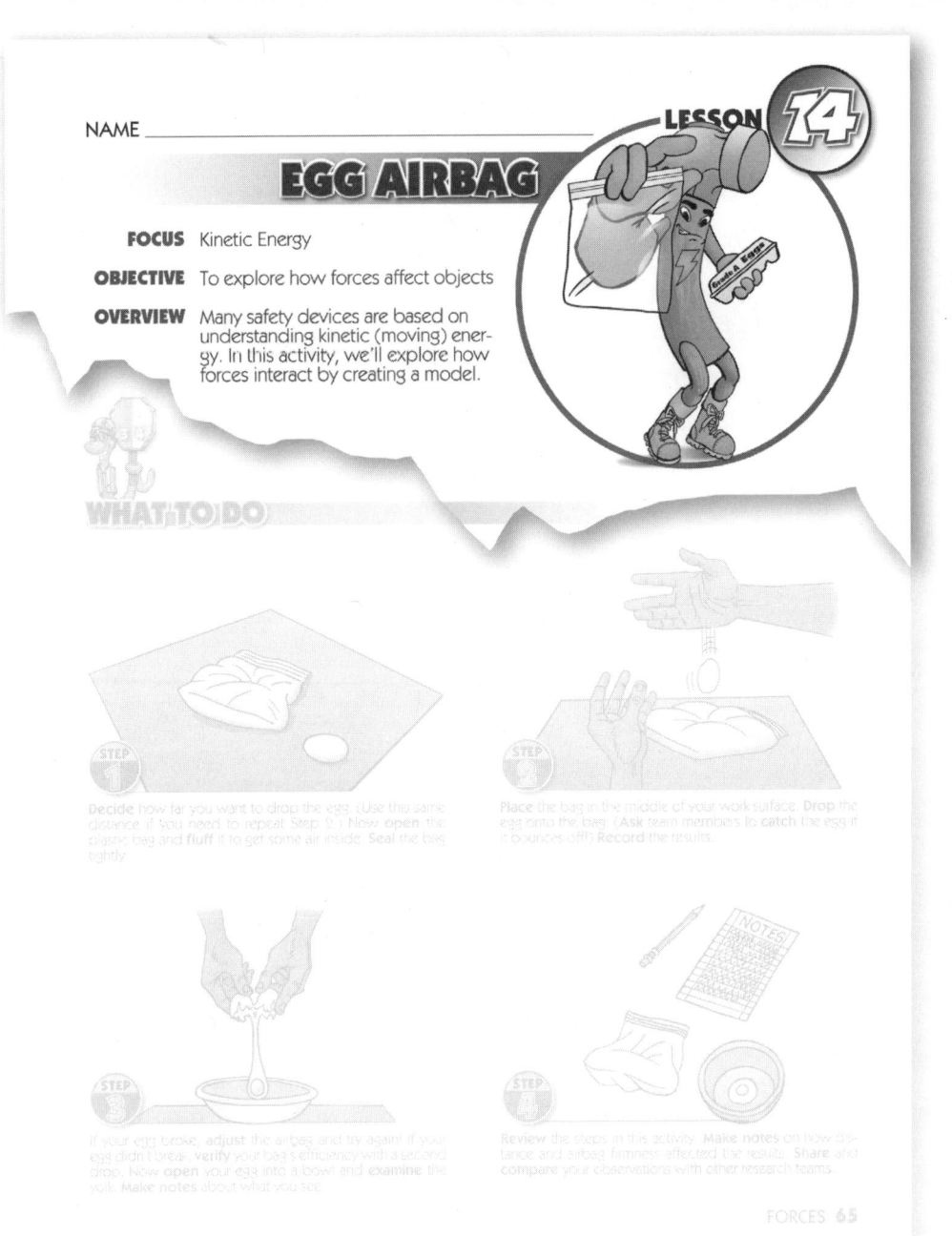

LESSON 14

EGG AIRBAG

FOCUS Kinetic Energy

OBJECTIVE To explore how forces affect objects

OVERVIEW Many safety devices are based on understanding kinetic (moving) energy. In this activity, we'll explore how forces interact by creating a model.

WHAT TO DO

STEP 1 Decide how far you want to drop the egg. (Use this same distance if you need to repeat Step 2.) Now open the plastic bag and fluff it to get some air inside. Seal the bag tightly.

STEP 2 Place the bag in the middle of your work surface. Drop the egg onto the bag. (Ask team members to catch the egg if it bounces off.) Record the results.

STEP 3 If your egg broke, adjust the airbag and try again! If your egg didn't break, verify your bag's efficiency with a second drop. Now open your egg into a bowl and examine the yolk. Make notes about what you see.

STEP 4 Review the steps in this activity. Make notes on how distance and airbag firmness affected the results. Share and compare your observations with other research teams.

FORCES 65

Category
Physical Science
Forces

Focus
Kinetic Energy

Objective
To explore how forces affect objects

National Standards
A1, A2, B1, B2, B3, E1, E2, F1, F4, F5, G1, G2

Materials Needed
egg
large sealable bag

Safety Concerns

3. Hygiene
Remind students to wash hands thoroughly after touching the egg.

4. Slipping
Remind students to exercise caution with the eggs. Clean up egg breakage immediately.

Additional Comments

Since this activity will definitely get messy, it's a good idea to do it outdoors. Keep plenty of paper towels and cleaning items handy! Keep extra eggs on hand to replace broken ones. Completely disinfect the area when done, and have students wash their hands thoroughly.

Overview

Read the overview aloud to your students. The goal is to create an atmosphere of curiosity and inquiry.

Lesson 14 · **69**

WHAT TO DO

Monitor student research teams as they complete each step.

NAME _____

EGG AIRBAG

LESSON 14

FOCUS Kinetic Energy

OBJECTIVE To explore how forces affect objects

OVERVIEW Many safety devices are based on understanding kinetic (moving) energy. In this activity, we'll explore how forces interact by creating a model.

WHAT TO DO

STEP 1
Decide how far you want to drop the egg. (Use this same distance if you need to repeat Step 2.) Now **open** the plastic bag and **fluff** it to get some air inside. **Seal** the bag tightly.

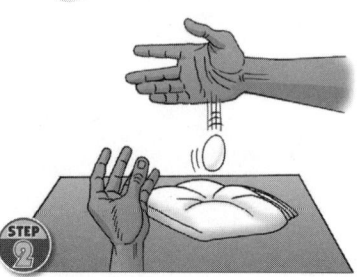

STEP 2
Place the bag in the middle of your work surface. **Drop** the egg onto the bag. (**Ask** team members to **catch** the egg if it bounces off!) **Record** the results.

STEP 3
If your egg broke, **adjust** the airbag and try again! If your egg didn't break, **verify** your bag's efficiency with a second drop. Now **open** your egg into a bowl and **examine** the yolk. **Make notes** about what you see.

STEP 4
Review the steps in this activity. **Make notes** on how distance and airbag firmness affected the results. **Share** and **compare** your observations with other research teams.

FORCES **65**

Teacher to Teacher

Newton's Third Law of Motion states that for every action there is a reaction. When the egg was dropped, its potential energy was converted into kinetic energy. Hitting the bag was an action. The bag pushing back was a reaction. If the egg was unharmed, the two forces cancelled each other out. If forces were unbalanced, the egg probably broke.

What Happened

Review the section with students. Emphasize bold-face words that identify key concepts and introduce new vocabulary.

*When you lifted the egg, you gave it **potential energy** (energy that's not moving). When you dropped the egg, you **converted** the potential energy into **kinetic energy** (energy that moves). **Gravity** was the **force** involved in both **storing** and **releasing** this energy.*

*Your bag used a principle similar to a car's airbag. The idea is to minimize damage to a moving object. The falling egg **pushes** on the air in the bag. The air in the bag pushes right back. Control comes from adjusting the force of the air. Too much air and the bag is too hard, cracking the egg's shell. Too little air and the bag is too limp, allowing the egg to hit the floor. The correct amount of air provides just the right amount of **opposing force**, cushioning the egg's fall to minimize damage.*

What We Learned

Answers will vary. Suggested responses are shown at left.

WHAT HAPPENED?

When you lifted the egg, you gave it **potential energy** (energy that's not moving). When you dropped the egg, you **converted** the potential energy into **kinetic energy** (energy that moves). **Gravity** was the **force** involved in both **storing** and **releasing** this energy.

Your bag used a principle similar to a car's airbag. The idea is to minimize damage to a moving object. The falling egg **pushes** on the air in the bag. The air in the bag pushes right back. Control comes from adjusting the force of the air. Too much air and the bag is too hard, cracking the egg's shell. Too little air and the bag is too limp, allowing the egg to hit the floor. The correct amount of air provides just the right amount of **opposing force**, cushioning the egg's fall to minimize damage.

WHAT WE LEARNED

1) How far did you drop the egg in Step 1? How would increasing or decreasing this distance affect the results?

a) answers will vary

b) increasing: more likely to break; decreasing: less likely to break

2) Why must the bag be tightly sealed in Step 2? How might a poorly sealed bag affect the results?

a) to keep the air inside

b) sudden loss of air would probably break the egg

3) Compare the yolk of your egg (Step 3) with the yolk of other teams' eggs. How were they similar? How were they different? What caused these differences?

Answers will vary, but some yolks may be broken; differences caused by efficiency of "air bag".

4) Name two kinds of energy involved in this activity. How are they similar? How are they different?

a) potential, kinetic

b) similar: both are forms of energy; different: potential = non-moving, kinetic = moving

5) Based on what you've learned, how does a car's airbag protect you in an accident? List potential problems airbag designers might face.

a) the air in the bag pushes in the opposite direction of force

b) answers should reflect the need for "just the right amount" of force

---

Lesson 14 • 71

Conclusion

Read this section aloud to the class to summarize the concepts learned in this activity.

Food for Thought

Read the Scripture aloud to the class. Talk about the awesome power of God's love. Discuss how God is always there to protect those who love and serve him.

Journal

If time permits, have a general class discussion about notes and drawings various students added to their journal pages. Discuss correct and incorrect predictions, and remind students that this "trial and error" process is part of the scientific process.

CONCLUSION

Potential energy is non-moving energy. Kinetic energy is moving energy. Moving energy contains force which can cause injury unless an appropriate opposing force is applied.

FOOD FOR THOUGHT

Romans 8:38-39 Thanks to an appropriate use of opposing force, your egg suffered only minimal damage. It was rushing downward toward certain destruction when the airbag intervened. It saved your egg from serious harm.

This Scripture talks about a similar kind of protection. Paul reminds us that nothing in Heaven or Earth can separate us from God's endless love. Even in those times when we're willfully rushing toward certain destruction, God is always listening for our call for help. His power can provide the opposing force that counteracts the evil actions of Satan, protecting our souls from a disastrous crash.

JOURNAL — My Science Notes

68 FORCES

Extended Teaching

1. Repeat this activity, only this time place water, packing pellets, or similar materials inside the bag. Compare the results to the original activity. How were they similar? How were they different?

2. Organize a "seat belt day" in front of your school. When someone drives in to the parking lot with their seatbelt fastened, have students give them a sticker or a prize!

3. Invite a doctor or nurse to your classroom. Have him/her talk about the affects of head injuries and how to avoid them. Have students write a paragraph about one thing they learn.

4. Take a field trip to a physical therapy clinic. Ask a therapist to demonstrate tools and techniques used to help people with brain injuries. Have students write a paragraph about one thing they learn.

5. Have teams research the importance of safety equipment. Challenge each team to create a poster about seat belts, air bags, or helmets, and how they protect us from head injuries.

NAME _____

BUOYANT BALL

LESSON 15

FOCUS Buoyancy

OBJECTIVE To explore why some objects float

OVERVIEW Punch a hole in an air mattress, and it sinks. Punch a hole in a life-preserver and it still floats! What's the difference? In this activity, we'll explore how buoyancy works.

WHAT TO DO

STEP 1 Fill the clear jar with water to within 1/2 inch of the top. Gently drop a washer into the jar. Record the results. Remove the washer and refill the jar if necessary.

STEP 2 Drop the small Styrofoam® ball in the water. Record the results. Remove the ball and poke the wire through it. Bend one end down against the ball. Bend the other end into a fish-hook shape.

STEP 3 Hang a washer on the end of the wire. Place the ball in the water. Record the results. Add washers one at a time until the top of the ball is at the water's surface. Record the total number of washers used.

STEP 4 Repeat Steps 2 and 3 with the larger ball. Record the results. Now review each step in this activity and make notes about what you discovered. Share and compare observations with your research team.

FORCES 69

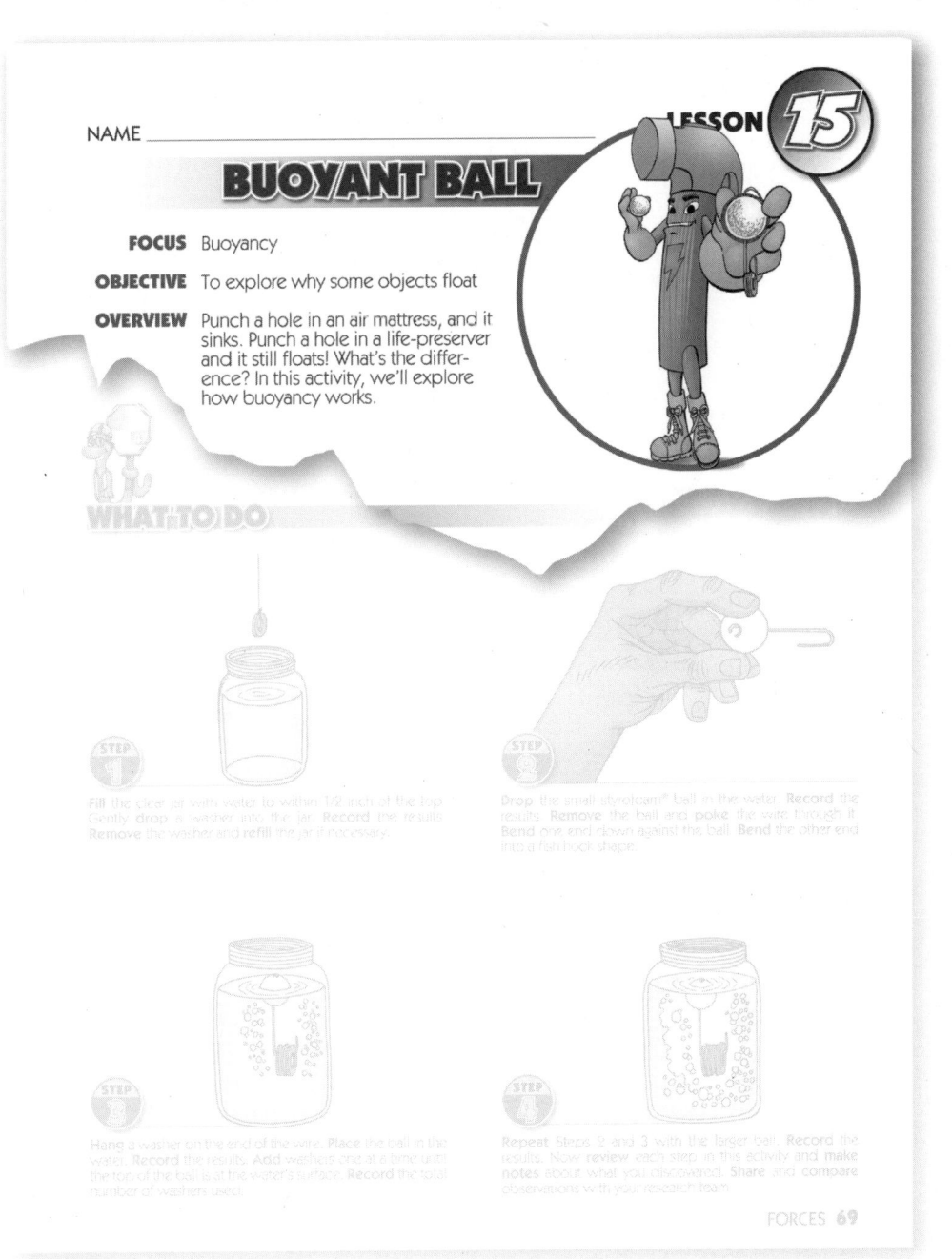

Category
Physical Science
Forces

Focus
Buoyancy

Objective
To explore why some objects float

National Standards
A1, A2, B1, B2, E1, E2, F5, G1, G2

Materials Needed
washer
small Styrofoam® ball
large Styrofoam® ball
wire
clear jar
water

Safety Concerns
4. Slipping
There is a potential for slipping. Clean up any spills immediately.

Additional Comments

Although any clear container will work, a large beaker or jar will show water displacement more clearly. It also makes for a better demonstration if students can see the activity from the side.

Overview

Read the overview aloud to your students. The goal is to create an atmosphere of curiosity and inquiry.

Lesson 15 · **73**

WHAT TO DO

Monitor student research teams as they complete each step.

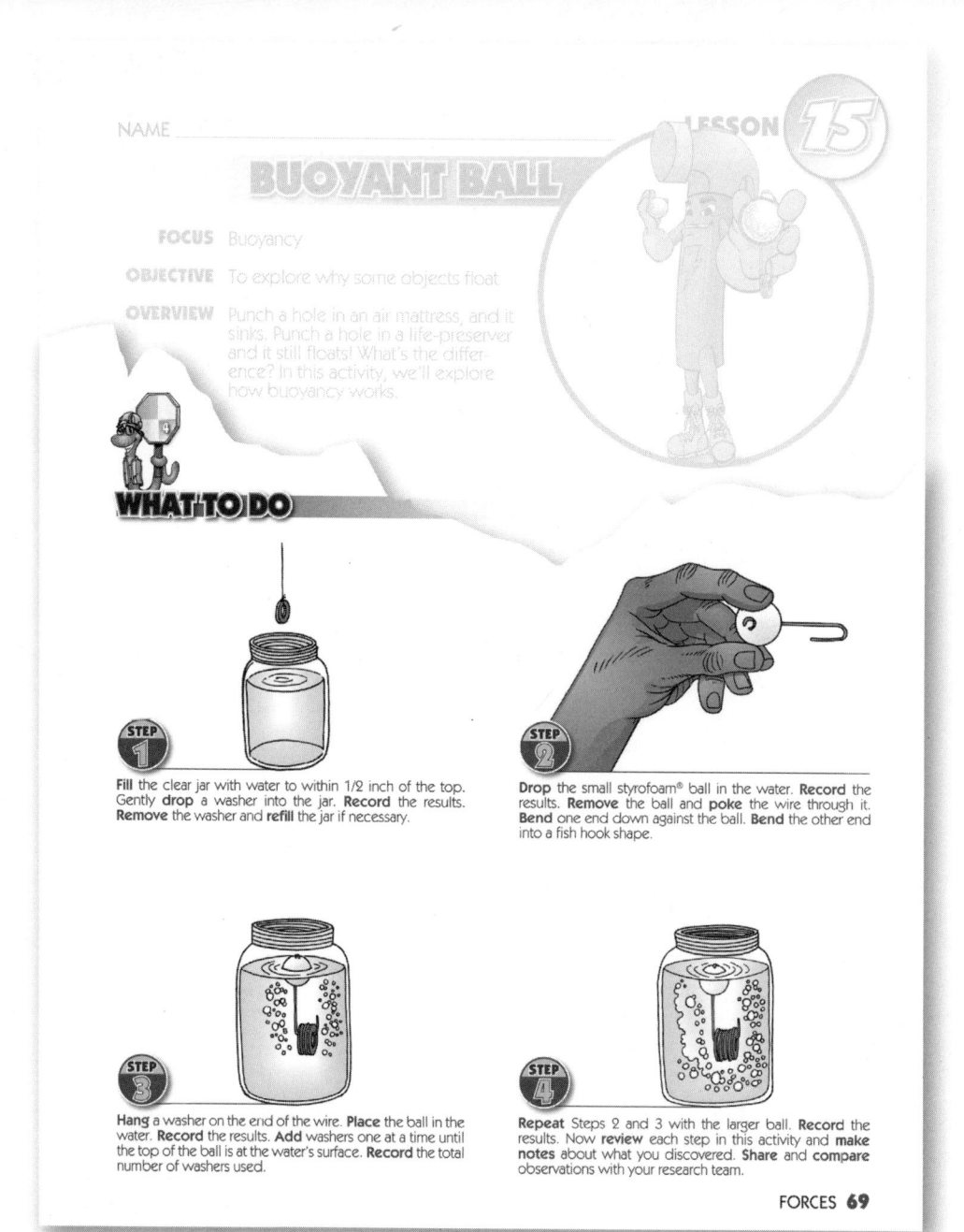

NAME _____

BUOYANT BALL

LESSON 15

FOCUS Buoyancy

OBJECTIVE To explore why some objects float.

OVERVIEW Punch a hole in an air mattress, and it sinks. Punch a hole in a life-preserver and it still floats! What's the difference? In this activity, we'll explore how buoyancy works.

WHAT TO DO

STEP 1
Fill the clear jar with water to within 1/2 inch of the top. Gently **drop** a washer into the jar. **Record** the results. **Remove** the washer and **refill** the jar if necessary.

STEP 2
Drop the small styrofoam® ball in the water. **Record** the results. **Remove** the ball and **poke** the wire through it. **Bend** one end down against the ball. **Bend** the other end into a fish hook shape.

STEP 3
Hang a washer on the end of the wire. **Place** the ball in the water. **Record** the results. **Add** washers one at a time until the top of the ball is at the water's surface. **Record** the total number of washers used.

STEP 4
Repeat Steps 2 and 3 with the larger ball. **Record** the results. Now **review** each step in this activity and **make notes** about what you discovered. **Share** and **compare** observations with your research team.

FORCES 69

Teacher to Teacher

A submarine provides a great example of balance between buoyancy and gravity. On the surface, it has equilibrium. To sink, its tanks are filled with water. To rise, compressed air replaces the water in the tanks. Adjusting the amounts of air or water allows a sub to "hover" at the depth chosen.

WHAT HAPPENED?

All **matter** on Earth is constantly being **pulled** downward by **gravity**. To keep an object from sinking, gravity has to be overcome (**pushed**) by another force. The **opposing force** pushing in this activity is called **buoyancy**.

An object's buoyancy primarily depends on its **density**. Steel is very dense, so it sinks. But steel boats float because their shape **displaces** water with air. The air is less dense than water, so the boat floats (unless a hole lets water in!). Like many life preservers, the ball in this activity is made of Styrofoam® — a material that's full of trapped air. Unlike an air mattress, punching a hole in Styrofoam® doesn't let the air out. In fact, if you grind Styrofoam® into small pieces (not recommended), every tiny piece will still float because it's still full of air!

WHAT WE LEARNED

1 Describe what happened to the washer in Step 1. Why did this happen?

a) it sank

b) a washer is more dense than water

2 Describe what happened to the styrofoam ball in Step 2? Why did this happen?

a) it floated

b) Styrofoam® is less dense than water

3 How did adding washers change the ball's buoyancy in Step 3? Compare this with the behavior of the larger ball in Step 4.

a) adding washers made the ball heavier

b) it took more washers to sink the larger ball

4 Buoyancy depends primarily on what characteristic? Explain why steel ships float.

a) density

b) their shape displaces water with air. Air is less dense than water, so the boat floats

5 Based on what you've learned, could a life preserver be made from steel? Why or why not?

a) not a good idea, but it is possible

b) a sealed steel container could hold air, which is less dense than water, and thus would float

What Happened

Review the section with students. Emphasize bold-face words that identify key concepts and introduce new vocabulary.

*All **matter** on Earth is constantly being **pulled** downward by **gravity**. To keep an object from sinking, gravity has to be overcome (**pushed**) by another force. The **opposing force** pushing in this activity is called **buoyancy**.*

*An object's buoyancy primarily depends on its **density**. Steel is very dense, so it sinks. But steel boats float because their shape **displaces** water with air. The air is less dense than water, so the boat floats (unless a hole lets water in!). Like many life preservers, the ball in this activity is made of Styrofoam® — a material that's full of trapped air. Unlike an air mattress, punching a hole in Styrofoam® doesn't let the air out. In fact, if you grind Styrofoam® into small pieces (not recommended), every tiny piece will still float because it's still full of air!*

What We Learned

Answers will vary. Suggested responses are shown at left.

Conclusion

Read this section aloud to the class to summarize the concepts learned in this activity.

Food for Thought

Read the Scripture aloud to the class. Talk about God's promises of care and protection. Discuss how a relationship with God can strengthen us and keep us safe.

Journal

If time permits, have a general class discussion about notes and drawings various students added to their journal pages. Discuss correct and incorrect predictions, and remind students that this "trial and error" process is part of the scientific process.

CONCLUSION
Buoyancy is a force that opposes gravity. An object's buoyancy depends primarily on its density. Buoyancy can also be seen as the amount of liquid an object can displace.

FOOD FOR THOUGHT
Isaiah 41:10 The Styrofoam® ball in this activity held up a lot of weight. Its buoyancy was able to overcome the force of gravity that was pulling the washers down. In fact, it held up a great deal compared to what it weighed!

In a way, this activity represents the continual battle between good and evil. God holds us up while evil constantly tries to drag us down. This Scripture reminds us that God's power and love conquer all. He promises to strengthen us and hold us up in his arms of love. In the truest sense, God is our ultimate life preserver!

JOURNAL My Science Notes

72 FORCES

Extended Teaching

1. Repeat this activity, only this time use very salty water. Compare the results with the original activity. How were they similar? How were they different?

2. Take a field trip to a facility where scuba is taught. Ask a diver to explain the equipment and how it works. Get an instructor to demonstrate buoyancy. Have students write a paragraph about one thing they learn.

3. Using the Internet, have students research fish that have a swim bladder (an air-filled structure inside their body). Discuss how this structure helps fish hover and swim. Challenge teams to create posters with examples.

4. Invite someone from the Coast Guard or Lake Patrol to visit your classroom. Find out about safety equipment and floatation devices on boats. Challenge each team to create a poster showing one device and how it works.

5. Challenge each team to create a set of water safety posters. Sponsor a "boating safety" week and display the safety posters around the community or school.

76 · Lesson 15

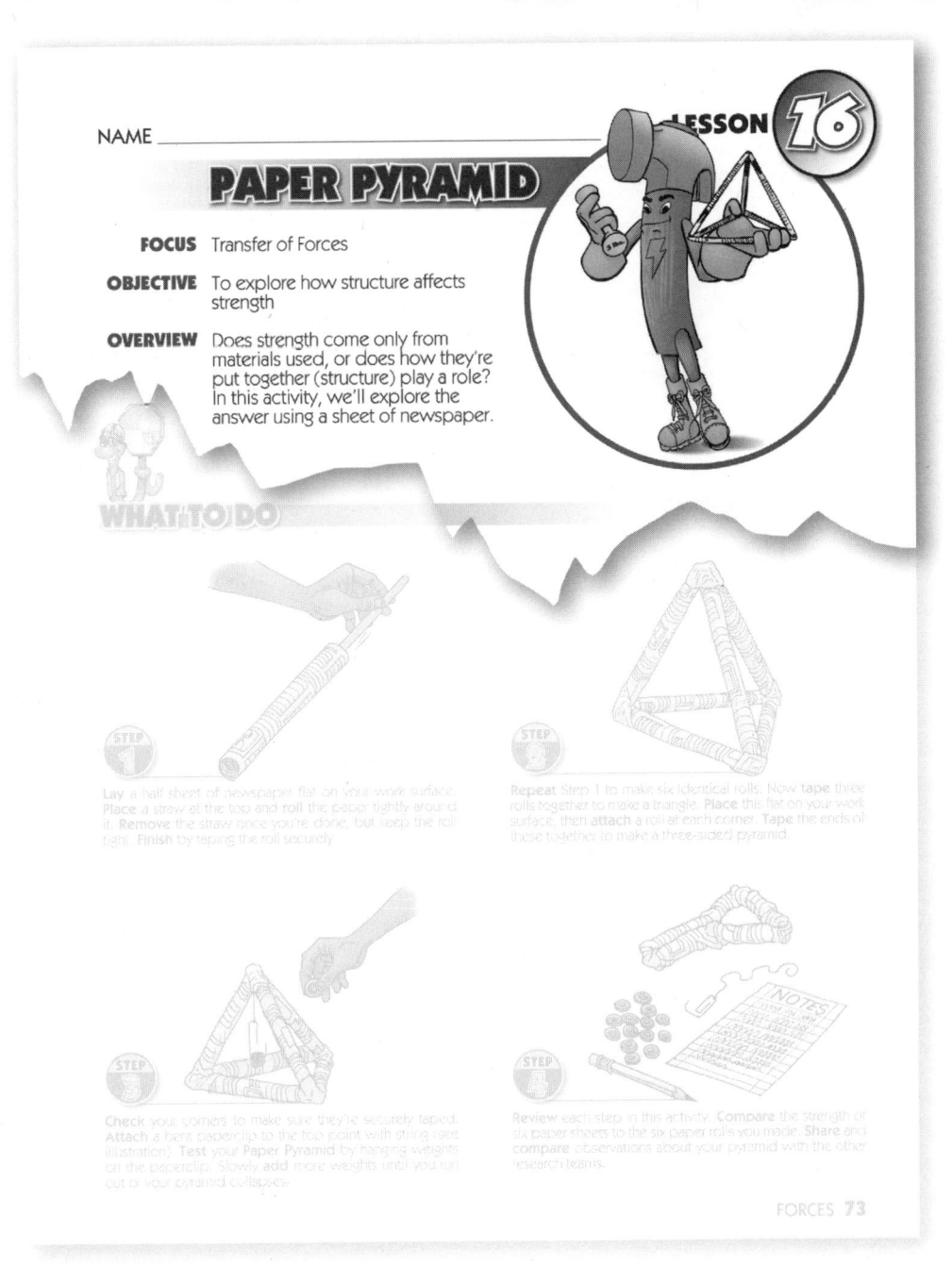

PAPER PYRAMID

LESSON 16

FOCUS Transfer of Forces

OBJECTIVE To explore how structure affects strength

OVERVIEW Does strength come only from materials used, or does how they're put together (structure) play a role? In this activity, we'll explore the answer using a sheet of newspaper.

What To Do

STEP 1 Lay a half sheet of newspaper flat on your work surface. Place a straw at the top and roll the paper tightly around it. Remove the straw once you're done, but keep the roll tight. Finish by taping the roll securely.

STEP 2 Repeat Step 1 to make six identical rolls. Now tape three rolls together to make a triangle. Place this flat on your work surface, then attach a roll at each corner. Tape the ends of these together to make a three-sided pyramid.

STEP 3 Check your corners to make sure they're securely taped. Attach a bent paperclip to the top point with string (see illustration). Test your Paper Pyramid by hanging weights on the paperclip. Slowly add more weights until you run out or your pyramid collapses.

STEP 4 Review each step in this activity. Compare the strength of six paper sheets to the six paper rolls you made. Share and compare observations about your pyramid with the other research teams.

FORCES 73

Category
Physical Science
Forces

Focus
Transfer of Forces

Objective
To explore how structure affects strength

National Standards
A1, A2, B1, B2, B3, E1, E2, F5, G1, G2

Materials Needed
paperclip
string
straw
newspaper
tape
weights

Safety Concerns
4. Sharp Objects
Remind students to exercise caution when using scissors.

Additional Comments

Cut a newspaper down the middle fold so each full sheet produces two equal half sheets. The sheets must be the same size and only a single sheet thick. Students should roll these single sheets from the narrow end to make their tubes. If they're having difficulty rolling, have them use the straw to start the rolling process.

Overview

Read the overview aloud to your students. The goal is to create an atmosphere of curiosity and inquiry.

WHAT TO DO

Monitor student research teams as they complete each step.

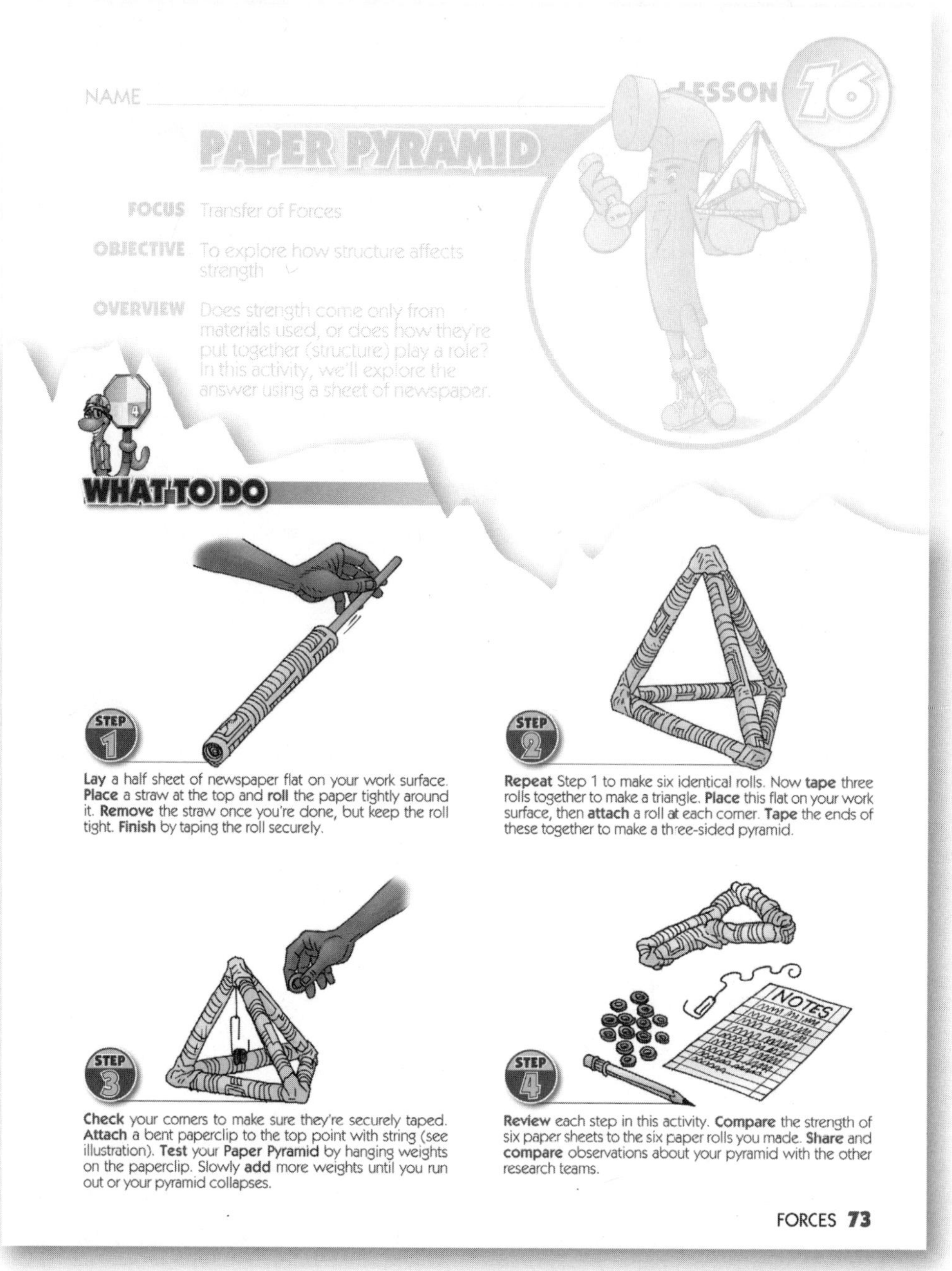

NAME _____

PAPER PYRAMID

LESSON 16

FOCUS Transfer of Forces

OBJECTIVE To explore how structure affects strength

OVERVIEW Does strength come only from materials used, or does how they're put together (structure) play a role? In this activity, we'll explore the answer using a sheet of newspaper.

WHAT TO DO

STEP 1
Lay a half sheet of newspaper flat on your work surface. **Place** a straw at the top and **roll** the paper tightly around it. **Remove** the straw once you're done, but keep the roll tight. **Finish** by taping the roll securely.

STEP 2
Repeat Step 1 to make six identical rolls. Now **tape** three rolls together to make a triangle. **Place** this flat on your work surface, then **attach** a roll at each corner. **Tape** the ends of these together to make a three-sided pyramid.

STEP 3
Check your corners to make sure they're securely taped. **Attach** a bent paperclip to the top point with string (see illustration). **Test** your Paper Pyramid by hanging weights on the paperclip. Slowly **add** more weights until you run out or your pyramid collapses.

STEP 4
Review each step in this activity. **Compare** the strength of six paper sheets to the six paper rolls you made. **Share** and **compare** observations about your pyramid with the other research teams.

FORCES 73

Teacher to Teacher

A structure's shape is an essential part of its support. In a house, for instance, the weight of the roof is transferred by the shape of the rafters to the walls. The force is then transferred but the shape of the walls to the foundation, and from there into the Earth itself. If these shapes are not well designed, the house will collapse.

WHAT HAPPENED?

Most paper is made from **wood fibers**. Trees are strong because the wood fibers are all connected together. When wood is ground up and treated with chemicals to make paper, the fibers are separated and smoothed into sheets. This helps make paper easy to write on, read, and fold. (Imagine doing this with a piece of bark!)

One sheet of newspaper is pretty flimsy. But when you roll it up, you're putting **layers** of separated wood fibers back together again. Then when you attach rolls together, you create a **structure** that has a lot of strength!

As you saw, **force** (weight) is easily **transferred** through the rolls by the design of the structure. Transferring force allows all parts of the structure to share the **load**.

WHAT WE LEARNED

1. Compare a sheet of newspaper with the newspaper roll you made in Step 1. How were they similar? How were they different?

Answers will vary, but should reflect the idea of similar material, but different shape.

2. Compare one newspaper roll with the pyramid you made in Step 2. How were they similar? How were they different?

Answers should be similar to #1 above.

3. When your pyramid finally collapsed, what was its weakest point? How could you have made this stronger?

Answers will vary, but should reflect logical conclusions.

4. What geometric shape is a pyramid made from? Compare the pyramid's ability to support weight to that of a cube. Which is stronger? Why?

a) _triangle_

b) _pyramid_

c) _cube uses squares, pyramid uses triangles, which are stronger_

5. Based on what you've learned, why are diagonal braces used at the corners of fences?

To create a triangle, which provides support and strength.

What Happened

Review the section with students. Emphasize bold-face words that identify key concepts and introduce new vocabulary.

*Most paper is made from **wood fibers**. Trees are strong because the wood fibers are all connected together. When wood is ground up and treated with chemicals to make paper, the fibers are separated and smoothed into sheets. This helps make paper easy to write on, read, and fold. (Imagine doing this with a piece of bark!)*

*One sheet of newspaper is pretty flimsy. But when you roll it up, you're putting **layers** of separated wood fibers back together again. Then when you attach rolls together, you create a **structure** that has a lot of strength!*

*As you saw, **force** (weight) is easily **transferred** through the rolls by the design of the structure. Transferring force allows all parts of the structure to share the **load**.*

What We Learned

Answers will vary. Suggested responses are shown at left.

Lesson 16 • 79

Conclusion

Read this section aloud to the class to summarize the concepts learned in this activity.

Food for Thought

Read the Scripture aloud to the class. Talk about what it means to "wrap yourself in God's love." Discuss how working together makes Christians stronger.

Journal

If time permits, have a general class discussion about notes and drawings various students added to their journal pages. Discuss correct and incorrect predictions, and remind students that this "trial and error" process is part of the scientific process.

CONCLUSION

Materials are usually stronger in layers. Layered materials can help transfer forces from one part of a structure to another one.

FOOD FOR THOUGHT

1 Thessalonians 5:11 The flimsy sheet of newspaper couldn't hold very much on its own. But when you rolled it into a tight cylinder, it gained a lot of strength. Then when you attached it to other cylinders, it became part of a strong, unified structure.

On our own we can't do much. In our weakness, it's easy to fail. Yet when we wrap ourselves in God's love, we gain needed strength. This Scripture reminds us of another important step. We must learn to encourage and support one another in Christian love. When God's children begin to work together, they become part of a strong, unified "structure" that helps spread God's goodness throughout the world.

JOURNAL — My Science Notes

Extended Teaching

1. Extend this activity by building other structures from paper rolls (bridges, log cabins, scaffolds, etc). Test for strength and compare results with the original activity. How were they similar? How were they different?

2. Take a field trip to a construction site. Have students examine the framework of the structure being built. Challenge teams to identify how weight is transferred to the ground. Have them write a paragraph about one thing they learn.

3. Invite the manager of a home improvement center to visit your classroom. Discuss products made from wood scraps and other by-products. What gives them their strength? Have students write a paragraph about one thing they learn.

4. Using the Internet, have teams research how wood is turned into paper. Challenge each team to make a poster depicting at least one thing they learn.

5. Have teams research how archeologists think the Pyramids of Giza were made. What materials were used? Where did they come from? How were they moved into place? Discuss student findings.

80 · Lesson 16

Category

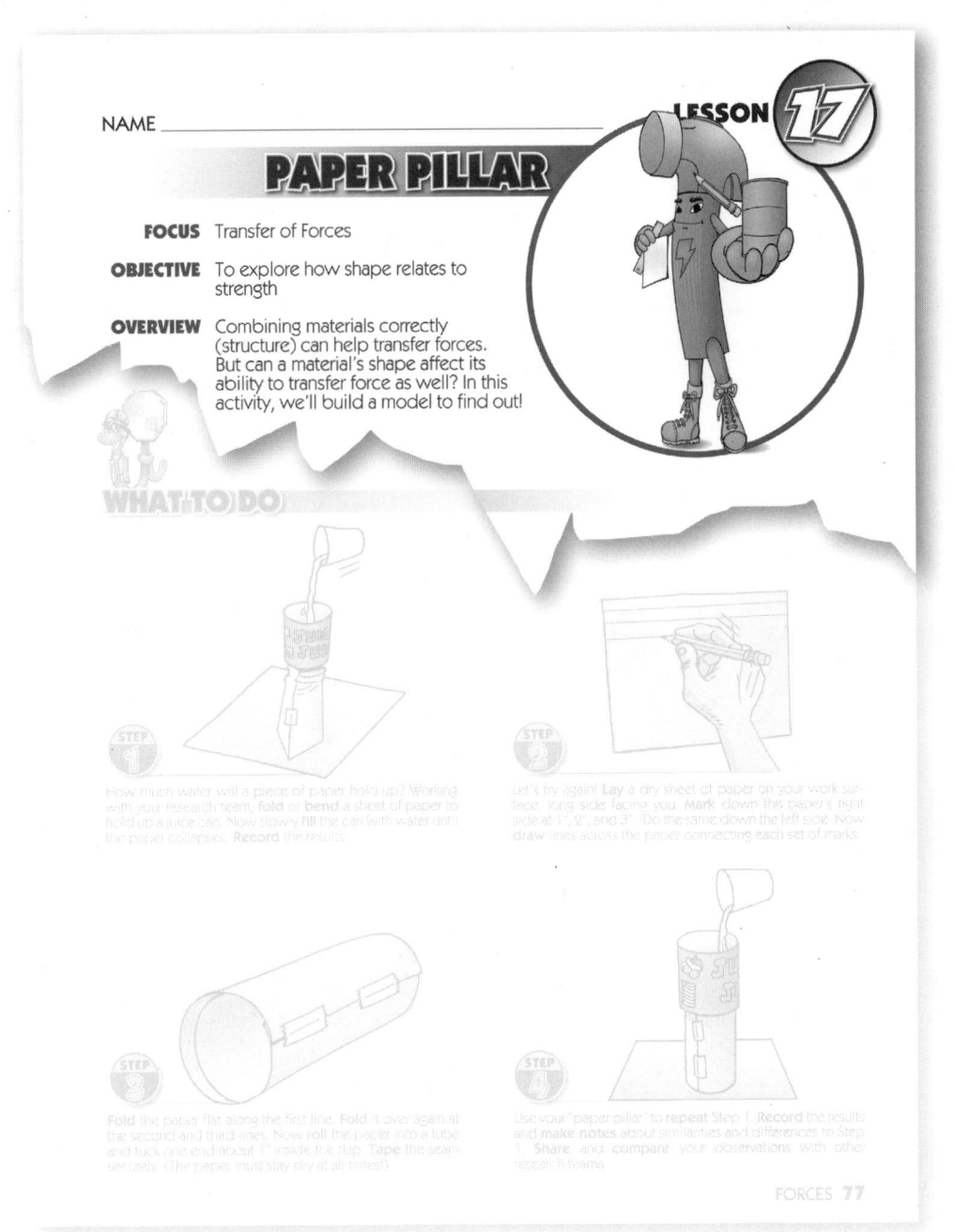

Physical Science
Forces

Focus

Transfer of Forces

Objective

To explore how shape relates to strength

National Standards

A1, A2, B1, B2, E1, E2, F5, G1, G2

Materials Needed

water
paper
juice can
ruler
tape

Safety Concerns

4. Slipping
There is a potential for spills with this activity. Remind students to exercise caution.

Additional Comments

To avoid nicked fingers, make sure the edges of the juice can are smooth. For extra safety, cover the can's edge with tape. Some teams will completely fill the can and may require a second one. Keep extra cans on hand, and use cardboard squares for spacers between cans.

Overview

Read the overview aloud to your students. The goal is to create an atmosphere of curiosity and inquiry.

Lesson 17 · **81**

WHAT TO DO

Monitor student research teams as they complete each step.

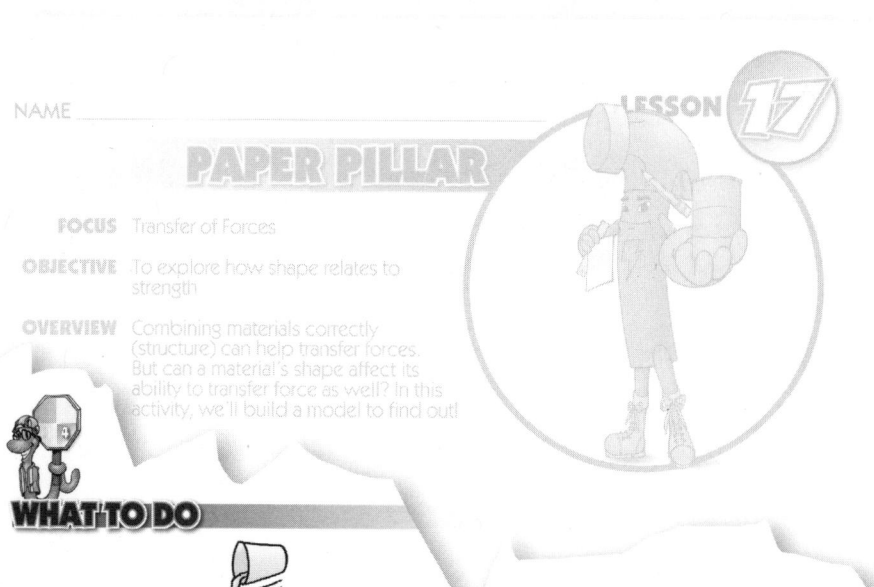

NAME _____

PAPER PILLAR

LESSON 17

FOCUS Transfer of Forces

OBJECTIVE To explore how shape relates to strength

OVERVIEW Combining materials correctly (structure) can help transfer forces. But can a material's shape affect its ability to transfer force as well? In this activity, we'll build a model to find out!

WHAT TO DO

STEP 1
How much water will a piece of paper hold up? Working with your research team, **fold** or **bend** a sheet of paper to hold up a juice can. Now slowly **fill** the can with water until the paper collapses. **Record** the results.

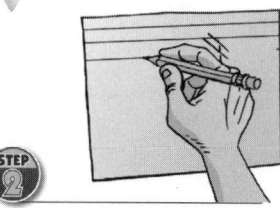

STEP 2
Let's try again! **Lay** a dry sheet of paper on your work surface, long side facing you. **Mark** down the paper's right side at 1", 2", and 3". Do the same down the left side. Now **draw** lines across the paper connecting each set of marks.

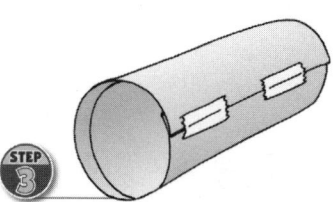

STEP 3
Fold the paper flat along the first line. **Fold** it over again at the second and third lines. Now **roll** the paper into a tube and tuck one end about 1" inside the flap. **Tape** the seam securely. (The paper must stay dry at all times!)

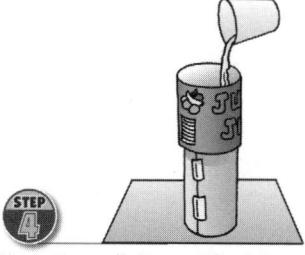

STEP 4
Use your "paper pillar" to **repeat** Step 1. **Record** the results and **make notes** about similarities and differences to Step 1. **Share** and **compare** your observations with other research teams.

FORCES **77**

Teacher to Teacher

A force in a given direction (with magnitude) is called a vector. The interaction of vectors determines what happens. When you're sitting in a chair, vector (gravity) pulls you straight down. There are also four upward vectors (the chair legs). If the upward vectors are not as strong as the downward vector, the chair collapses!

---

82 · Lesson 17

WHAT HAPPENED?

Generally the more **material** you use the stronger the **structure**. But there's a problem! More material creates greater **weight** and also drives up costs. Not enough material, however, makes for a weak and possibly unsafe structure. That's why engineers try to design structures with materials and **shapes** that offer great strength, but are also lighter and less expensive.

That was the focus of this activity. Although it used the same amount of material, the reinforced tube you created was a much stronger shape. This different shape allowed the paper's **molecules** to work together in a more efficient fashion. More efficient shapes help **transfer** the **forces**. In this case, the weight of the water was transferred to your work surface, which transferred the weight to the floor, which transferred the weight to the ground.

WHAT WE LEARNED

1 Describe what happened in Step 1. How much water (weight) did your first structure hold?

a) the paper collasped

b) answers will vary, but probably very little

2 What was the purpose of the folds in Step 2? What effect did the folds have on the paper's molecules?

a) to reinforce the tube

b) made the tube stronger

78 FORCES

3 Why did the seams have to be taped securely? What might have happened if the tape's adhesive was weak? Why?

a) to hold the tube together

b) the tube might have fallen apart

c) it couldn't hold its shape

4 Describe a building component that's similar to the Paper Pillar you created. What does this component support? Why is this support important?

a) posts, columns, walls, etc.

b) answers will vary

c) answers will vary

5 Based on what you've learned, how does shape help transfer force? Give at least three common examples of a column or pillar shape transferring force.

a) certain shapes support weight better

b) the post on a porch, a column inside a building, etc.

FORCES 79

What Happened

Review the section with students. Emphasize bold-face words that identify key concepts and introduce new vocabulary.

*Generally the more **material** you use the stronger the **structure**. But there's a problem! More material creates greater **weight** and also drives up costs. Not enough material, however, makes for a weak and possibly unsafe structure. That's why engineers try to design structures with materials and **shapes** that offer great strength, but are also lighter and less expensive.*

*That was the focus of this activity. Although it used the same amount of material, the reinforced tube you created was a much stronger shape. This different shape allowed the paper's **molecules** to work together in a more efficient fashion. More efficient shapes help **transfer** the **forces**. In this case, the weight of the water was transferred to your work surface, which transferred the weight to the floor, which transferred the weight to the ground.*

What We Learned

Answers will vary. Suggested responses are shown at left.

Lesson 17 · 83

Conclusion

Read this section aloud to the class to summarize the concepts learned in this activity.

Food for Thought

Read the Scripture aloud to the class. Talk about a time something seemed impossible. Discuss how amazing things can happen in our lives when we're in a right relationship with God.

Journal

If time permits, have a general class discussion about notes and drawings various students added to their journal pages. Discuss correct and incorrect predictions, and remind students that this "trial and error" process is part of the scientific process.

CONCLUSION

The shape of a material can affect its strength, helping it to more efficiently transfer force.

FOOD FOR THOUGHT

Psalms 18:16-18 It didn't seem like a simple sheet of paper could hold up even an empty can, let alone the weight of all that water. But once everything was in the right relationship, it worked! The paper was able to hold up an amazing amount of water.

This Scripture reminds us that God often accomplishes seemingly impossible tasks. When we're drowning in troubles, when we're surrounded by those who would do us harm, when we're at our very weakest — God steps in and lifts us up in his loving arms. Always remember, when you're in a right relationship with God, amazing things can happen!

JOURNAL — My Science Notes

80 FORCES

Extended Teaching

1. Repeat this activity using smaller or larger sheets of paper. Compare the results with the original activity. How were they similar? How were they different?

2. Using the Internet, have students research construction methods used in building skyscrapers. How are the forces of weight transmitted into the Earth? Challenge each team to make a poster depicting what they find.

3. Have students research construction methods used to help prevent earthquake damage. Challenge each team to contribute drawings and descriptions for a bulletin board on this topic.

4. Arrange a field trip to a multi-story building. Have an architect describe the structure of the building and how it works. Have students write a paragraph about one thing they learn.

5. Watch a video of buildings being demolished by timed explosions that weaken structural supports. Find out how the "imploding" process works. Have students write a paragraph about one thing they learn.

84 · Lesson 17

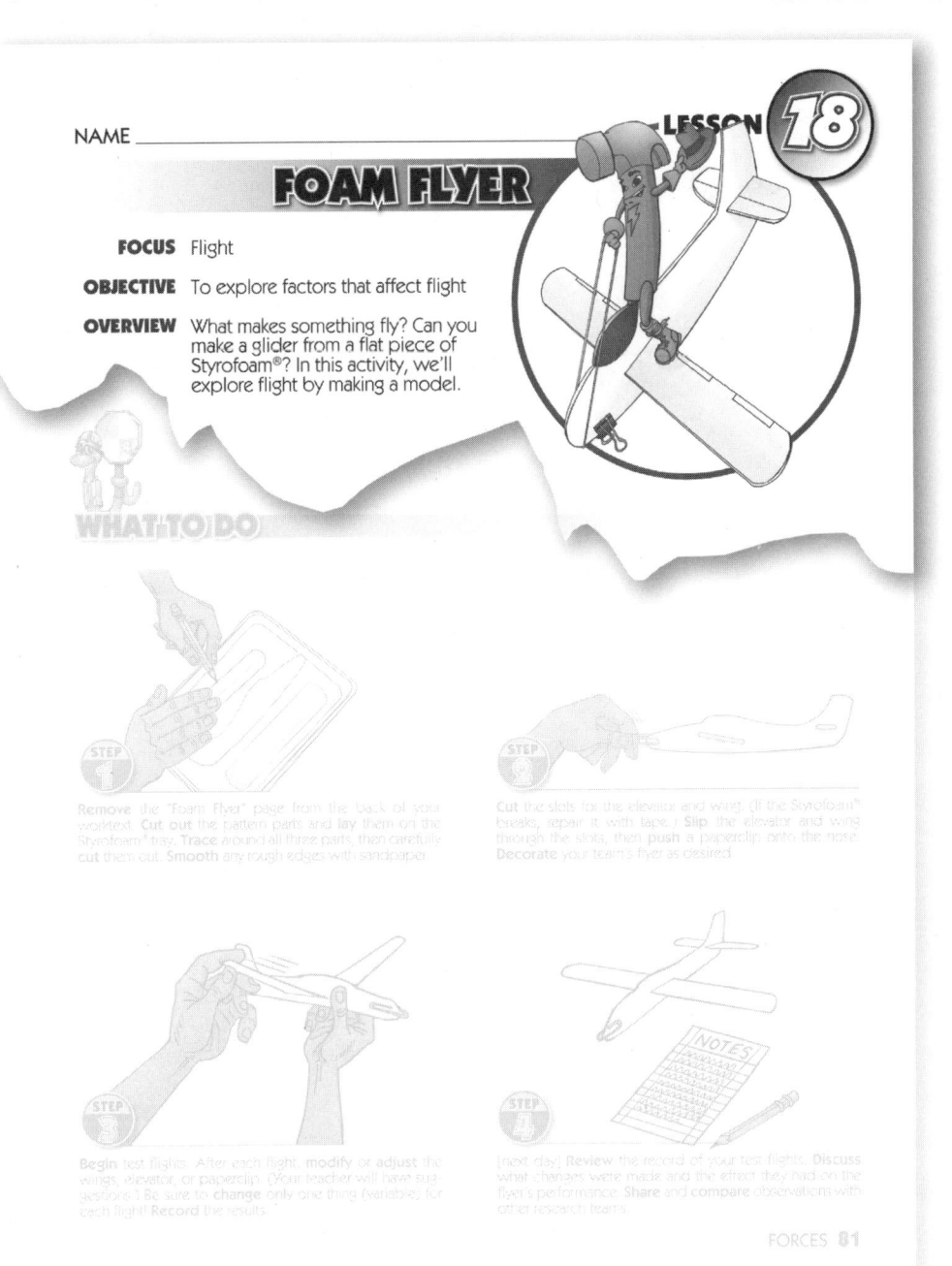

NAME _____

FOAM FLYER

LESSON 18

FOCUS Flight

OBJECTIVE To explore factors that affect flight

OVERVIEW What makes something fly? Can you make a glider from a flat piece of Styrofoam®? In this activity, we'll explore flight by making a model.

WHAT TO DO

STEP 1 Remove the "Foam Flyer" page from the back of your worktext. Cut out the pattern parts and lay them on the Styrofoam® tray. Trace around all three parts, then carefully cut them out. Smooth any rough edges with sandpaper.

STEP 2 Cut the slots for the elevator and wing. (If the Styrofoam® breaks, repair it with tape.) Slip the elevator and wing through the slots, then push a paperclip onto the nose. Decorate your team's flyer as desired.

STEP 3 Begin test flights. After each flight, modify or adjust the wings, elevator, or paperclip. (Your teacher will have suggestions.) Be sure to change only one thing (variable) for each flight. Record the results.

STEP 4 [next day] Review the record of your test flights. Discuss what changes were made and the effect they had on the flyer's performance. Share and compare observations with other research teams.

FORCES 81

Category
Physical Science
Forces

Focus
Flight

Objective
To explore factors that affect flight

National Standards
A1, A2, B1, B2, E1, E2, F5, G1, G2

Materials Needed
Foam Flyer worksheet *(Student Worktext, p. 165)*
Styrofoam® tray
sandpaper
paperclip
scissors
tape

Safety Concerns
4. Sharp Objects
Remind students to be exercise caution when using the scissors.

Additional Comments

Ordinary Styrofoam® meat trays work well for this activity. (Local supermarkets with meat departments often are willing to donate these.) Make sure the trays are disinfected before use. Students will need to experiment with the location of the paperclip. Don't expect perfect flights right off the bat.

Overview

Read the overview aloud to your students. The goal is to create an atmosphere of curiosity and inquiry.

Lesson 18 · **85**

WHAT TO DO

Monitor student research teams as they complete each step.

LESSON 18 — FOAM FLYER

FOCUS Flight

OBJECTIVE To explore factors that affect flight

OVERVIEW What makes something fly? Can you make a glider from a flat piece of Styrofoam®? In this activity, we'll explore flight by making a model.

WHAT TO DO

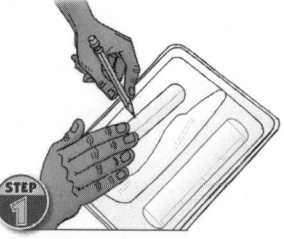

STEP 1 — **Remove** the "Foam Flyer" page from the back of your worktext. **Cut out** the pattern parts and **lay** them on the Styrofoam® tray. **Trace** around all three parts, then carefully **cut** them out. **Smooth** any rough edges with sandpaper.

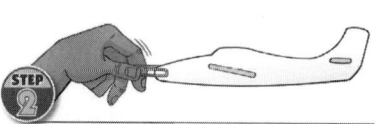

STEP 2 — **Cut** the slots for the elevator and wing. (If the Styrofoam® breaks, repair it with tape.) **Slip** the elevator and wing through the slots, then **push** a paperclip onto the nose. **Decorate** your team's flyer as desired.

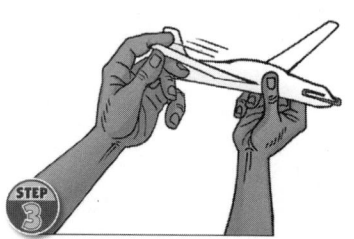

STEP 3 — **Begin** test flights. After each flight, **modify** or **adjust** the wings, elevator, or paperclip. (Your teacher will have suggestions.) Be sure to **change** only one thing (variable) for each flight! **Record** the results.

STEP 4 — [next day] **Review** the record of your test flights. **Discuss** what changes were made and the effect they had on the flyer's performance. **Share** and **compare** observations with other research teams.

FORCES **81**

Teacher to Teacher

Since they don't have motors, gliders need large wing surfaces to take advantage of Bernoulli's Principle. A bigger wing surface means greater lift, but a loss of maneuverability. By contrast, fighter jets have smaller wings which allow them to change directions rapidly, but they must compensate for the loss of lift with huge engines.

WHAT HAPPENED?

Flight is possible because fast-moving air has lower **air pressure**. This is called the **Bernoulli Principle** (named after the man who discovered this). Because of a wing's **shape** (or angle), air moves faster over the top than it does under the bottom, creating **low air pressure** on top of the wing. This causes the **higher air pressure** under the wing to **push** up. The result is known as **lift**.

So why don't sitting planes just rise into the sky? Because air isn't moving fast enough to create the large air pressure differences needed for lift. Some kind of **force** must be applied. Usually the force is provided by a motor with a propeller or by a jet engine. This makes the plane move faster until air **speeds** are high enough to provide lift. In this activity, you provided the force by flinging your **Foam Flyer** toward the sky!

WHAT WE LEARNED

1. Why was it important to smooth the rough edges in Step 1? What effect could rough edges have on air flow?

a) smoother surface = better air flow

b) more friction leading to less lift

2. What characteristic of a wing creates lift on an airplane? Explain how this works.

a) its shape or angle

b) air moves faster over the top, creating lower air pressure and lift

3. Describe the test flights in Step 3. What variables did you change? What effect did these changes have?

Answers will vary, but should reflect logical conclusions.

4. What is the name of the effect that fast-moving air has on air pressure? How is this important for flight?

a) Bernoulli Principle

b) it creates lift, an essential component of flight for fixed wing aircraft

5. Based on what you've learned, how are hawks, eagles, seagulls, and similar birds able to fly for long periods of time without flapping their wings? Explain your answer.

a) the shape of their wings provide lift

b) wind flowing over the curved wing creates lift

What Happened

Review the section with students. Emphasize bold-face words that identify key concepts and introduce new vocabulary.

*Flight is possible because fast-moving air has lower **air pressure**. This is called the **Bernoulli Principle** (named after the man who discovered this). Because of a wing's **shape** (or angle), air moves faster over the top than it does under the bottom, creating **low air pressure** on top of the wing. This causes the **higher air pressure** under the wing to **push** up. The result is known as **lift**.*

*So why don't sitting planes just rise into the sky? Because air isn't moving fast enough to create the large air pressure differences needed for lift. Some kind of **force** must be applied. Usually the force is provided by a motor with a propeller or by a jet engine. This makes the plane move faster until air **speeds** are high enough to provide lift. In this activity, you provided the force by flinging your Foam Flyer toward the sky!*

What We Learned

Answers will vary. Suggested responses are shown at left.

Conclusion

Read this section aloud to the class to summarize the concepts learned in this activity.

Food for Thought

Read the Scripture aloud to the class. Talk about the power of Jesus' love. Discuss ways we can reach out to others and share his love.

Journal

If time permits, have a general class discussion about notes and drawings various students added to their journal pages. Discuss correct and incorrect predictions, and remind students that this "trial and error" process is part of the scientific process.

CONCLUSION

Fast-moving air creates lower air pressure. This is called the Bernoulli Principle. The curved surface of a wing uses this principle to create lift, which leads to flight.

FOOD FOR THOUGHT

2 Corinthians 5:17 Who would have thought you could turn a plain styrofoam® tray into something that could fly? With a little time and effort, you were able to create something brand-new!

In this Scripture, Paul reminds us that God can make us brand-new. The bad things in our past are forgiven, and we begin a clean, new life. Through the power of Jesus' love, our hearts are changed, and we begin to reach out to others in care and compassion. Remember that God can take anyone, no matter how plain or ordinary, and turn them into something special!

JOURNAL — My Science Notes

84 FORCES

Extended Teaching

1. Repeat this activity, allowing students to modify their "flyer" any way they think will improve distance or time aloft. Compare the results to the original activity. How were they similar? How were they different?

2. Discuss the four forces of flight — lift, drag, thrust, weight (see http://www.fi.edu/flights/own2/forces.html). Challenge each team to create a flight poster with an outline of an airplane and the forces affecting it.

3. Invite a pilot to visit your classroom. Have him/her talk about what makes an airplane fly, and why he/she likes flying. Have students write a paragraph about one thing they learn.

4. Take a field trip to an aircraft maintenance hanger. Ask the mechanics to describe the parts of various planes and how they work together to achieve flight. Have students write a paragraph about one thing they learn.

5. Find out if students or their parents have a flight simulator game. Ask him/her to demonstrate the game for the class. Have students write a paragraph about one thing they learn about the four forces of flight.

88 · Lesson 18

NAME _____

OCEAN OF AIR

LESSON 19

FOCUS Atmospheric Pressure

OBJECTIVE To explore the force of air pressure

OVERVIEW Everyone knows we're surrounded by an "ocean" of air. You may think of air as weightless. But is it? In this activity, we'll explore this idea by trying to break a toothpick with air!

WHAT TO DO

STEP 1 Lay a flat toothpick on your work surface so that about a third of it is sticking out over the edge. Make sure the area is clear, then try to break the toothpick by flipping the end with your index finger. Record the results.

STEP 2 Lay the toothpick back on your work surface and cover it with six sheets of newspaper. Make sure the papers are very flat and even with the edge. Now push down quickly, but gently, on the end of the toothpick. Record the results.

STEP 3 Repeat Step 2, but instead of pushing gently, flip the end with your index finger as in Step 1. Hit the end hard! Record the results.

STEP 4 Review each step in this activity. Make notes about what you discovered. Predict how air pressure may have played a role in the results of Step 3. Share and compare observations with your research team.

EARTH 87

Category
Earth Science

Focus
Atmospheric Pressure

Objective
To explore the force of air pressure

National Standards
A1, A2, B1, B2, B3, D1, G1, G2

Materials Needed
toothpick
newspaper - 6 sheets

Safety Concerns
4. Sharp Objects
Remind students to exercise caution with toothpicks.

Additional Comments

Some students can be a bit over-enthusiastic with this activity. For safety reasons, monitor students closely for any signs of horseplay.

Overview

Read the overview aloud to your students. The goal is to create an atmosphere of curiosity and inquiry.

WHAT TO DO

Monitor student research teams as they complete each step.

NAME _____

OCEAN OF AIR

FOCUS Atmospheric Pressure

OBJECTIVE To explore the force of air pressure

OVERVIEW Everyone knows we're surrounded by an "ocean" of air. You may think of air as weightless. But is it? In this activity, we'll explore this idea by trying to break a toothpick with air!

WHAT TO DO

STEP 1
Lay a flat toothpick on your work surface so that about a third of it is sticking out over the edge. Make sure the area is clear, then try to break the toothpick by flipping the end with your index finger. **Record** the results.

STEP 2
Lay the toothpick back on your work surface and cover it with six sheets of newspaper. Make sure the papers are very flat and even with the edge. Now **push** down quickly, but gently, on the end of the toothpick. **Record** the results.

STEP 3
Repeat Step 2, but instead of pushing gently, **flip** the end with your index finger as in Step 1. **Hit** the end hard! **Record** the results.

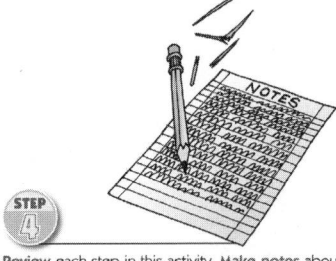

STEP 4
Review each step in this activity. **Make** notes about what you discovered. **Predict** how air pressure may have played a role in the results of Step 3. **Share** and **compare** observations with your research team.

EARTH 87

Teacher to Teacher

Although we're surrounded every moment with an "ocean" of air, we don't feel it since our body is pushing back with equal force. The pressure of air is usually measured in pounds per square inch (psi). The scientific formula is P=F/A (pressure equals force divided by the area the force is pushing on).

90 · Lesson 19

WHAT HAPPENED?

In Step 1, the toothpick shot off the table. In Step 2, the toothpick raised the papers and fell off the table. But in Step 3, the toothpick broke! What happened? Obviously some kind of **force** was holding the toothpick back.

The force pushing down was **air pressure**. The large **surface area** of the newspaper **transferred** this pressure to surface of the toothpick. (Step 2 proved it wasn't just the newspaper's **weight**.) When you **pushed** the toothpick slowly, the **air molecules** had time to shift their weight aside. But when you moved rapidly, the toothpick pushed against the full pressure of the air. The resulting **resistance** (force) of the air broke the toothpick.

WHAT WE LEARNED

1. In Step 1, why didn't the toothpick break? How much surface area was the air pressure pushing on?

a) there was no force holding it down

b) only the surface of the toothpick

2. In Step 2, why didn't the toothpick break? How was the speed you pushed on the toothpick a factor?

The newspaper increased surface area, but the slow push gave the air molecules time to move aside.

3. In Step 3, why did the toothpick break? How much surface area was the air pressure pushing on?

a) fast movement and large force holding toothpick down

b) the entire surface area of the newspaper

4. Explain how force was transferred in this activity.

The large surface area of the newpaper transferred the force of the air pressure to the toothpick's surface.

5. Based on what you've learned, variations in what characteristic of air might affect weather? Why?

a) moisture or humidity

b) moist air is heavier, harder to move, harder to stop

What Happened

Review the section with students. Emphasize bold-face words that identify key concepts and introduce new vocabulary.

In Step 1, the toothpick shot off the table. In Step 2, the toothpick raised the papers and fell off the table. But in Step 3, the toothpick broke! What happened? Obviously some kind of **force** *was holding the toothpick back.*

The force pushing down was **air pressure**. *The large* **surface area** *of the newspaper* **transferred** *this pressure to the surface of the toothpick. (Step 2 proved it wasn't just the newspaper's* **weight**.*) When you* **pushed** *the toothpick slowly, the* **air molecules** *had time to shift their weight aside. But when you moved rapidly, the toothpick pushed against the full pressure of the air. The resulting* **resistance** *(force) of the air broke the toothpick.*

What We Learned

Answers will vary. Suggested responses are shown at left.

Conclusion

Read this section aloud to the class to summarize the concepts learned in this activity.

Food for Thought

Read the Scripture aloud to the class. Talk about how trust increases as a relationship deepens. Discuss specific ways to a deeper relationship with God.

Journal

If time permits, have a general class discussion about notes and drawings various students added to their journal pages. Discuss correct and incorrect predictions, and remind students that this "trial and error" process is part of the scientific process.

CONCLUSION

We're surrounded by an ocean of air. Its pressure is constantly pushing on us — but we don't notice because our bodies are pushing back with equal force.

FOOD FOR THOUGHT

James 1:5-8 At first, you may have doubted that air could break a toothpick. Certainly at first glance, it seemed impossible! But you trusted your teacher, followed the instructions, and SNAP! Mission accomplished.

Many times in life we have to act based on our faith. We have to trust God, follow his instructions, and know that the results are in his hands. This Scripture reminds us that God is always ready to help us, ready to lead in the plan of our lives. As our relationship with God deepens, we will learn to trust him more and more, no matter how impossible the situation seems.

JOURNAL My Science Notes

Extended Teaching

1. As a demonstration, repeat this activity using a wooden ruler or painter's stir stick. Students are usually amazed when it breaks! Have them compare your demonstration with the original activity, discussing similarities and differences.

2. Have teams research air pressure at high altitudes and compare it to air pressure at sea level. Challenge each team to make a poster showing what they learn.

3. Take a field trip to a local television station. Ask a meteorologist to explain how high and low pressure areas affect the weather. Have students write a paragraph about one thing they learn.

4. Have a pilot or a flight attendant visit your classroom. Ask him/her to discuss pressurized cabins, how they work, and related safety procedures. Have students write a paragraph about one thing they learn.

5. Using the Internet, have teams research altitude sickness. Find out what causes it and ways to prevent it. Have each team give a report to the class on what they find.

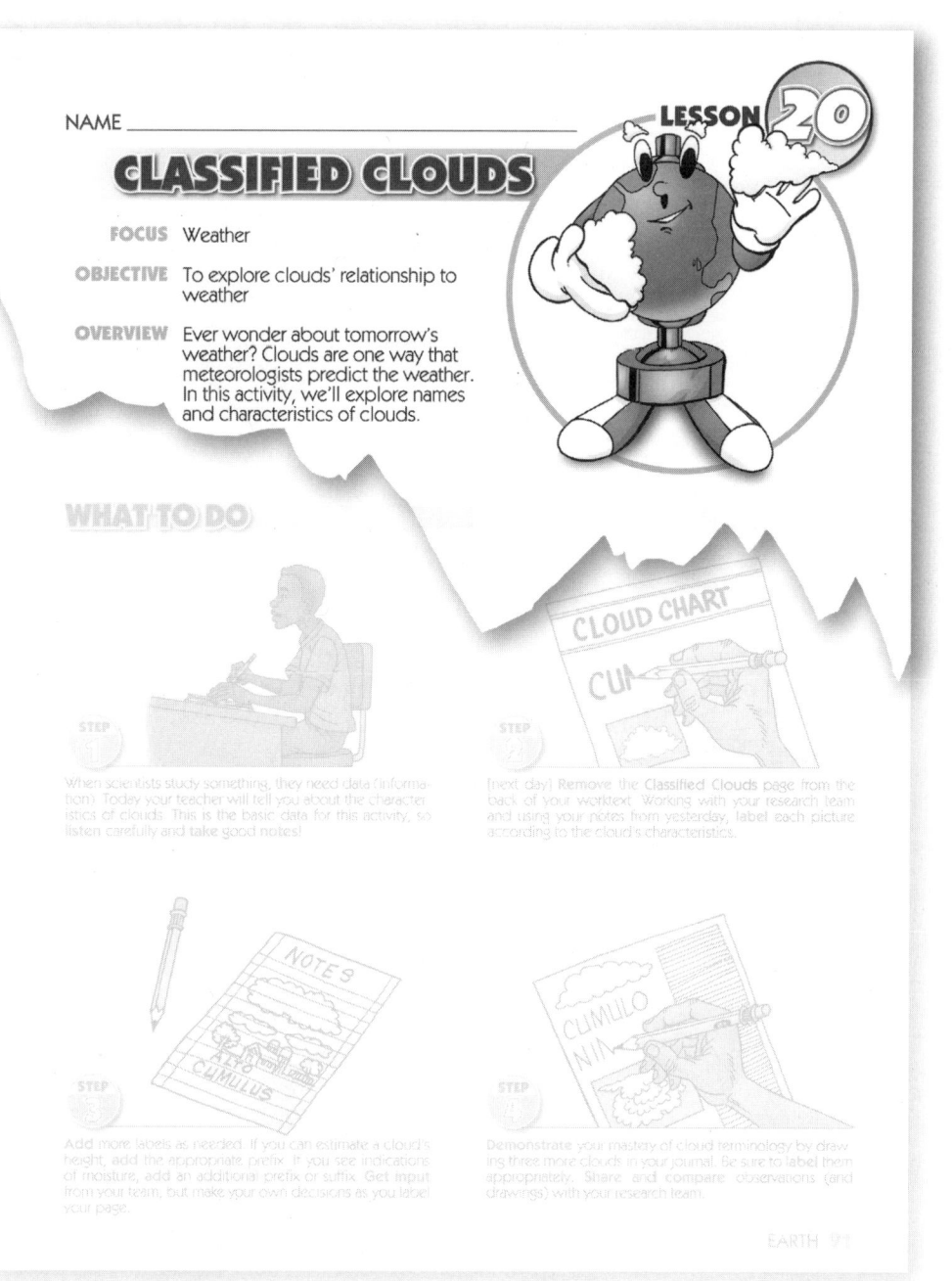

Category
Earth Science

Focus

Weather

Objective

To explore clouds' relationship to weather

National Standards

A1, A2, B1, D1, G1, G2

Materials Needed

Classified Cloud Worksheet *(student worktext, p. 167)*

Safety Concerns

none

Additional Comments

This activity offers a basic overview of cloud formations, but meteorologists often use much more complex terminology. Don't be surprised if you run across a few terms in your research that don't translate well.

Overview

Read the overview aloud to your students. The goal is to create an atmosphere of curiosity and inquiry.

Lesson 20 · 93

WHAT TO DO

Monitor student research teams as they complete each step.

Step 1

This is a mini-lecture about clouds. Feel free to supplement the following information with overheads of cloud pictures clipped from magazines or downloaded off the Internet. The "Classified Clouds" worksheet can also be made into an overhead.

Clouds can be classified in many ways. The most common classifications are based on their characteristic shapes, and by their height above the Earth. Cirrus clouds appear very thin and wispy. Stratus clouds are in layers, somewhat like a cake. Cumulus clouds are lumpy, puffy, or fluffy clouds. Nimbus is the term used for clouds causing precipitation. Regarding heights, a "cirro-" prefix indicates very high clouds (over 18,000 feet). An "alto-" prefix indicates medium height clouds (6,000 to 18,000 feet). No prefix indicates low level clouds (under 6,000 feet). For example, cirrostratus are very high clouds that are in layers; altocumulus are lumpy "cotton-ball" clouds of medium height.

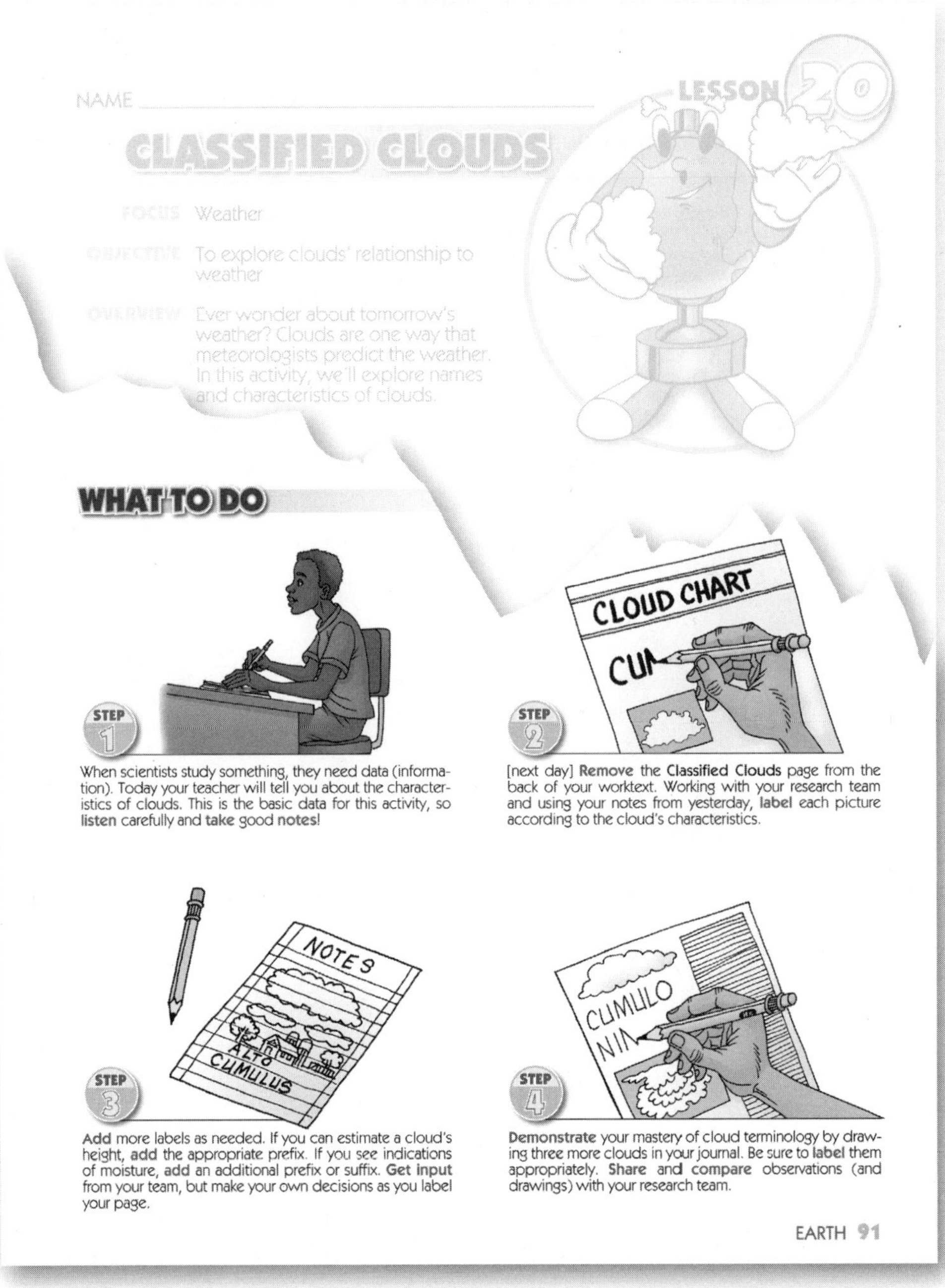

Teacher to Teacher

Clouds move moisture and heat energy around the atmosphere. Nobody disagrees that Earth's climate is warming — the disagreement is over the current *rate* of global warming. Depending on the group of scientists and the data entered, computer models can vary widely, making this complex issue even more difficult!

WHAT HAPPENED?

Clouds are a visible form of water in the air. Although we usually think of clouds in a **gaseous** (water vapor) state, they can also be a **liquid** (suspended rain) or even a **solid** (tiny ice crystals). Most weather involves clouds and the various forms of moisture they carry.

The **Sun** provides the **energy** that creates **weather**. The amount of **solar energy** varies depending on the location and season. In northern **climates** or winter months, the low **heat energy** can cause moisture in the air to **freeze**, creating ice, snow, and sleet. In southern climates or summer months, high heat energy can cause moisture to **evaporate**.

These changes in **temperature** and moisture mix the **atmosphere's** energy, helping it **circulate** around the planet.

WHAT WE LEARNED

1) What three specific terms describe clouds based on their height? What does each term mean?

cirro = very high, over 18,000 feet
alto = medium; no prefix = below 6,000 feet

2) Which of the three "states of matter" apply to clouds? Give examples.

gaseous, water vapor; liquid, suspended rain; solid, tiny ice crystals

3) Compare stratonimbus and cumlonimbus clouds. How are they similar? How are they different?

a) similar: both produce precipitation

b) different: stratonimubus = layered; cumulonimbus = lumpy

4) Based on what you've learned, describe the characteristics of an "altostratusnimbus" cloud.

medium height, layered, produces precipitation

5) If changes in temperature and moisture didn't circulate around the Earth, what would countries around the equator be like? What would far northern countries be like?

a) extremely hot, high level of evaporation

b) extremely cold, heavy snow and ice

What Happened

Review the section with students. Emphasize bold-face words that identify key concepts and introduce new vocabulary.

*Clouds are a visible form of water in the air. Although we usually think of clouds in a **gaseous** (water vapor) state, they can also be a **liquid** (suspended rain) or even a **solid** (tiny ice crystals). Most weather involves clouds and the various forms of moisture they carry.*

*The **Sun** provides the **energy** that creates **weather**. The amount of **solar energy** varies depending on the location and season. In northern **climates** or winter months, the low **heat energy** can cause moisture in the air to **freeze**, creating ice, snow, and sleet. In southern climates or summer months, high heat energy can cause moisture to **evaporate**.*

*These changes in **temperature** and moisture mix the **atmosphere's** energy, helping it **circulate** around the planet.*

What We Learned

Answers will vary. Suggested responses are shown at left.

Conclusion

Read this section aloud to the class to summarize the concepts learned in this activity.

Food for Thought

Read the Scripture aloud to the class. Talk about the importance of trusting God to lead in our lives. Discuss how God can keep us safe from the "storms of life."

Journal

If time permits, have a general class discussion about notes and drawings various students added to their journal pages. Discuss correct and incorrect predictions, and remind students that this "trial and error" process is part of the scientific process.

CONCLUSION

The sun provides the energy that produces weather. Weather changes are usually indicated by clouds. Weather changes help distribute moisture and atmospheric energy around the Earth.

FOOD FOR THOUGHT

Psalm 104:5-13 Clouds are wonderful indicators of the weather to come. This can be helpful when we're making plans for an afternoon picnic or a day at the lake. But weather forecasting isn't an exact science. Sometimes weather doesn't turn out to be what we'd hoped for!

When making plans for your life, wouldn't you prefer something more reliable than a weather forecast? This Scripture reminds us that God is the master planner! When the storms of life rage around you, God can keep you safe from harm. Why not let God take control of your life?

JOURNAL — My Science Notes

Extended Teaching

1. Using the Internet, have teams research historic tornadoes, hurricanes, and blizzards. Challenge each team to make a poster depicting one of these major disasters.

2. Invite a pilot to visit your classroom. Have him/her talk about what clouds look like from above, and how knowing cloud types helps them avoid problems. Have students write a paragraph about one thing they learn.

3. Take a field trip to a local television station. Ask the meteorologist how cloud information helps him/her to predict the weather. Have students write a paragraph about one thing they learn.

4. Using what they've learned, challenge teams to predict each day's weather. Have them keep track of how accurate their forecasts were. Use graph paper to compare actual and predicted temperatures.

5. Keep a classroom weather log for several weeks. Challenge teams to identify the cloud types that are over your school each day.

MARVELOUS MAPPING

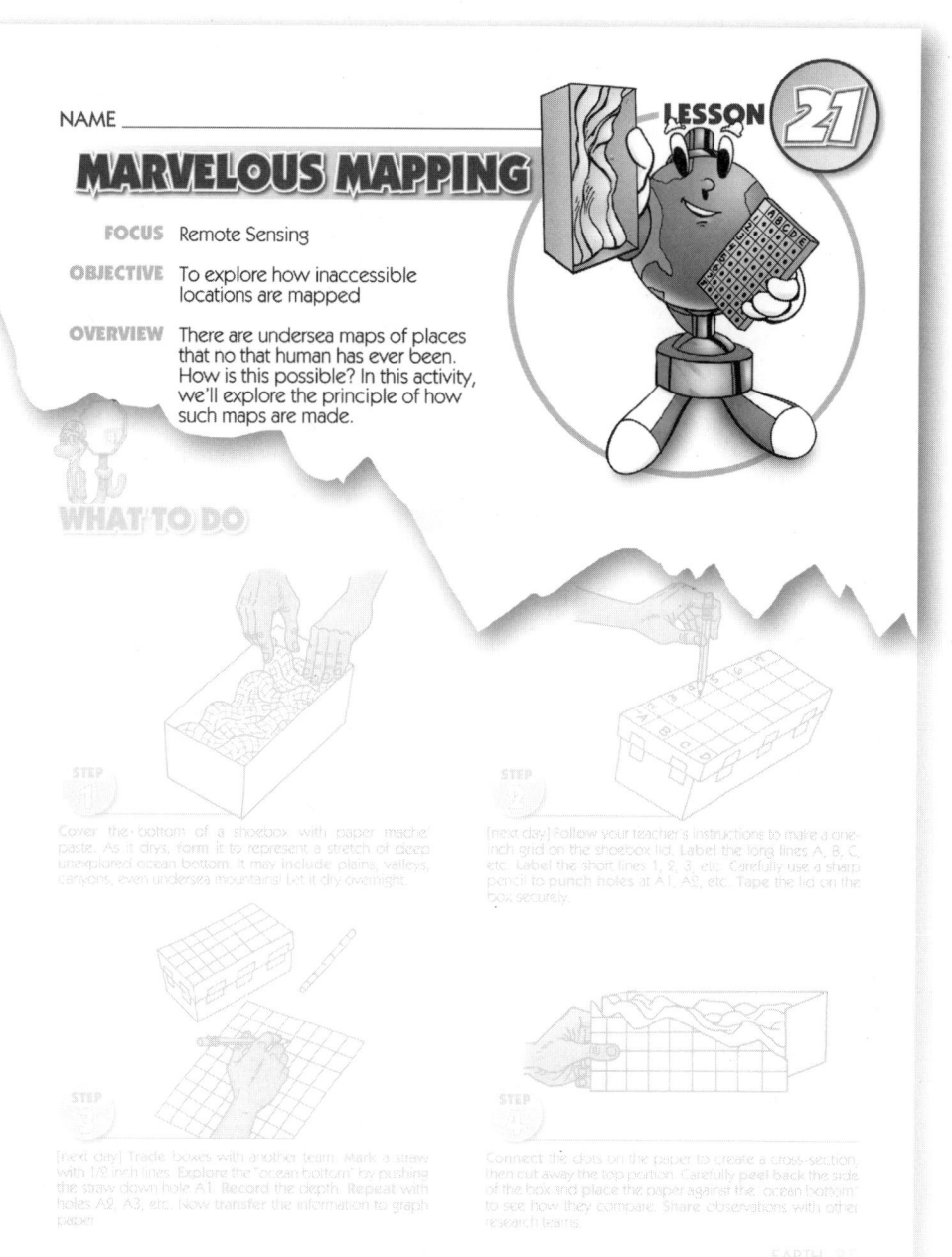

NAME _____

LESSON 21

FOCUS Remote Sensing

OBJECTIVE To explore how inaccessible locations are mapped

OVERVIEW There are undersea maps of places that no human has ever been. How is this possible? In this activity, we'll explore the principle of how such maps are made.

WHAT TO DO

STEP 1
Cover the bottom of a shoebox with paper mache paste. As it dries, form it to represent a stretch of deep unexplored ocean bottom. It may include plains, valleys, canyons, even undersea mountains. Let it dry overnight.

STEP 2
[next day] Follow your teacher's instructions to make a one-inch grid on the shoebox lid. Label the long lines A, B, C, etc. Label the short lines 1, 2, 3, etc. Carefully use a sharp pencil to punch holes at A1, A2, etc. Tape the lid on the box securely.

STEP 3
[next day] Trade boxes with another team. Mark a straw with 1/2 inch lines. Explore the "ocean bottom" by pushing the straw down hole A1. Record the depth. Repeat with holes A2, A3, etc. Now transfer the information to graph paper.

STEP 4
Connect the dots on the paper to create a cross-section, then cut away the top portion. Carefully peel back the side of the box and place the paper against the "ocean bottom" to see how they compare. Share observations with other research teams.

EARTH

Category
Earth Science

Focus
Remote Sensing

Objective
To explore how in-accessible locations are mapped

National Standards
A1, A2, B1, B3, D1, G1, G2

Materials Needed
straw
shoe box with lid
paper machè paste
ruler
permanent marker
tape
graph paper

Safety Concerns
4. Sharp Objects
Remind students to use caution when they punch holes with the pencil.

Additional Comments

It's easy to bend the lid while poking holes, so encourage students to be gentle. One option is to take a cordless drill to class and drill holes for teams after they mark the lids. Have them use a permanent marker on the straws so the marks don't rub off. Buy paper mache' paste in bulk at a craft store, or students can make their own using flour and water.

Overview

Read the overview aloud to your students. The goal is to create an atmosphere of curiosity and inquiry.

Lesson 21 · 97

WHAT TO DO

Monitor student research teams as they complete each step.

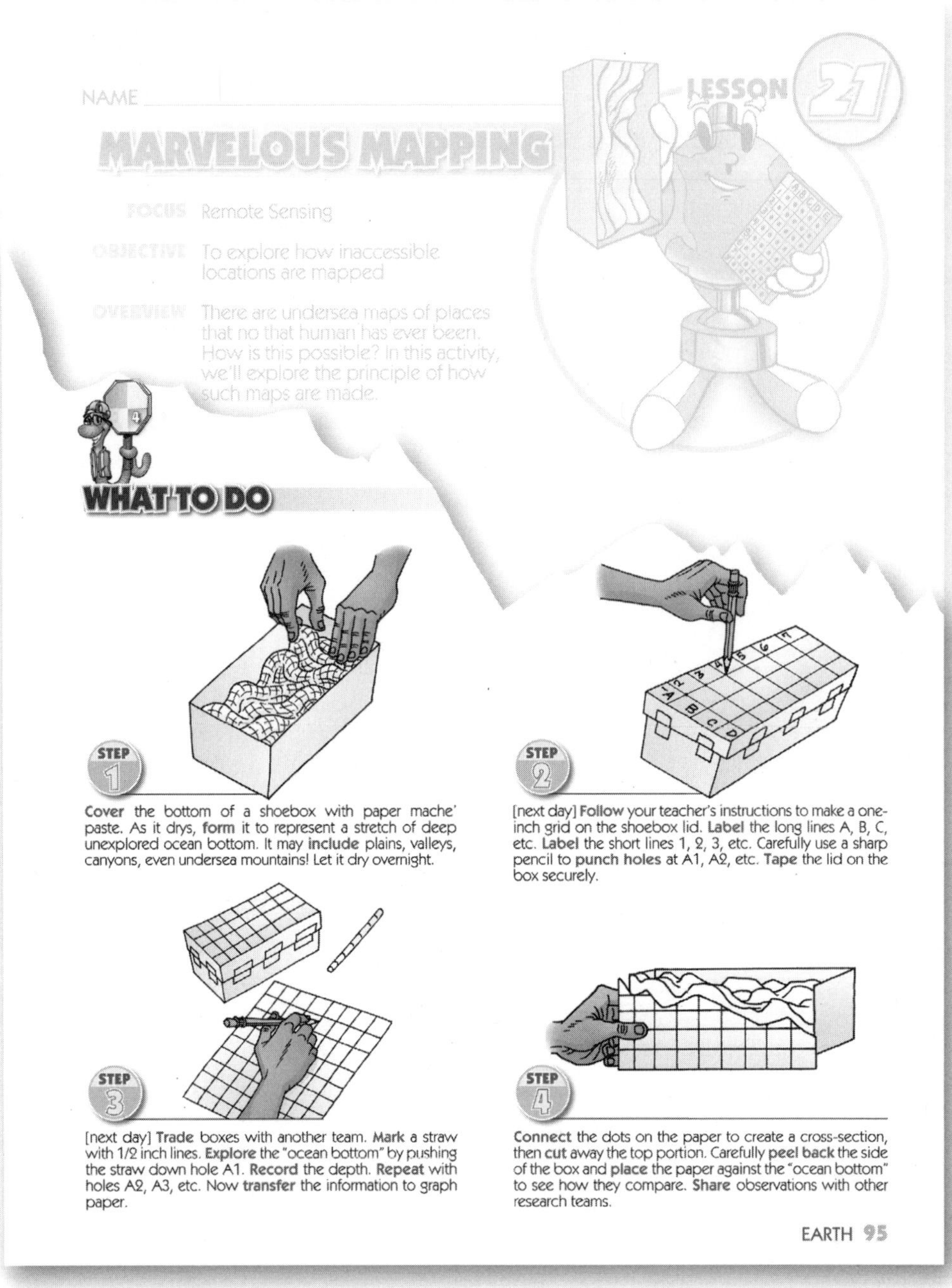

NAME _____

MARVELOUS MAPPING

LESSON 21

FOCUS Remote Sensing

OBJECTIVE To explore how inaccessible locations are mapped

OVERVIEW There are undersea maps of places that no that human has ever been. How is this possible? In this activity, we'll explore the principle of how such maps are made.

WHAT TO DO

STEP 1
Cover the bottom of a shoebox with paper mache' paste. As it drys, form it to represent a stretch of deep unexplored ocean bottom. It may include plains, valleys, canyons, even undersea mountains! Let it dry overnight.

STEP 2
[next day] Follow your teacher's instructions to make a one-inch grid on the shoebox lid. Label the long lines A, B, C, etc. Label the short lines 1, 2, 3, etc. Carefully use a sharp pencil to punch holes at A1, A2, etc. Tape the lid on the box securely.

STEP 3
[next day] Trade boxes with another team. Mark a straw with 1/2 inch lines. Explore the "ocean bottom" by pushing the straw down hole A1. Record the depth. Repeat with holes A2, A3, etc. Now transfer the information to graph paper.

STEP 4
Connect the dots on the paper to create a cross-section, then cut away the top portion. Carefully peel back the side of the box and place the paper against the "ocean bottom" to see how they compare. Share observations with other research teams.

EARTH 95

Teacher to Teacher

Oceanographers provide vital information for many fields. Their research helps geologists better understand plate tectonics. Their maps help petroleum companies locate off-shore drilling sites. Their work offers clues for discovering valuable mineral deposits. Even salvage/recovery operations depend on the data they provide.

WHAT HAPPENED?

The method you used to make your map is called **remote sensing**. Using an **energy beam** (radar, sonar, laser, etc.) as a **probe**, scientists can measure distances between points very accurately. This **technology** was originally developed by NASA for the space program. Long-range probes help scientists collect information about places that humans may never go.

However, the map you made wasn't nearly as accurate as actually viewing the contour of your model's surface. This is because your **data points** (the places you took measurements) were relatively far apart. The more data points you sample, the better picture you get.

Even though they provide only an incomplete picture, remote sensing maps can help us gain a much better understanding of Earth's surface.

WHAT WE LEARNED

1. Describe the surface you created in Step 1. What were its most notable features?

Answers will vary, but should reflect logical descriptions.

2. Explain how the letters and numbers added in Step 2 help identify a specific hole.

Answers should reflect the "grid" concept.

3. What was the purpose of the 1/2" lines on the straw? Explain how they relate to the graph you produced in Step 4.

a) depth markers

b) combining straw with grid helps show depth at various locations

4. Compare the features of the surface you created in Step 1 with actual surface features. Other than under the ocean, where might you find similar contours on Earth?

Steep mountains, deep valleys, but also some plains and rolling hills.

5. How was your graph similar to the actual bottom contours? How was it different? How could you have made it more accurate?

a) answers will vary

b) answers will vary

c) smaller grid, more depth marks on straw

What Happened

Review the section with students. Emphasize bold-face words that identify key concepts and introduce new vocabulary.

*The method you used to make your map is called **remote sensing**. Using an **energy beam** (radar, sonar, laser, etc.) as a **probe**, scientists can measure distances between points very accurately. This **technology** was originally developed by NASA for the space program. Long-range probes help scientists collect information about places that humans may never go.*

*However, the map you made wasn't nearly as accurate as actually viewing the contour of your model's surface. This is because your **data points** (the places you took measurements) were relatively far apart. The more data points you sample, the better picture you get.*

Even though they provide only an incomplete picture, remote sensing maps can help us gain a much better understanding of Earth's surface.

What We Learned

Answers will vary. Suggested responses are shown at left.

Conclusion

Read this section aloud to the class to summarize the concepts learned in this activity.

Food for Thought

Read the Scripture aloud to the class. Talk about how God sees the "whole picture" while we often see only a fraction of what's there. Discuss how this relates to letting God control our lives.

Journal

If time permits, have a general class discussion about notes and drawings various students added to their journal pages. Discuss correct and incorrect predictions, and remind students that this "trial and error" process is part of the scientific process.

CONCLUSION

Remote sensing provides a way to map places humans can't go. Even though such maps provide less detail (inaccuracy of scale), they still help increase scientists' understanding of an area.

FOOD FOR THOUGHT

Genesis 1:9-10 Can you imagine what a huge job it would be to accurately sample the bottom of a large lake? Even data points a few yards apart could miss ledges and rock outcroppings. How much more difficult would it be to accurately map the world's oceans?

This Scripture reminds us God created both the oceans and dry land. He knows their every detail. It's the same way with our lives. At best, we can see only a limited number of life's data points, and sometimes it's hard to make good decisions. But when we trust God to direct our lives, we're guided by one who sees the whole picture!

JOURNAL — My Science Notes

98 EARTH

Extended Teaching

1. Using the Internet, have teams research WWII to discover how SONAR was used to detect and destroy enemy submarines. Challenge each team to make a poster based on their findings.

2. Have teams research the different kinds of waves used to explore space, oceans, and even our bodies. Challenge each team to contribute material for a classroom bulletin board on this topic.

3. Take a field trip to a surgical clinic. Find out about non-invasive surgical testing, how it's done, and what forms of energy are used. Have students write a paragraph about one thing they learn.

4. Invite a surveyor to visit your school. Ask him/her to bring equipment and demonstrate its use. Discuss how modern tools have changed the profession. Have students write a paragraph about one thing they learn.

5. Read students the "Blind Men and the Elephant" poem. Have teams compare this concept to the use of remote sensing for data collection. What does this tell us about the need for cooperative data sharing?

NAME _____

COOKED COAL

LESSON 22

FOCUS Earth Materials

OBJECTIVE To explore the properties of coal

OVERVIEW Heat a rock and you'll get . . . a hot rock. But not all "rocks" are the same. In this activity, we'll explore a rock-like material that's a major source of energy!

WHAT TO DO

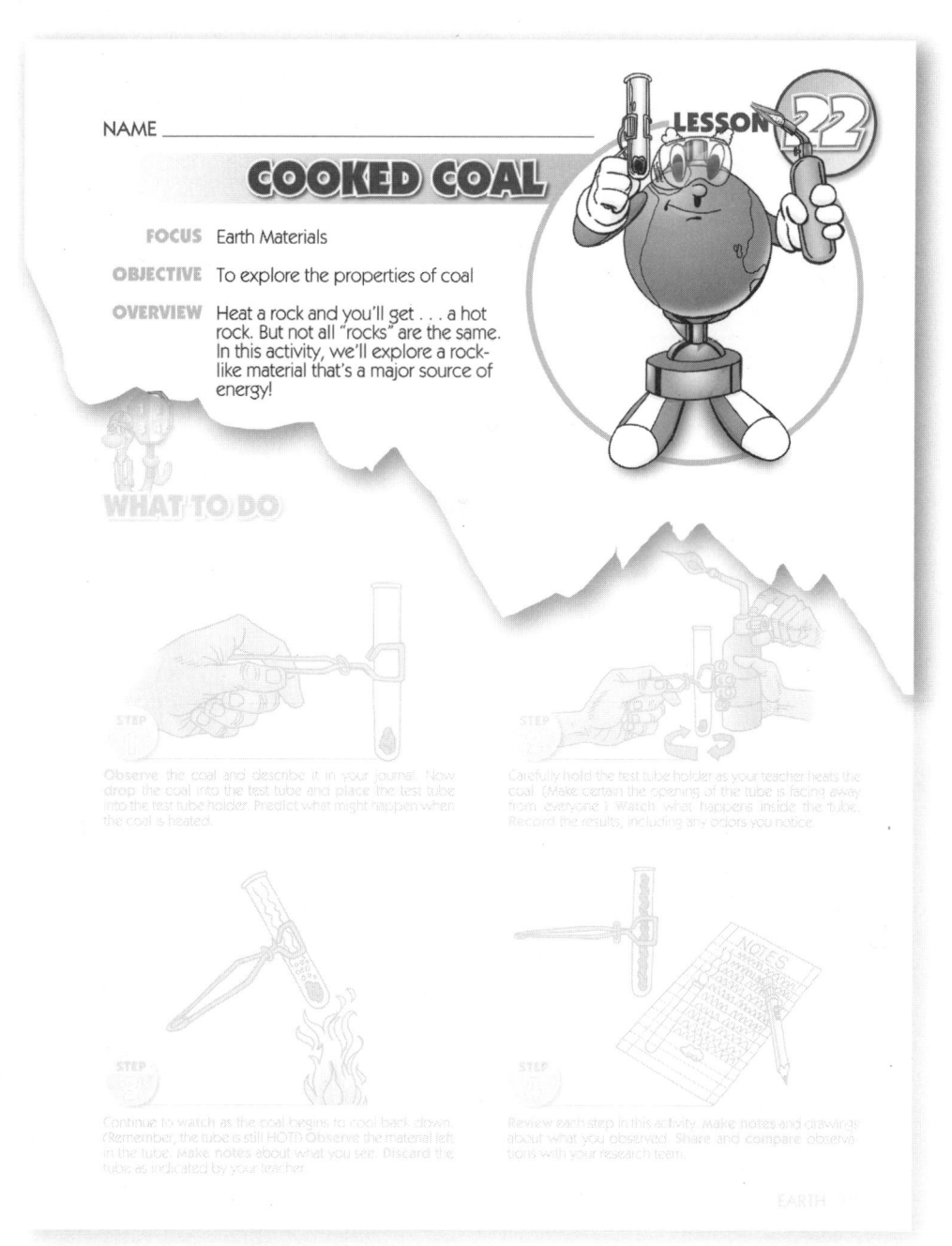

STEP 1 Observe the coal and describe it in your journal. Now drop the coal into the test tube and place the test tube into the test tube holder. Predict what might happen when the coal is heated.

STEP 2 Carefully hold the test tube holder as your teacher heats the coal. (Make certain the opening of the tube is facing away from everyone.) Watch what happens inside the tube. Record the results, including any odors you notice.

STEP 3 Continue to watch as the coal begins to cool back down. (Remember, the tube is still HOT!) Observe the material left in the tube. Make notes about what you see. Discard the tube as indicated by your teacher.

STEP 4 Review each step in this activity. Make notes and drawings about what you observed. Share and compare observations with your research team.

Additional Comments

Break coal samples into quarter inch pieces. Heating coal too long will set it on fire. If that happens, place a thick cloth over the top of the tube. Remind students that test tubes can be hot even though they may not look like it! Use the "wafting" method to smell contents. Never smell any chemical directly! Discard test tubes after use.

Overview

Read the overview aloud to your students. The goal is to create an atmosphere of curiosity and inquiry.

Category
Earth Science

Focus
Earth Materials

Objective
To explore the properties of coal

National Standards
A1, A2, B1, B2, B3, D2, E1, E2, F1, F2, F3, F4, F5, G1, G2

Materials Needed
coal
test tube
test tube holder
propane torch
 (teacher only)

Safety Concerns

1. Goggles/Gloves
Goggles and gloves are a reasonable safety precaution.

2. Open Flame
Remind students to exercise caution with open flame.

3. Vapor
Keep eyes, nose, and face away from vapor emitted from tube.

4. Breakage
Remind students to exercise caution when handling the glass test tube.

WHAT TO DO

Monitor student research teams as they complete each step.

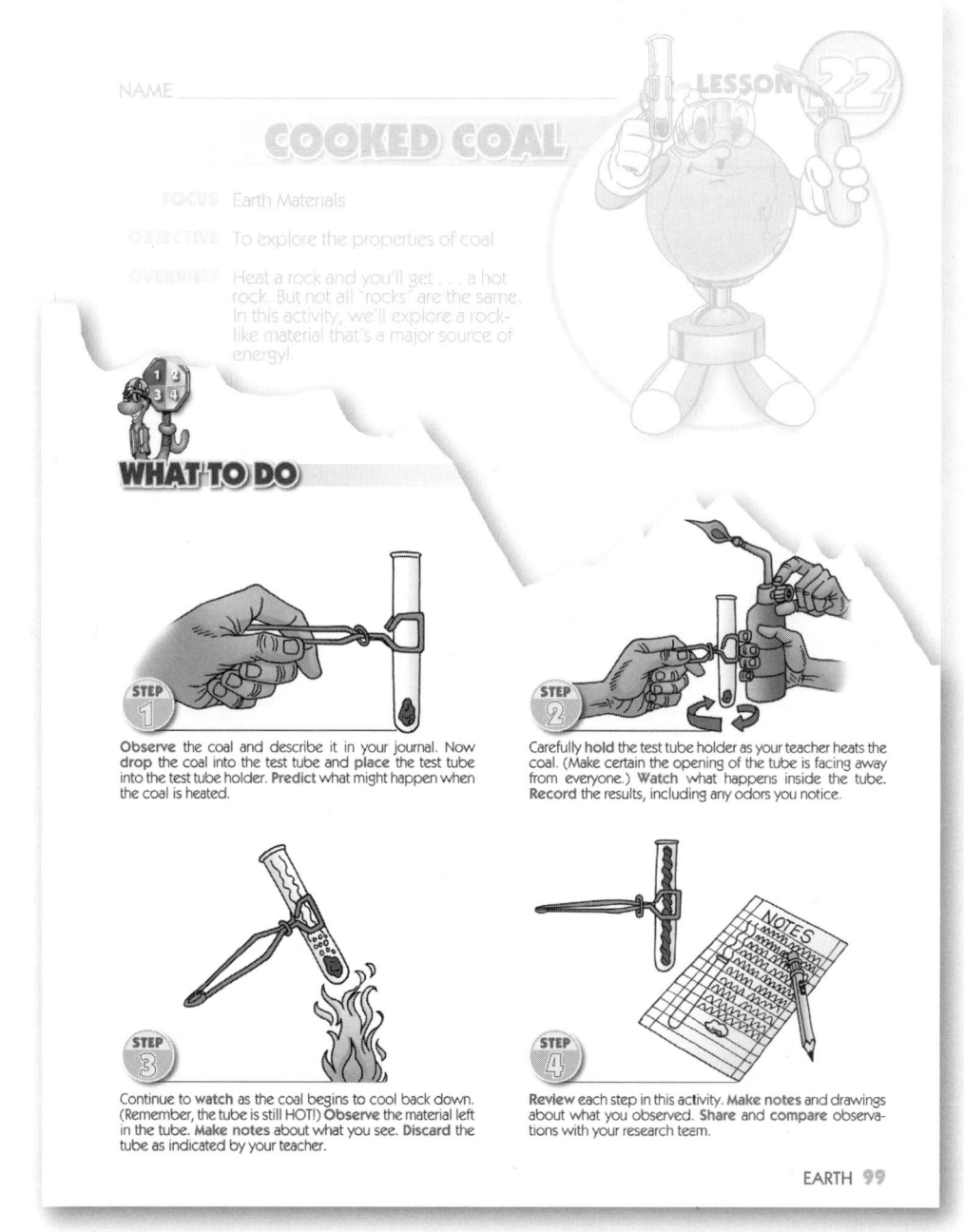

NAME _____

COOKED COAL

LESSON 22

FOCUS Earth Materials

OBJECTIVE To explore the properties of coal

OVERVIEW Heat a rock and you'll get . . . a hot rock. But not all "rocks" are the same. In this activity, we'll explore a rock-like material that's a major source of energy!

WHAT TO DO

STEP 1
Observe the coal and describe it in your journal. Now drop the coal into the test tube and place the test tube into the test tube holder. Predict what might happen when the coal is heated.

STEP 2
Carefully hold the test tube holder as your teacher heats the coal. (Make certain the opening of the tube is facing away from everyone.) Watch what happens inside the tube. Record the results, including any odors you notice.

STEP 3
Continue to watch as the coal begins to cool back down. (Remember, the tube is still HOT!) Observe the material left in the tube. Make notes about what you see. Discard the tube as indicated by your teacher.

STEP 4
Review each step in this activity. Make notes and drawings about what you observed. Share and compare observations with your research team.

EARTH 99

Teacher to Teacher

Coal is composed of plants covered by mud, silt, or similar materials. Oxygen can't reach such plants, so they don't decompose completely. Over time, the weight of the covering soil produces pressure and heat, creating the material we call coal. Since coal is made from once living things and is formed by a sedimentary process, it can be classified as "organic sedimentary rock."

WHAT HAPPENED?

Coal looks a lot like rock (or even dirt or dust), but it certainly reacts in a different way! When you "cook" coal, complicated things happen. The coal changes states from **solid** to **liquid** to **gas** back to a liquid. These are **physical** changes.

The coal also goes through a **chemical** change. As it's heated, it gives off **coal gas** and leaves behind **coal tar**. Coal gas was once a major source of **energy**, similar to natural gas or propane. People used it to light their homes and businesses. Coal tar is a complex stew of chemicals used in such diverse products as medicine and plastic!

As the coal cools, the residue it leaves behind is called **coke**. Coke is a very concentrated energy source used in the production of iron and steel.

WHAT WE LEARNED

1. Describe the coal in Step 1. How was it similar to the material left in Step 3? How was it different?

Answers should reflect descriptions of color, shape, hardness, etc.

2. What did you predict in Step 1? How did this prediction reflect what actually happened?

Answers will vary, but should reflect logical comparisons.

3. Describe what happened in Step 2. What did the coal do as it was heated? Describe any odors you detected.

a) descriptions will vary

b) began to bubble and melt

c) a smell like hot tar or asphalt

4. What "states of matter" occurred during this activity. Were these chemical or physical changes? Explain your answer.

a) solid, liquid, gas

b) both

c) part was still coal in a different form, but part changed into coal tar

5. Based on what you observed in Step 3, why is coal gas not an ideal residential energy source? What energy source do most American homes now use for light? How does this relate to coal?

a) smelly, flammable, etc.

b) electricity

c) coal is often used in power plants that generate electricity

---

What Happened

Review the section with students. Emphasize bold-face words that identify key concepts and introduce new vocabulary.

Coal looks a lot like rock (or even dirt or dust), but it certainly reacts in a different way! When you "cook" coal, complicated things happen. The coal changes states from solid to liquid to gas back to a liquid. These are physical changes.

The coal also goes through a chemical change. As it's heated, it gives off coal gas and leaves behind coal tar. Coal gas was once a major source of energy, similar to natural gas or propane. People used it to light their homes and businesses. Coal tar is a complex stew of chemicals used in such diverse products as medicine and plastic!

As the coal cools, the residue it leaves behind is called coke. Coke is a very concentrated energy source used in the production of iron and steel.

What We Learned

Answers will vary. Suggested responses are shown at left.

Conclusion

Read this section aloud to the class to summarize the concepts learned in this activity.

Food for Thought

Read the Scripture aloud to the class. Share a time when you've faced a challenge. Discuss how God uses these obstacles to help make us more valuable in serving him.

Journal

If time permits, have a general class discussion about notes and drawings various students added to their journal pages. Discuss correct and incorrect predictions, and remind students that this "trial and error" process is part of the scientific process.

CONCLUSION

Properties of similar-looking earth materials can vary widely. Coal is an earth material used as an energy source. Coal is composed of useful and complicated chemicals that can be released by heating.

FOOD FOR THOUGHT

2 Corinthians 5:17 Some serious changes took place inside that test tube when heat was applied! The coal experienced both physical and chemical changes in its nature. These changes made the coal into several much more valuable substances.

Scripture tells us that major changes take place in our natures when God takes control of our hearts. As we get closer to God, we better reflect his love. Our selfish natures begin to be replaced with a spirit of compassion and caring. Although God may put us through the fires of trials and trouble, these obstacles only serve to make us more valuable in his service.

JOURNAL — My Science Notes

102 EARTH

Extended Teaching

1. Using the Internet, have teams research how coal and coal tar is used in making different materials. Challenge each team to make a poster or bulletin board depicting at least one use that they have found.

2. Invite a power company representative to come to your classroom. Have him/her discuss energy production and distribution. Discuss environmental concerns. Have students write a paragraph about one thing they learn.

3. Visit a coal-fired electrical generating plant. Have a representative talk about how coal is burned to produce power. Have students write a paragraph about one thing they learn.

4. Have a class discussion about the pros and cons of coal mining. Talk about the environmental problems associated with mining coal. Find out how mining companies are trying to reduce environmental damage.

5. Discuss the role that coal plays in our society. Challenge students to write a story about how our lives might be different if coal mining suddenly ceased.

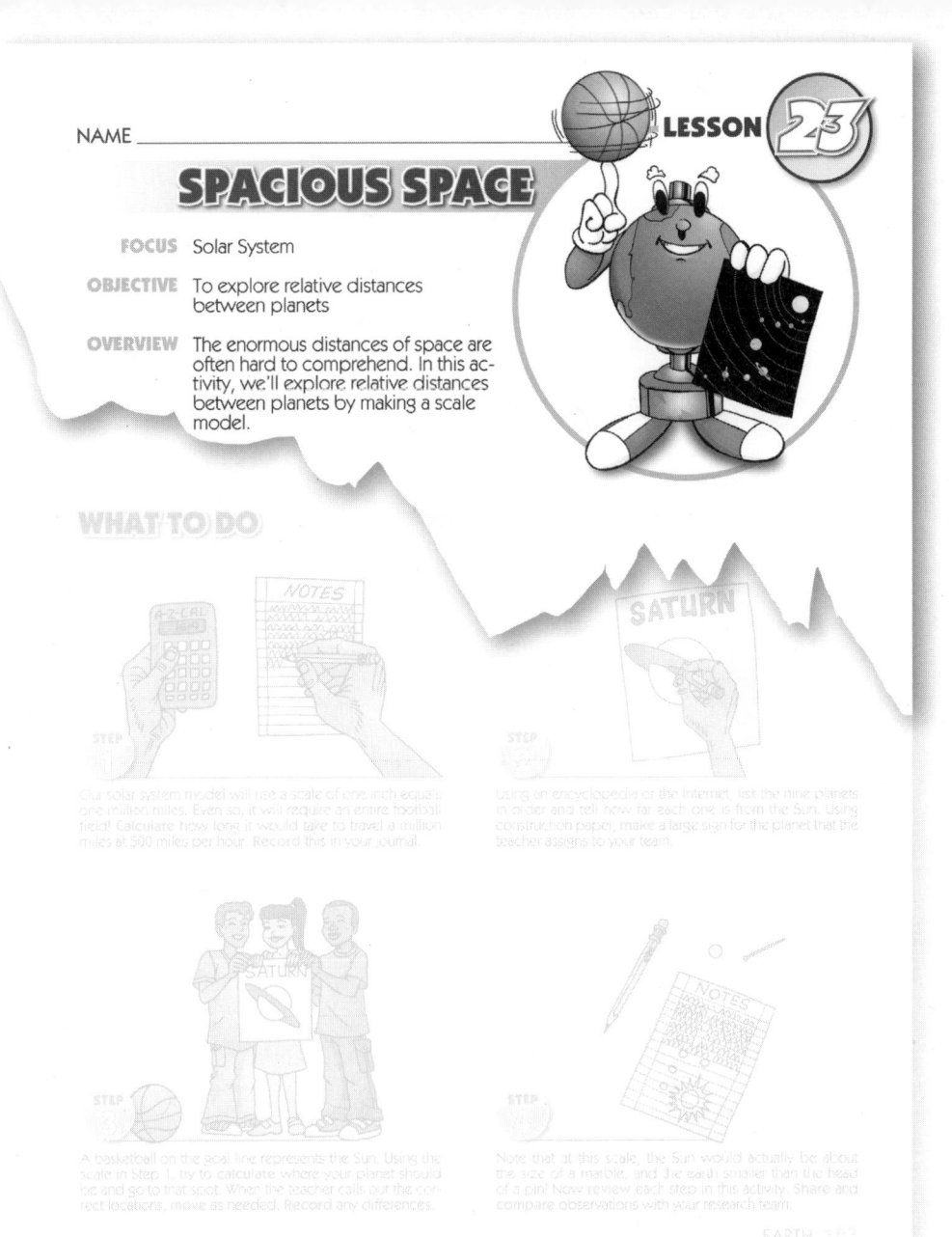

NAME _____

SPACIOUS SPACE

LESSON 23

FOCUS Solar System

OBJECTIVE To explore relative distances between planets

OVERVIEW The enormous distances of space are often hard to comprehend. In this activity, we'll explore relative distances between planets by making a scale model.

WHAT TO DO

STEP 1
Our solar system model will use a scale of one inch equals one million miles. Even so, it will require an entire football field! Calculate how long it would take to travel a million miles at 500 miles per hour. Record this in your journal.

STEP 2
Using an encyclopedia or the Internet, list the nine planets in order and tell how far each one is from the Sun. Using construction paper, make a large sign for the planet that the teacher assigns to your team.

STEP 3
A basketball on the goal line represents the Sun. Using the scale in Step 1, try to calculate where your planet should be and go to that spot. When the teacher calls out the correct locations, move as needed. Record any differences.

STEP 4
Note that at this scale, the Sun would actually be about the size of a marble, and the earth smaller than the head of a pin! Now review each step in this activity. Share and compare observations with your research team.

Category
Earth Science

Focus
Solar System

Objective
To explore relative distances between planets

National Standards
A1, A2, D3, G1, G2

Materials Needed
football field
calculator
construction paper
basketball

Safety Concerns
none

Additional Comments

In Step 3, stagger the inner groups (Mercury, Venus, Earth, and Mars), rather than having them stand in a straight line. This will make the signs easier to read, and keep groups from stepping on each other.

Overview

Read the overview aloud to your students. The goal is to create an atmosphere of curiosity and inquiry.

WHAT TO DO

Monitor student research teams as they complete each step.

Step 2

Distance of planets from the Sun: Mercury (35,983,610), Venus (67,232,360), Earth (92,957,100), Mars (141,635,300), Jupiter (483,632,000), Saturn (888,188,000), Uranus (1,783,950,000), Neptune (2,798,842,000) and Pluto (3,674,491,000). Note: The order of planets given here is based on average distances since most orbits are elliptical. In fact, Pluto's orbit is so elliptical it's actually closer than Neptune some years!

Step 3

Using a "one inch = one million miles" scale, distances from the goal line should be: Mercury - 36 inches; Venus - 68 inches; Earth - 93 inches; Mars - 142 inches (3.9 yards); Jupiter - 484 inches (13.5 yards); Saturn - 888 inches (24.6 yards); Uranus - 1,784 inches (49.5 yards); Neptune - 2,799 inches (77.7 yards); and Pluto - 3,675 inches (102 yards).

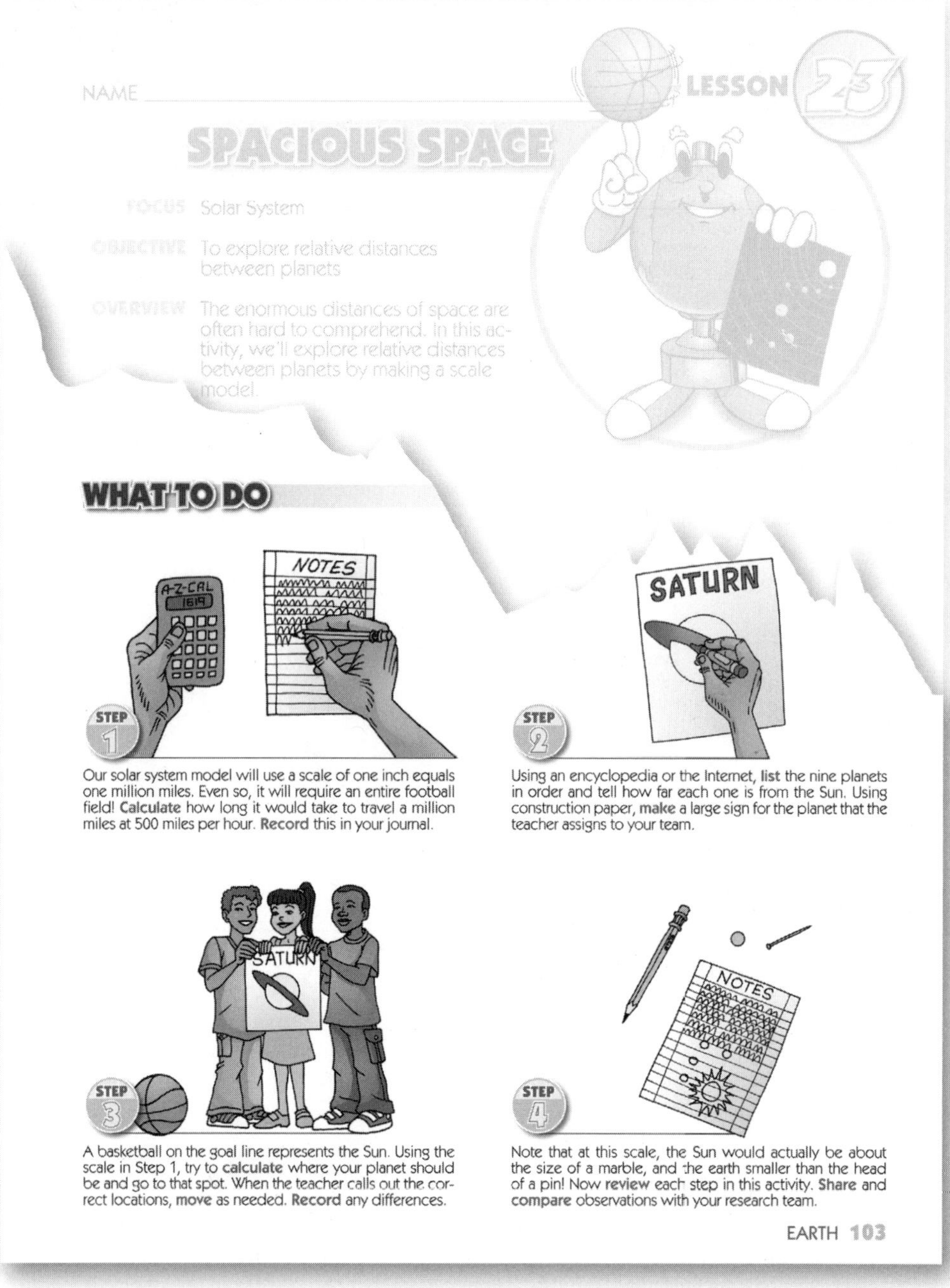

Teacher to Teacher

The inner planets (Mercury, Venus, and Mars) have structural similarities to Earth. By contrast, the outer planets (Jupiter, Saturn, Uranus, and Neptune) are "gas giants" with very unstable surfaces. What about Pluto? It's mostly rock and ice, and so small that as recently as 1999, there was a major move to declassify it as a planet!

WHAT HAPPENED?

A group of **planets** that **orbit** (circle) a **star** is called a **solar system**. A group of solar systems (and other space bodies) that rotate around together are called a **galaxy**. The galaxy that contains our solar system is the **Milky Way**. Scientists estimate that the Milky Way contains over four hundred billion solar systems.

The **scale model** we made represents only the planets orbiting our **Sun**. The distance between other objects in the **universe** is almost unimaginable! For this activity, we used average distances since the paths planets follow are not really circles. Some orbits are so different that there are times Neptune is closer to the Sun than Pluto!

WHAT WE LEARNED

1) What two planets are Earth's closest neighbors? What is the relationship of these planets and Earth to the Sun?

a) Venus and Mars

b) Venus is closest, then Earth, then Mars

2) In the scale we used, what distance does a foot represent? What distance does a yard represent? Traveling ten thousand miles per hour, about how far could you go in one day?

a) 12 million miles

b) 36 million miles

c) only 240,000 miles

3) Why couldn't we show the planets in the correct scale on this model? Based on distance to the sun, which two planets would be the coldest? Which two planets would be the hottest?

a) not enough room

b) Neptune and Pluto

c) Mercury and Venus

4) What is a group of planets orbiting a star called? What is a group of solar systems rotating together called? What is the name of the galaxy that contains our solar system?

a) solar system

b) galaxy

c) Milky Way

5) If you could fly through space at ten thousand miles per hour, how likely would you be to run into another planet? Explain your answer.

a) extremely unlikely

b) planets are incredibly far apart, space is mostly emptiness

---

What Happened

Review the section with students. Emphasize bold-face words that identify key concepts and introduce new vocabulary.

*A group of **planets** that **orbit** (circle) a **star** is called a **solar system**. A group of solar systems (and other space bodies) that rotate around together is called a **galaxy**. The galaxy that contains our solar system is the **Milky Way**. Scientists estimate that the Milky Way contains over 400 billion solar systems.*

*The **scale model** we made represents only the planets orbiting our **Sun**. The distance between other objects in the **universe** is almost unimaginable! For this activity, we used average distances since the paths planets follow are not really circles. Some orbits are so different that there are times Neptune is closer to the Sun than Pluto!*

What We Learned

Answers will vary. Suggested responses are shown at left.

Conclusion

Read this section aloud to the class to summarize the concepts learned in this activity.

Food for Thought

Read the Scripture aloud to the class. Talk about some of the things that people have a tendancy to put before God. Discuss ways we can keep God at the center of our lives.

Journal

If time permits, have a general class discussion about notes and drawings various students added to their journal pages. Discuss correct and incorrect predictions, and remind students that this "trial and error" process is part of the scientific process.

CONCLUSION
A group of planets orbiting a star is called a solar system. A group of solar systems rotating together is called a galaxy. The distance between a star and a planet determines the amount of energy it receives.

FOOD FOR THOUGHT
Psalm 89:11 It's hard to imagine a solar system without the sun. Imagine what would happen to the planets! They would be barren and cold, wandering aimlessly through space. The sun not only keeps the planets in their appointed orbits, but also provides the energy that allows for life.

Just as the sun is the center of the solar system, so God should be the center of our lives. His power is what keeps us headed in the right direction. His love provides the force that gives us life. Keep God at the center of your universe!

JOURNAL, My Science Notes

106 EARTH

Extended Teaching

1. Assign each team a planet or two. Have them draw pictures of their planet(s) and write descriptions. Use these materials to create a classroom bulletin board.

2. Invite an amateur astronomer to visit your classroom. Have him/her show or talk about how they use their telescope to study the solar system. Have students write a paragraph about one thing they learn.

3. Visit the NASA website to learn more about the planets and our voyages of discovery. Challenge each team to create a poster that compares these explorations to the early discovery voyages of the Europeans or Polynesians.

4. Have teams research the Hubbell Telescope. What has it discovered about our solar system, how does it work, when was it created, etc.? Challenge each team to create a poster showing one interesting aspect of this device.

5. Have a class discussion about what conditions (gravity, heat, moisture, atmosphere, etc.) allow for life on Earth. What conditions on other planets will not allow life to exist there?

PLANET PERSPECTIVE

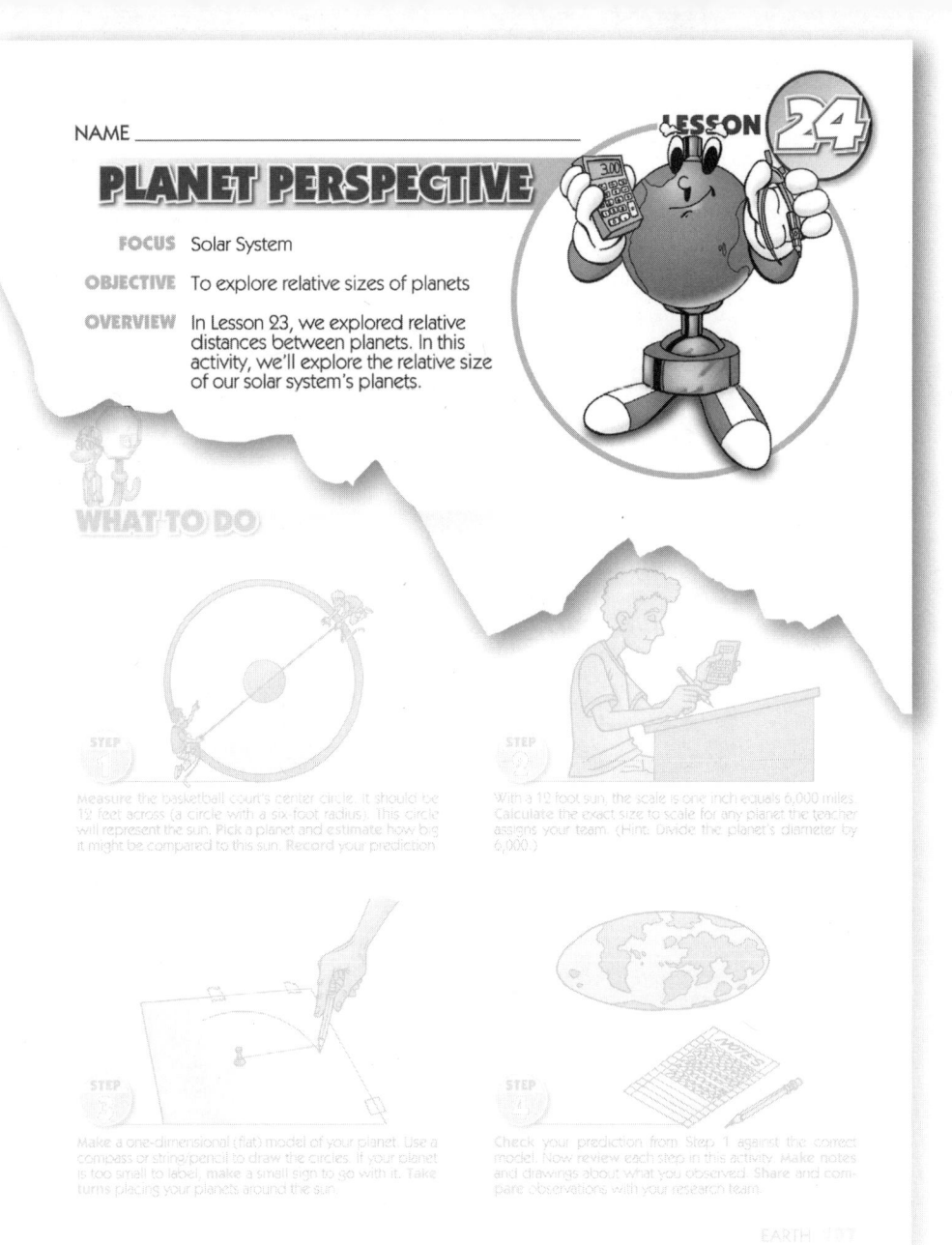

FOCUS Solar System

OBJECTIVE To explore relative sizes of planets

OVERVIEW In Lesson 23, we explored relative distances between planets. In this activity, we'll explore the relative size of our solar system's planets.

WHAT TO DO

STEP 1 Measure the basketball court's center circle. It should be 12 feet across (a circle with a six-foot radius). This circle will represent the sun. Pick a planet and estimate how big it might be compared to this sun. Record your prediction.

STEP 2 With a 12 foot sun, the scale is one inch equals 6,000 miles. Calculate the exact size to scale for any planet the teacher assigns your team. (Hint: Divide the planet's diameter by 6,000.)

STEP 3 Make a one-dimensional (flat) model of your planet. Use a compass or string/pencil to draw the circles. If your planet is too small to label, make a small sign to go with it. Take turns placing your planets around the sun.

STEP 4 Check your prediction from Step 1 against the correct model. Now review each step in this activity. Make notes and drawings about what you observed. Share and compare observations with your research team.

Category
Earth Science

Focus
Solar System

Objective
To explore relative sizes of planets

National Standards
A1, A2, D3, G1, G2

Materials Needed
basketball court
compass
tape measure
calculator

Safety Concerns
4. Sharp Objects
Remind students to exercise caution when using the compass.

Additional Comments

If the center circle of your basketball court isn't standard size (or you don't have access to a basketball court), make a 12 foot diameter circle from poster paper or cardboard. Use this on the playground.

Overview

Read the overview aloud to your students. The goal is to create an atmosphere of curiosity and inquiry.

WHAT TO DO

Monitor student research teams as they complete each step.

Step 2

Have teams take notes as you share the following planet diameters: Mercury (3,032 miles), Venus (7,521 miles), Earth (7,926 miles), Mars (4,222 miles), Jupiter (88,846 miles), Saturn (74,898 miles), Uranus (31,763 miles), Neptune (30,778 miles) and Pluto (1,413 miles). Be sure to give your students the diameters of the Sun (about 865,000 miles) and Moon (2,162 miles) too, since they'll need these for questions in "What We Learned."

At a scale of "1 inch = 6,000 miles" the approximate sizes would be: Mercury (1/2 inch), Venus (1 1/4 inches), Earth (1 3/8 inches), Mars (3/4 inch), Jupiter (14 3/4 inches), Saturn (12 1/2 inches), Uranus (5 1/4 inches), Neptune (5 1/8 inches) and Pluto (1/4 inch).

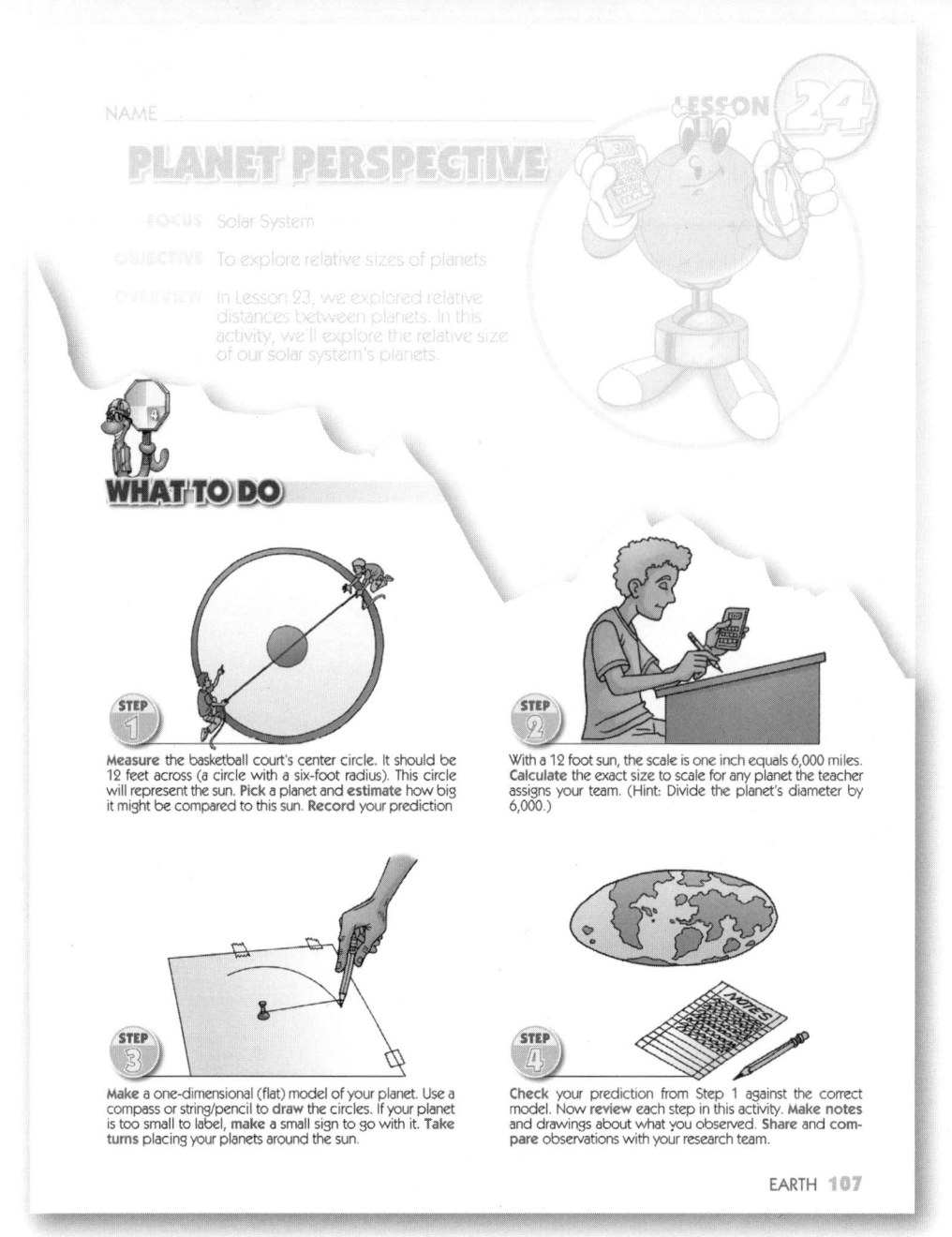

PLANET PERSPECTIVE

FOCUS Solar System

OBJECTIVE To explore relative sizes of planets

OVERVIEW In Lesson 23, we explored relative distances between planets. In this activity, we'll explore the relative size of our solar system's planets.

WHAT TO DO

STEP 1 Measure the basketball court's center circle. It should be 12 feet across (a circle with a six-foot radius). This circle will represent the sun. Pick a planet and estimate how big it might be compared to this sun. Record your prediction

STEP 2 With a 12 foot sun, the scale is one inch equals 6,000 miles. Calculate the exact size to scale for any planet the teacher assigns your team. (Hint: Divide the planet's diameter by 6,000.)

STEP 3 Make a one-dimensional (flat) model of your planet. Use a compass or string/pencil to draw the circles. If your planet is too small to label, make a small sign to go with it. Take turns placing your planets around the sun.

STEP 4 Check your prediction from Step 1 against the correct model. Now review each step in this activity. Make notes and drawings about what you observed. Share and compare observations with your research team.

EARTH 107

Teacher to Teacher

The power plant for any solar system is the star at its center. Our star (the sun) consists of an ongoing nuclear fusion reaction, which constantly converts one element into another, releasing enormous amounts of energy in the process. Without this energy, our planet would just be a frozen, lifeless lump floating in space.

What Happened

Review the section with students. Emphasize bold-face words that identify key concepts and introduce new vocabulary.

Since **planets** are too large to fit in the gym, we used a **scale model** to compare relative sizes. (If you've ever made a model airplane or model car, you understand the concept of scale models.) Scientists and engineers make models all the time to teach, to test ideas, and to enhance their understanding of an object or idea.

In this model, it was obvious that the planets varied enormously in size! But in addition to size, planets can vary in **composition**, **temperature**, **atmosphere**, and other major ways. For instance, Venus is similar in size to Earth, but the average surface temperature is 900 degrees Fahrenheit, and the atmosphere is filled with clouds of sulfuric acid. Not a place designed to support life as we know it!

What We Learned

Answers will vary. Suggested responses are shown at left.

WHAT HAPPENED?

Since planets are too large to fit in the gym, we used a scale model to compare relative sizes. (If you've ever made a model airplane or model car, you understand the concept of scale models.) Scientists and engineers make models all the time to teach, to test ideas, and to enhance their understanding of an object or idea.

In this model, it was obvious that the planets varied enormously in size! But in addition to size, planets can vary in composition, temperature, atmosphere, and other major ways. For instance, Venus is similar in size to Earth, but the average surface temperature is 900 degrees Fahrenheit, and the atmosphere is filled with clouds of sulfuric acid. Not a place designed to support life as we know it!

WHAT WE LEARNED

1. What did you predict in Step 1? How did this prediction reflect the correct answer?

Answers will vary, but should reflect logical comparisons.

2. America is about 3,000 miles across. In the scale you used for this activity, about how far would that be?

about half an inch

3. In your model, what two planets were the smallest? What two planets were the biggest? How does this compare to the real planets in our solar system? Why?

a) Pluto and Mercury

b) Jupiter and Saturn

c) the same since this is a scale model

4. "Planets of the same size are similar in most ways." Is this statement true or false? Explain your answer.

a) not true

b) Earth and Venus are similar in size, but very different atmospheres!

5. How does the size of the moon compare to that of Earth? How does it compare to the Sun? Why does the Moon look about the same size as the Sun when viewed from Earth?

a) Earth is roughly 4 times larger

b) the Sun is roughly 400 times larger

c) it's much, much closer

Conclusion

Read this section aloud to the class to summarize the concepts learned in this activity.

Food for Thought

Read the Scripture aloud to the class. Talk about some of the amazing things that God has created. Discuss how God's love for us is as infinate as the universe!

Journal

If time permits, have a general class discussion about notes and drawings various students added to their journal pages. Discuss correct and incorrect predictions, and remind students that this "trial and error" process is part of the scientific process.

CONCLUSION

Planets vary significantly in size as well as other characteristics. Scale models help scientists to study relationships between objects.

FOOD FOR THOUGHT

Matthew 10:29 The scale model you made helped you visualize the relative sizes of the planets in our solar system. It's amazing how insignificant the Earth looks in comparison to the Sun. A human being on this scale would be much smaller than the tiniest grain of sand!

Yet even though we're very small in comparison to the mighty, marvelous things God has made, God still knows each one of us individually. This Scripture tells us that God even notices the fall of a tiny bird. Next time you look at the night sky and contemplate the immensity of the stars, remember that God's love for you is as infinite as the universe.

JOURNAL   My Science Notes

Extended Teaching

1. Using the Internet, have teams research the Sun. Find out what it's made up of, how it gives off energy, etc. Challenge teams to contribute material for a classroom bulletin board on this topic.

2. Have teams research different types of stars. Find out how they are classified by color, temperature, and other characteristics. Challenge each team to create a poster about a specific star.

3. Take a field trip to a University astronomy lab. Ask a grad student to give you a tour and explain the various equipment and exhibits. Have students write a few paragraphs about one thing they learn.

4. Host a "star party" on a clear night. Invite amateur astronomers to bring their equipment, and let students look at Mars, Venus, or the moon firsthand. Have students write a few paragraphs about one thing they learn.

5. Have teams visit the NASA web site to discover what the Hubbell Telescope is presently studying. Have them download pictures and information, and create a presentation for their classmates.

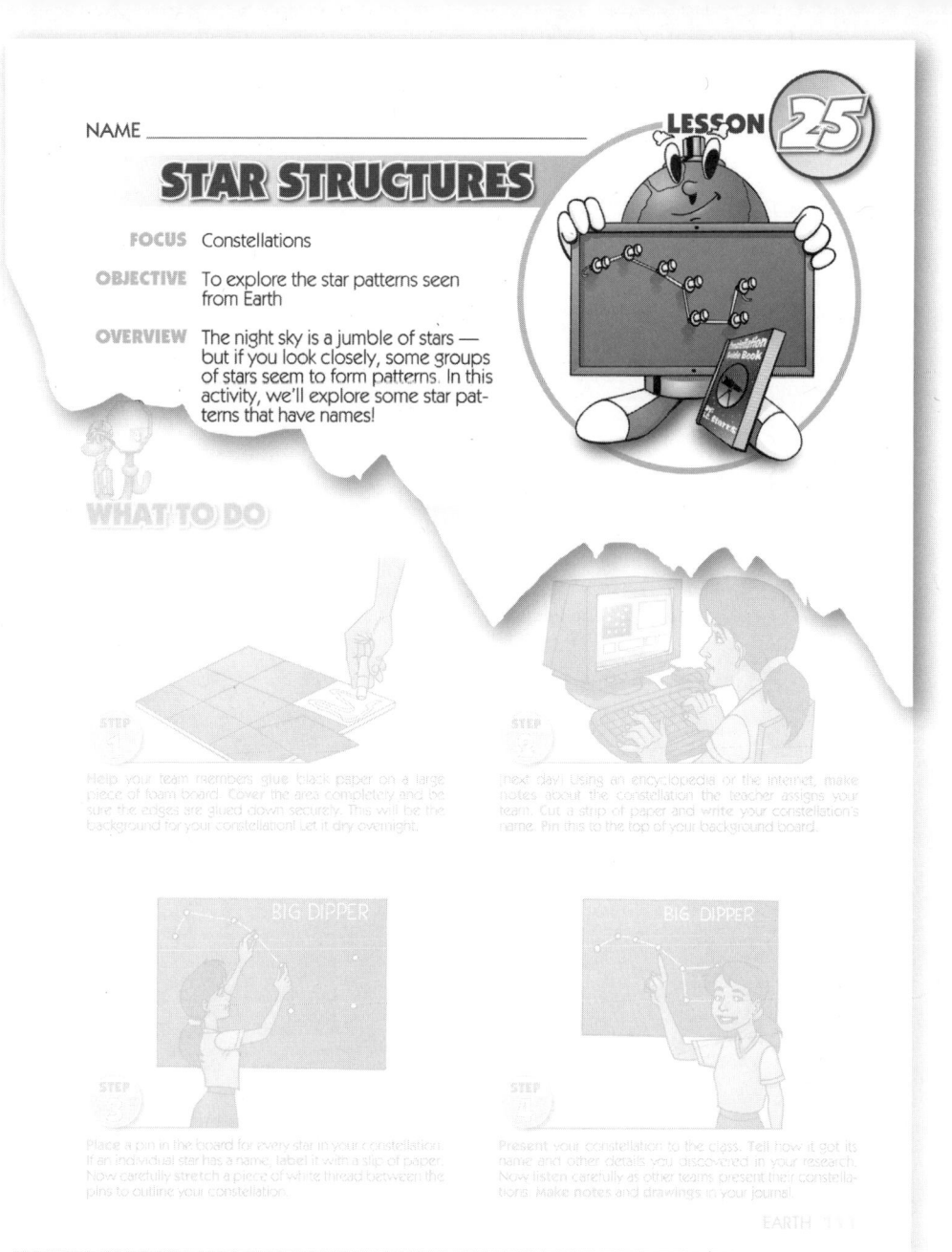

NAME _____

STAR STRUCTURES

LESSON 25

FOCUS Constellations

OBJECTIVE To explore the star patterns seen from Earth

OVERVIEW The night sky is a jumble of stars — but if you look closely, some groups of stars seem to form patterns. In this activity, we'll explore some star patterns that have names!

WHAT TO DO

STEP 1
Help your team members glue black paper on a large piece of foam board. Cover the area completely and be sure the edges are glued down securely. This will be the background for your constellation. Let it dry overnight.

STEP 2
(next day) Using an encyclopedia or the Internet, make notes about the constellation the teacher assigns your team. Cut a strip of paper and write your constellation's name. Pin this to the top of your background board.

STEP 3
Place a pin in the board for every star in your constellation. If an individual star has a name, label it with a slip of paper. Now carefully stretch a piece of white thread between the pins to outline your constellation.

STEP 4
Present your constellation to the class. Tell how it got its name and other details you discovered in your research. Now listen carefully as other teams present their constellations. Make notes and drawings in your journal.

EARTH

Category
Earth Science

Focus
Constellations

Objective
To explore the star patterns seen from Earth

National Standards
A1, A2, D3, G1, G2

Materials Needed
glue
scissors
black paper
foam board
encyclopedia/Internet
pushpins
white thread

Safety Concerns
4. Sharp Objects
Remind students to exercise caution when using scissors and pushpins.

Additional Comments

If you have limited Internet access or few reference books, assign Step 2 as an independent project for students with Internet access at home. Have them print what they find and share it with their team members.

Overview

Read the overview aloud to your students. The goal is to create an atmosphere of curiosity and inquiry.

Lesson 25 · 113

WHAT TO DO

Monitor student research teams as they complete each step.

NAME _____

STAR STRUCTURES

LESSON 25

FOCUS Constellations

OBJECTIVE To explore the star patterns seen from Earth

OVERVIEW The night sky is a jumble of stars — but if you look closely, some groups of stars seem to form patterns. In this activity, we'll explore some star patterns that have names!

WHAT TO DO

STEP 1
Help your team members **glue** black paper on a large piece of foam board. **Cover** the area completely and be sure the edges are glued down securely. This will be the background for your constellation! Let it **dry** overnight.

STEP 2
[next day] Using an encyclopedia or the internet, **make notes** about the constellation the teacher assigns your team. **Cut** a strip of paper and **write** your constellation's name. **Pin** this to the top of your background board.

STEP 3
Place a pin in the board for every star in your constellation. If an individual star has a name, **label** it with a slip of paper. Now carefully **stretch** a piece of white thread between the pins to outline your constellation.

STEP 4
Present your constellation to the class. **Tell** how it got its name and other details you discovered in your research. Now **listen** carefully as other teams present their constellations. **Make notes** and **drawings** in your journal.

EARTH 111

Teacher to Teacher

Although our Sun is pretty average, there are many other kinds of stars. Double stars are pairs that circle each other. White Dwarfs are small and hot. Red Giants are huge, relatively cool stars. Quasars constantly emit huge amounts of energy, while super dense Pulsars release energy in spurts. There are even invisible collapsed stars (Black Holes) with gravity so intense it even traps light!

114 · Lesson 25

WHAT HAPPENED?

Sometimes groups of stars appear to form **patterns**. Such a grouping is called a **constellation**. Ancient people from various cultures often named constellations for the shapes they saw there. The constellation models you made represent certain portions of Earth's night sky.

If you were on the other side of the galaxy, however, these same stars would form different groupings. Some would be closer; some farther away. Some might not even be visible! The thick band of stars we call the **Milky Way**, for instance, is just the edge of our own **galaxy** as seen from Earth. From another part of the universe, our galaxy might appear as a disk or even a spiral!

WHAT WE LEARNED

1. What constellation did your team research in Step 2? Describe what you discovered about this constellation.

Answers will vary, but should reflect logical descriptions.

2. How would you locate your constellation in the night sky? Would it require a telescope or a certain time of year? Explain.

Answers will vary, but should be supported with some sort of data.

3. Did individual stars in your constellation have names? If so, what were their names or labels?

answers will vary

4. Pick a constellation researched by another team. What did you learn from their presentation about this constellation?

answers will vary

5. Would your constellation look different from the other side of the galaxy? Explain your answer.

a) *yes*

b) *a different viewing location creates different groupings*

What Happened

Review the section with students. Emphasize bold-face words that identify key concepts and introduce new vocabulary.

*Sometimes groups of **stars** appear to form **patterns**. Such a grouping is called a **constellation**. Ancient people from various cultures often named constellations for the shapes they saw there. The constellation models you made represent certain portions of Earth's night sky.*

*If you were on the other side of the galaxy, however, these same stars would form different groupings. Some would be closer; some farther away. Some might not even be visible! The thick band of stars we call the **Milky Way**, for instance, is just the edge of our own **galaxy** as seen from Earth. From another part of the universe, our galaxy might appear as a disk or even a spiral!*

What We Learned

Answers will vary. Suggested responses are shown at left.

Conclusion

Read this section aloud to the class to summarize the concepts learned in this activity.

Food for Thought

Read the Scripture aloud to the class. Talk about how the night sky can remind us of God's immense creative power. Discuss how God's love for us will outlast the heavens.

Journal

If time permits, have a general class discussion about notes and drawings various students added to their journal pages. Discuss correct and incorrect predictions, and remind students that this "trial and error" process is part of the scientific process.

CONCLUSION

A constellation is a pattern of stars as seen from Earth. Such patterns would look much different if they were viewed from another part of the galaxy.

FOOD FOR THOUGHT

Genesis 1:16 If you want to see how the night sky looked to people long ago, you have to get out of the cities and towns. Without the competition of man-made lights, each star is crisp, clear, and bright. On a clear summer night, the sky is filled with dazzling brilliance!

This Scripture reminds us that God created the universe. He placed the sun, moon, and stars in their appointed places. Looking at the night sky, we're amazed at the immense creative power it represents. Yet the mighty God who created the entire universe has room in his heart for you! Never forget that God loves you with a love that will outlast the heavens.

JOURNAL — My Science Notes

114 EARTH

Extended Teaching

1. Using the Internet, have teams research classes of stars: O, B, A, F, G, K, and M. Challenge each team to make a poster showing how this star classification system works.

2. Research the life cycle of a star (especially Supernovae). Notice that their life cycles vary due to the starting mass. Have students write a paragraph about what they learn.

3. Have teams visit the NASA website again. Find out what's new since the last visit, or explore portions of the site not visited last time. Challenge each team to create a poster about something they learn.

4. Have teams research other forms of telescopes used in Astronomy (especially Radio Telescopes). Find out how they work and why they're so important. Have students write a few paragraphs about one thing they learn.

5. If you live near a major metropolitan area, take a field trip to a planetarium. Challenge each team to find at least one thing of particular interest, then create a presentation for the class.

116 · Lesson 25

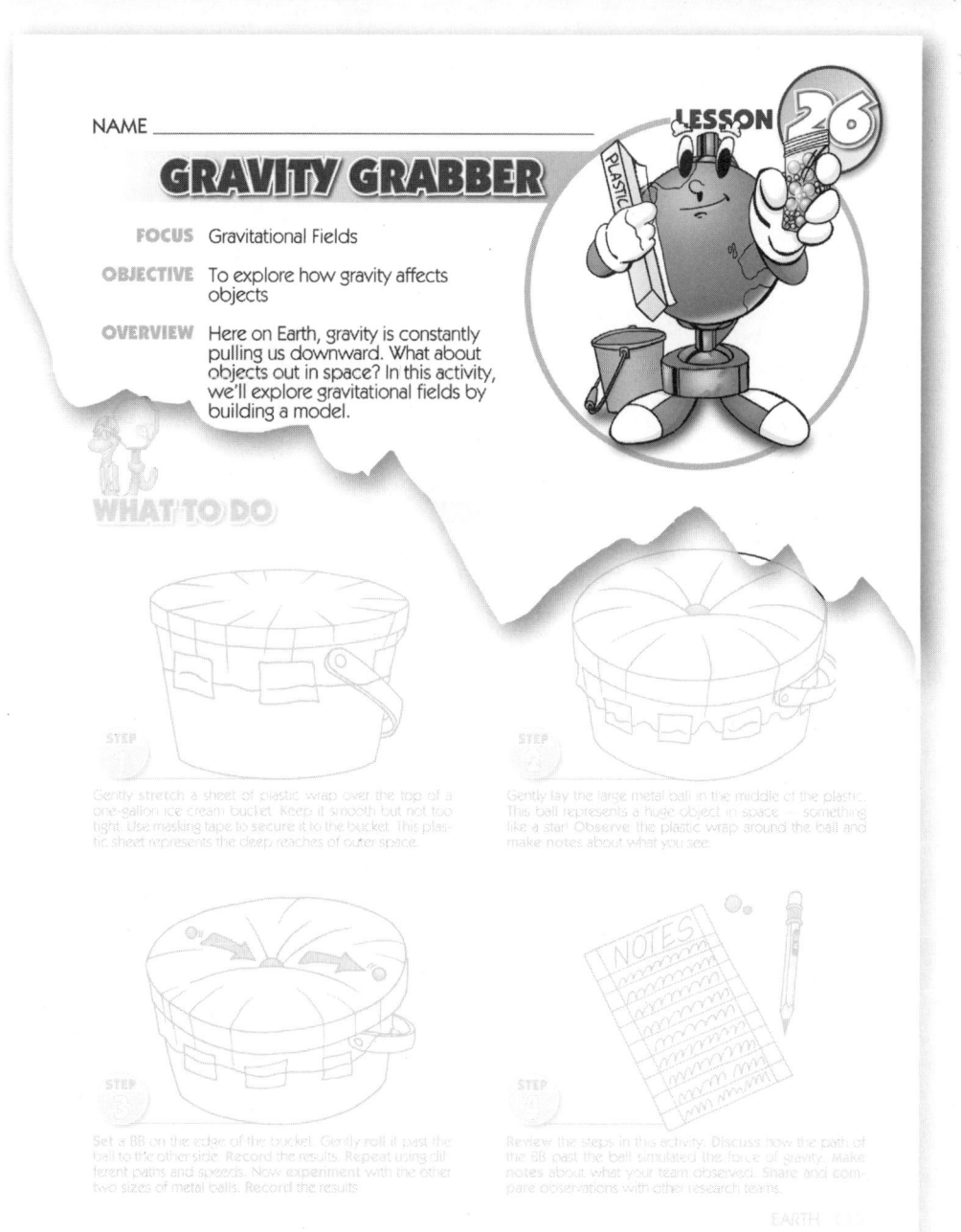

Category
Earth Science

Focus
Gravitational Fields

Objective
To explore how gravity affects objects

National Standards
A1, A2, B2, B3, D3, G1, G2

Materials Needed
masking tape
metal balls
BBs
plastic wrap
plastic bucket

Safety Concerns
4. Slipping
Metal balls and BBs can pose a slipping hazard if spilled.

Additional Comments

Use a high quality "cling-type" plastic wrap like Handiwrap®. A one-gallon ice cream bucket is perfect for this activity. Monitor students to make sure metal balls are on the bucket (or safely in the bag) at all times.

Overview

Read the overview aloud to your students. The goal is to create an atmosphere of curiosity and inquiry.

Lesson 26 · 117

WHAT TO DO

Monitor student research teams as they complete each step.

NAME _____

GRAVITY GRABBER

FOCUS Gravitational Fields

OBJECTIVE To explore how gravity affects objects

OVERVIEW Here on Earth, gravity is constantly pulling us downward. What about objects out in space? In this activity, we'll explore gravitational fields by building a model.

WHAT TO DO

STEP 1
Gently **stretch** a sheet of plastic wrap over the top of a one-gallon ice cream bucket. Keep it smooth but not too tight. Use masking tape to **secure** it to the bucket. This plastic sheet represents the deep reaches of outer space.

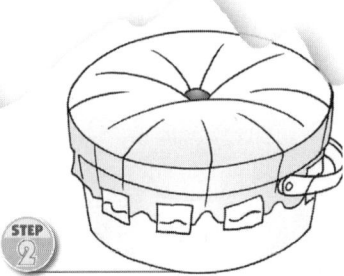

STEP 2
Gently **lay** the large metal ball in the middle of the plastic. This ball represents a huge object in space — something like a star! **Observe** the plastic wrap around the ball and **make notes** about what you see.

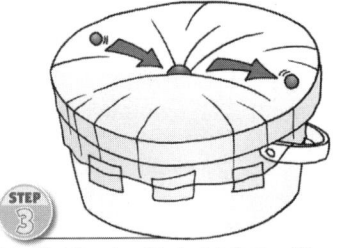

STEP 3
Set a BB on the edge of the bucket. Gently **roll** it past the ball to the other side. **Record** the results. **Repeat** using different paths and speeds. Now **experiment** with the other two sizes of metal balls. **Record** the results.

STEP 4
Review the steps in this activity. **Discuss** how the path of the BB past the ball simulated the force of gravity. **Make notes** about what your team observed. **Share** and compare observations with other research teams.

EARTH 115

Teacher to Teacher

The greater the mass, the greater the force of gravity. But a slightly different view is held by some scientists. They believe that gravity is not a "force" at all, but simply something that occurs when matter interacts with time and space. In other words, matter causes a change around itself that we call gravity.

WHAT HAPPENED?

The empty plastic sheet represents an area of **space** with no objects. When you added the large metal ball, it made a dent. The size of the dent represents the object's **gravitational field** — how far it can easily **attract** other objects. It also shows how **gravity** relates to **mass**. A large ball (greater mass) makes a big dent (large gravitational field). A small ball (less mass) makes a small dent (small gravitational field).

The large ball in the middle represents a **star**. Some of the balls you shot went right by the star. They were moving too fast or were too far away to be affected. Other balls were close enough, but still moving too fast. They passed by, but their **direction** and **speed** were changed. (NASA uses this gravitational "slingshot" effect to whip satellites deeper into space.) And some balls were close and slow, so gravity **pulled** them into the star.

WHAT WE LEARNED

1. Compare the plastic wrap in Step 1 with the plastic wrap in Step 2. How are they similar? How are they different?

a) similar: same material, same amount of stress, etc.

b) different: big dent in Step 2

2. What does the dent around the large ball represent? How did this dent affect the BB in Step 3?

a) a gravitational field

b) changed its path toward ball in center

3. What were the three possible paths the BB could have taken? List the factors that would cause it to take each of these paths.

straight: fast and far from ball
curved: fast but closer to ball
collision: slow and close to ball.

4. Describe how NASA uses the gravity of large planets to extend the range of their satellites.

Passing a satellite close to a large planet "slingshots" the satellite deeper into space.

5. Explain how mass relates to gravity. Give at least one example.

a) a larger ball (greater mass) makes a big dent (large gravitational field) and vice-versa

b) gravity is lower on the moon than on Earth

What Happened

Review the section with students. Emphasize bold-face words that identify key concepts and introduce new vocabulary.

The empty plastic sheet represents an area of **space** *with no objects. When you added the large metal ball, it made a dent. The size of the dent represents the object's* **gravitational field** *— how far it can easily* **attract** *other objects. It also shows how* **gravity** *relates to* **mass**. *A large ball (greater mass) makes a big dent (large gravitational field). A small ball (less mass) makes a small dent (small gravitational field).*

The large ball in the middle represents a **star**. *Some of the balls you shot went right by the star. They were moving too fast or were too far away to be affected. Other balls were close enough, but still moving too fast. They passed by, but their* **direction** *and* **speed** *were changed. (NASA uses this gravitational "slingshot" effect to whip satellites deeper into space.) And some balls were close and slow, so gravity* **pulled** *them into the star.*

What We Learned

Answers will vary. Suggested responses are shown at left.

Conclusion

Read this section aloud to the class to summarize the concepts learned in this activity.

Food for Thought

Read the Scripture aloud to the class. Talk about how bad companions and worthless amusements can pull us away from God. Discuss specific things we can do to stay close to God.

Journal

If time permits, have a general class discussion about notes and drawings various students added to their journal pages. Discuss correct and incorrect predictions, and remind students that this "trial and error" process is part of the scientific process.

CONCLUSION

The greater the mass of the object, the greater its gravitational field. The gravitational fields of planets affect passing objects in various ways.

FOOD FOR THOUGHT

Ezekiel 33:11 Objects in space can be attracted by a planet's gravity. The closer they get to the planet, the greater the pull. Some objects eventually come too close. They're trapped by the planet's gravitational field and may crash into the planet.

In a similar way, people are attracted by the tricks of Satan. The closer they get to bad companions and worthless amusements, the greater the pull. Before long, they find themselves trapped in a web of sin. Scripture warns us to turn away from such evil. Keep your eyes on Christ, and you can stay far from the pull of the evil one.

JOURNAL — My Science Notes

Extended Teaching

1. Repeat this activity using a bigger bucket and round objects of various sizes. Have your students compare the results to the original activity. How were they similar? How were they different?

2. Here's a great option if you have access to a trampoline. Repeat the activity using a bowling ball in the center and marbles to represent passing satellites. Have students compare the results with previous activities.

3. Using the Internet, have teams research Albert Einstein's views on gravity. Challenge each team to contribute materials (drawings, descriptions, etc.) for a classroom bulletin board on this topic.

4. Watch a video of astronauts in space. Discuss how lower gravity impacts mass, movement, and inertia. (Mass doesn't change!) Have students write a few paragraphs about one thing they learn.

5. Challenge teams to calculate their collective weight. Now calculate the collective weight of the class on a planet with half Earth's gravity. Discuss mass and weight in this context (similar on Earth, but not in space!).

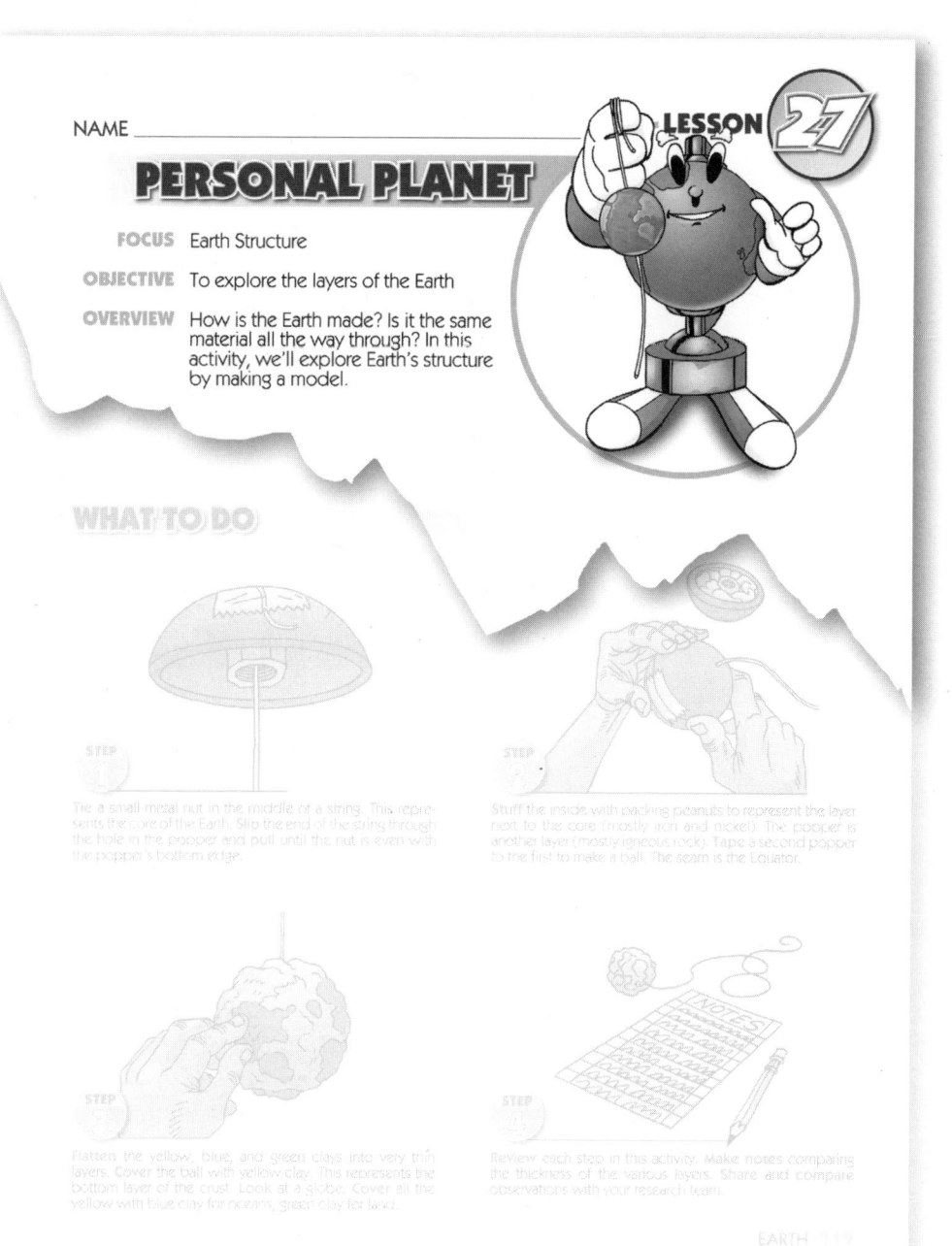

NAME _____

PERSONAL PLANET

LESSON 27

FOCUS Earth Structure

OBJECTIVE To explore the layers of the Earth

OVERVIEW How is the Earth made? Is it the same material all the way through? In this activity, we'll explore Earth's structure by making a model.

WHAT TO DO

STEP
Tie a small metal nut in the middle of a string. This represents the core of the Earth. Slip the end of the string through the hole in the popper and pull until the nut is even with the popper's bottom edge.

STEP
Stuff the inside with packing peanuts to represent the layer next to the core (mostly iron and nickel). The popper is another layer (mostly igneous rock). Tape a second popper to the first to make a ball. The seam is the Equator.

STEP
Flatten the yellow, blue, and green clays into very thin layers. Cover the ball with yellow clay. This represents the bottom layer of the crust. Look at a globe. Cover all the yellow with blue clay for oceans, green clay for land.

STEP
Review each step in this activity. Make notes comparing the thickness of the various layers. Share and compare observations with your research team.

EARTH

Category
Earth Science

Focus
Earth Structure

Objective
To explore the layers of the Earth

National Standards
A1, A2, D1, D2, G1, G2

Materials Needed
metal nut
string
large poppers - 2
packing pellets
clay
tape
globe

Safety Concerns
none

Additional Comments

Remind students that clay layers should be *very* thin. Working with clay can get messy, so have cleanup items handy. Poppers and nuts can be cleaned and used next year.

Overview

Read the overview aloud to your students. The goal is to create an atmosphere of curiosity and inquiry.

Lesson 27 · **121**

WHAT TO DO

Monitor student research teams as they complete each step.

NAME _____

PERSONAL PLANET

FOCUS Earth Structure

OBJECTIVE To explore the layers of the Earth

OVERVIEW How is the Earth made? Is it the same material all the way through? In this activity, we'll explore Earth's structure by making a model.

WHAT TO DO

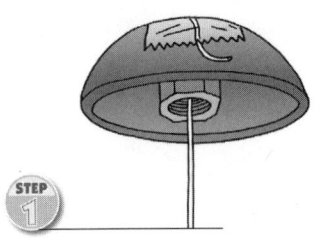

STEP 1
Tie a small metal nut in the middle of a string. This represents the core of the Earth. **Slip** the end of the string through the hole in the popper and **pull** until the nut is even with the popper's bottom edge.

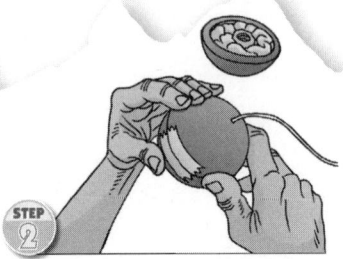

STEP 2
Stuff the inside with packing peanuts to represent the layer next to the core (mostly iron and nickel). The popper is another layer (mostly igneous rock). **Tape** a second popper to the first to make a ball. The seam is the Equator.

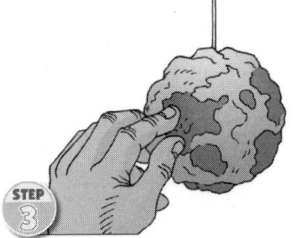

STEP 3
Flatten the yellow, blue, and green clays into very thin layers. **Cover** the ball with yellow clay. This represents the bottom layer of the crust. **Look** at a globe. **Cover** all the yellow with blue clay for oceans; green clay for land.

STEP 4
Review each step in this activity. **Make** notes comparing the thickness of the various layers. **Share** and **compare** observations with your research team.

EARTH 119

Teacher to Teacher

Scientists believe the inner core of the Earth is a sphere of iron (and some nickel) about 1,600 miles across. Even though temperatures are far beyond the melting point of these metals, tremendous pressure — 50 million psi compared to the surface's 15 psi — keeps the center of the core in a solid form.

122 · Lesson 27

WHAT HAPPENED?

This **model** represents the relative thickness of Earth's **layers**. The nut represents the inner **core** of the Earth. The packing peanuts represent the outer core. The popper represents the **mantle**. The layers of clay represent the **crust** of Earth.

Scientist believe Earth's core is mostly iron. Because of enormous pressure, the inner portion of the core is solid iron. The outer core is liquid (**molten**) iron.

The mantle is made of **minerals** in a state between molten and solid. These minerals are mostly melted **igneous rock** that scientists call **magma**.

The crust of the Earth (the part you walk on) is relatively **solid**. It has layers of its own, mostly made of rock, soil, sand, and similar materials.

WHAT WE LEARNED

1 Name the three primary parts of the model. How were they similar? How were they different?

a) core, mantle, crust

b) answers will vary, but should reflect logical comparisons

2 Name and describe the innermost (center) layer of Earth. What do scientists believe it is composed of? What are its two parts?

a) core

b) mostly iron

c) inner core is solid iron; outer core is liquid (molten) iron

3 Name the middle layer of Earth. What is it composed of? What do scientists call the melted rock?

a) mantle

b) melted igneous rock

c) magma

4 Name and describe the outer layer of Earth. What is it composed of? How does this layer compare to the other layers?

a) crust

b) rock, soil, sand, similar materials

c) it is relatively solid

5 What states of matter are represented in this model? Explain your answer.

solid (crust and inner core) and liquid (mantle and outer core)

What Happened

Review the section with students. Emphasize bold-face words that identify key concepts and introduce new vocabulary.

This **model** represents the relative thickness of Earth's **layers**. The nut represents the inner **core** of the Earth. The packing pellets represent the outer core. The popper represents the **mantle**. The layers of clay represent the **crust** of Earth.

Scientists believe Earth's core is mostly iron. Because of enormous pressure, the inner portion of the core is solid iron. The outer core is liquid (**molten**) iron.

The mantle is made of **minerals** in a state between molten and solid. These minerals are mostly melted **igneous rock** that scientists call **magma**.

The crust of the Earth (the part you walk on) is relatively **solid**. It has layers of its own, mostly made of rock, soil, sand, and similar materials.

What We Learned

Answers will vary. Suggested responses are shown at left.

Conclusion

Read this section aloud to the class to summarize the concepts learned in this activity.

Food for Thought

Read the Scripture aloud to the class. Talk about how the more time we spend with God, the better we reflect his character. Discuss specific ways we can show God's love through our treatment of others.

Journal

If time permits, have a general class discussion about notes and drawings various students added to their journal pages. Discuss correct and incorrect predictions, and remind students that this "trial and error" process is part of the scientific process.

CONCLUSION

The Earth is a series of complicated layers that contain tremendous energy. These layers can be divided into three major sections: the core, the mantle, and the crust.

FOOD FOR THOUGHT

2 Thessalonians 3:6-10 Models are very useful tools for helping us understand the world around us. In this Scripture, Paul writes about the importance of being a good model to others.

Think about the way you treat people around you. Are you being a good model? Does the way you relate to others reflect the love of God? The more time you spend learning about God, the more you'll be able to truly reflect God's character to the world.

JOURNAL — My Science Notes

Extended Teaching

1. Have teams repeat this activity by making a large paper mache' model of Earth. (Use a balloon for the mold.) Shape and color the continents as accurately as possible. Ask how this model compares to the original activity.

2. Using the Internet, have teams research earthquakes and their causes. What do earthquakes tell us about the Earth's layers? Challenge each team to create a poster depicting some of their findings.

3. If your area is prone to Earthquakes, invite a building inspector to visit your classroom. Ask him/her to talk about ways buildings can be made safer. Have students write a paragraph about one thing they learn.

4. Take a field trip to an interesting geological area (canyon, plateau, dunes, etc.). Discuss how this area differs from the Earth's crust at your school. Have students write a paragraph about one thing they learn.

5. Have teams research seismographs and how the "Richter scale" works. Gather information on historic earthquakes. Challenge each team to create a poster about one such event, including its Richter scale rating.

Reproduction of student page

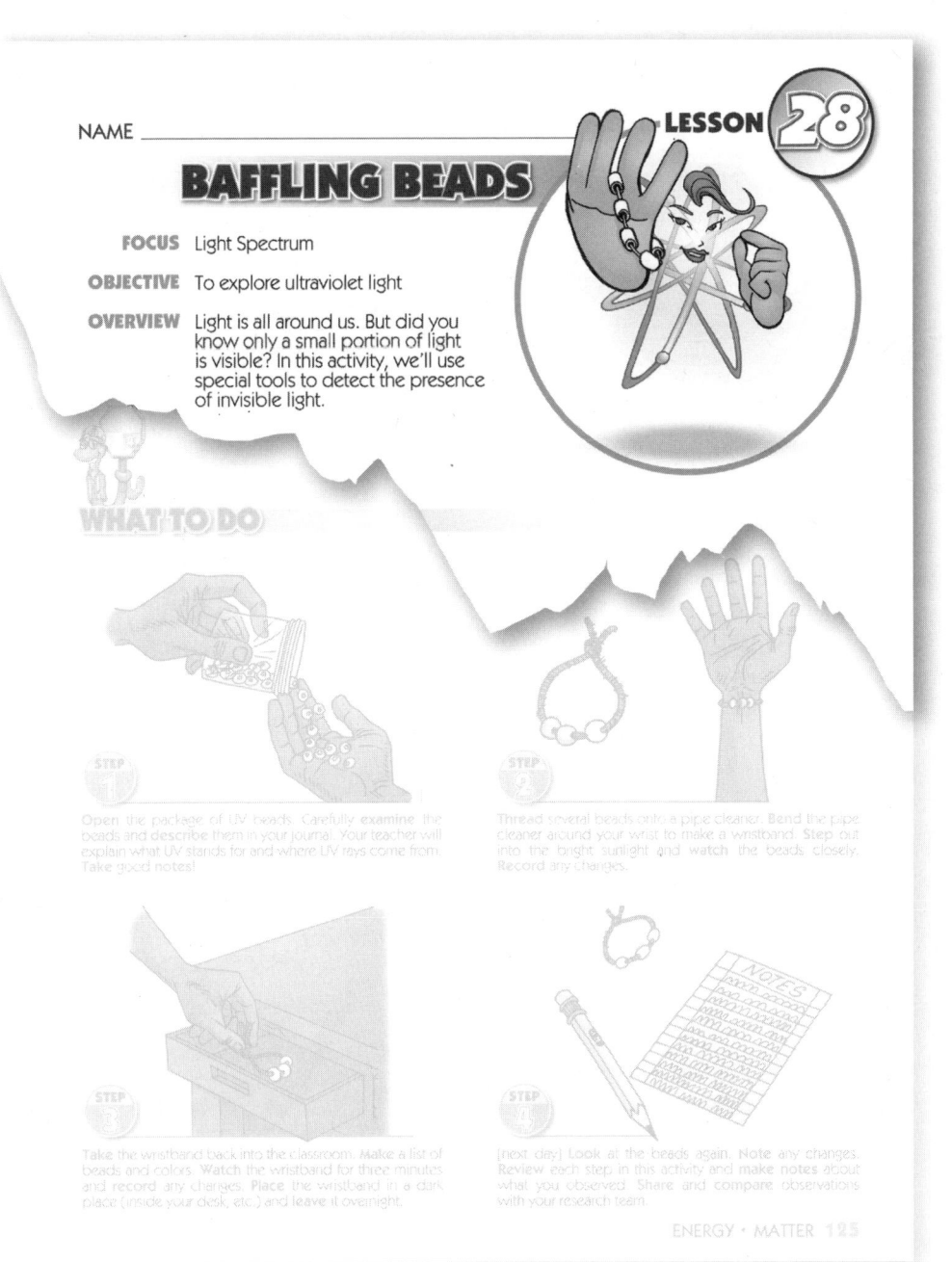

NAME _____

LESSON 28
BAFFLING BEADS

FOCUS Light Spectrum

OBJECTIVE To explore ultraviolet light

OVERVIEW Light is all around us. But did you know only a small portion of light is visible? In this activity, we'll use special tools to detect the presence of invisible light.

WHAT TO DO

STEP 1
Open the package of UV beads. Carefully examine the beads and describe them in your journal. Your teacher will explain what UV stands for and where UV rays come from. Take good notes!

STEP 2
Thread several beads onto a pipe cleaner. Bend the pipe cleaner around your wrist to make a wristband. Step out into the bright sunlight and watch the beads closely. Record any changes.

STEP 3
Take the wristband back into the classroom. Make a list of beads and colors. Watch the wristband for three minutes and record any changes. Place the wristband in a dark place (inside your desk, etc.) and leave it overnight.

STEP 4
[next day] Look at the beads again. Note any changes. Review each step in this activity and make notes about what you observed. Share and compare observations with your research team.

ENERGY · MATTER 125

Category
Physical Science
Energy/Matter

Focus
Light Spectrum

Objective
To explore ultraviolet light

National Standards
A1, A2, B1, B2, B3, E1, E2, F1, F3, F5, G1, G2

Materials Needed
UV beads
pipe cleaner

Safety Concerns
4. Other
Never allow students to look directly at the Sun.

Additional Comments

Without proper supervision, tiny parts can lead to horseplay. Make sure students are using beads correctly. Don't let them throw beads or put them in their mouths.

Overview

Read the overview aloud to your students. The goal is to create an atmosphere of curiosity and inquiry.

Lesson 28 · **125**

WHAT TO DO

Monitor student research teams as they complete each step.

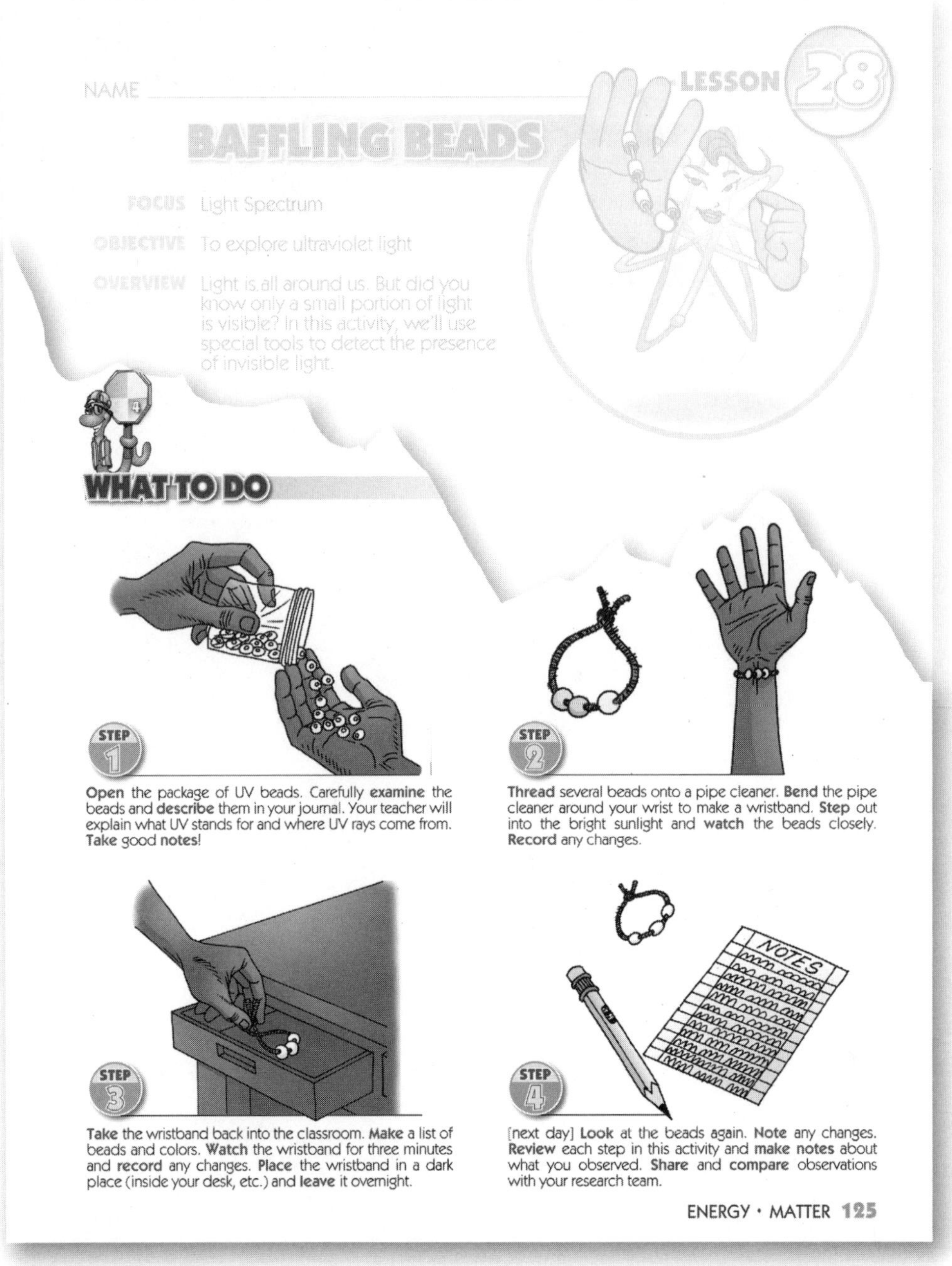

NAME _____

BAFFLING BEADS

LESSON 28

FOCUS Light Spectrum

OBJECTIVE To explore ultraviolet light

OVERVIEW Light is all around us. But did you know only a small portion of light is visible? In this activity, we'll use special tools to detect the presence of invisible light.

WHAT TO DO

STEP 1
Open the package of UV beads. Carefully **examine** the beads and **describe** them in your journal. Your teacher will explain what UV stands for and where UV rays come from. **Take** good **notes!**

STEP 2
Thread several beads onto a pipe cleaner. **Bend** the pipe cleaner around your wrist to make a wristband. **Step** out into the bright sunlight and **watch** the beads closely. **Record** any changes.

STEP 3
Take the wristband back into the classroom. **Make** a list of beads and colors. **Watch** the wristband for three minutes and **record** any changes. **Place** the wristband in a dark place (inside your desk, etc.) and **leave** it overnight.

STEP 4
[next day] **Look** at the beads again. **Note** any changes. **Review** each step in this activity and **make notes** about what you observed. **Share** and **compare** observations with your research team.

ENERGY · MATTER 125

Teacher to Teacher

Within the "visible light spectrum," human eyes have fantastic capabilities for vision and color discrimination. But we're completely blind to about 99% of the electromagnetic spectrum. In this activity, for instance, we couldn't see the ultraviolet light itself — only its effect on the beads when they radiated colors.

WHAT HAPPENED?

These special beads are made from a material that absorbs the ultraviolet light from sunlight. Ultraviolet light is colorless and invisible, but the beads help indicate its presence. After they've absorbed the light, they begin radiating (releasing) this light. Variations in the material the beads are made from cause the ultraviolet light to show up as different colors.

A rainbow shows you all the colors of visible light. But once you pass violet, the frequency (vibration rate) of light is too fast for your eyes to see. In fact, that's where ultraviolet light gets its name: ultra means "greater than" so ultra-violet means light whose frequency is greater than that of violet light!

WHAT WE LEARNED

1. Compare the beads in Step 1 with those in Step 2. How were they similar? How were the light sources different?

a) similar: same beads

b) different: white in Step 1, colors in Step 2

c) sunlight contains UV light

2. How many beads were on your wristband? How many colors were represented?

Answers will vary depending on combinations.

3. What combination created the colors in Step 3? How is this similar or different from a rainbow?

a) a material that could absorb UV light, then radiate visible light

b) both show only visible light, not UV

4. Describe the beads in Step 4 (no light). What happened to the color?

Beads went back to their original color.

5. Based on what you've learned, would your classroom be a good place to get a large dose of ultraviolet light? Explain your answer.

a) no

b) classroom lights don't give off UV light like sunlight does

---

What Happened

Review the section with students. Emphasize bold-face words that identify key concepts and introduce new vocabulary.

*These special beads are made from a material that **absorbs** the **ultraviolet light** from **sunlight**. Ultraviolet light is colorless and invisible, but the beads help indicate its presence. After they've absorbed the light, they begin **radiating** (releasing) this light. Variations in the material the beads are made from cause the ultraviolet light to show up as different colors.*

*A **rainbow** shows you all the **colors** of **visible light**. But once you pass violet, the **frequency** (vibration rate) of light is too fast for your eyes to see. In fact, that's where ultraviolet light gets its name: ultra means "greater than" so ultra-violet means light that has a frequency is greater than that of violet light!*

What We Learned

Answers will vary. Suggested responses are shown at left.

Lesson 28 · 127

Conclusion

Read this section aloud to the class to summarize the concepts learned in this activity.

Food for Thought

Read the Scripture aloud to the class. Talk about the analogy of absorbing, then radiating light. Discuss how this is similar to what happens in our lives when we let God's love shine in.

Journal

If time permits, have a general class discussion about notes and drawings various students added to their journal pages. Discuss correct and incorrect predictions, and remind students that this "trial and error" process is part of the scientific process.

CONCLUSION

Only a portion of the light spectrum is visible to the human eye. Invisible forms, like ultraviolet, can be detected with special tools. Light energy can be absorbed and released.

FOOD FOR THOUGHT

Psalm 27:1 When there was no light, the beads looked much the same — dull and featureless. But when they were placed in strong sunlight, they began to absorb ultraviolet light. They absorbed so much that they began to radiate that light back as color. As long as they continued to absorb light, the beads could really shine!

In this Scripture, David reminds us that God is the ultimate source of light. Like the beads, our lives can be pretty dull and featureless. But when we open our hearts to God, we begin to absorb his great love. As our lives are filled, we begin to radiate God's great love to others. But remember, this process can only continue if we stay close to God!

JOURNAL — My Science Notes

128 ENERGY • MATTER

Extended Teaching

1. Have teams research health risks associated with too much UV light. Challenge each team to make a safety poster based on what they learn.

2. Using the Internet, have teams research other forms of solar energy. How are they similar to UV light? How are they different? How are they used? Challenge teams to contribute material for a bulletin board on this topic.

3. Invite a telecommunications technician to visit your classroom. Find out what part of the electromagnetic spectrum is used in his/her field, and how it works. Have students write a paragraph about one thing they learn.

4. Have teams research what a photon is, how it works, and how it's used. Challenge each team to create a poster showing at least one aspect of what they learn about photons.

5. Invite a satellite television technician to visit your classroom. Ask him/her to show how waves are used to send information. Challenge students to write a paragraph about one thing they learn.

128 • Lesson 28

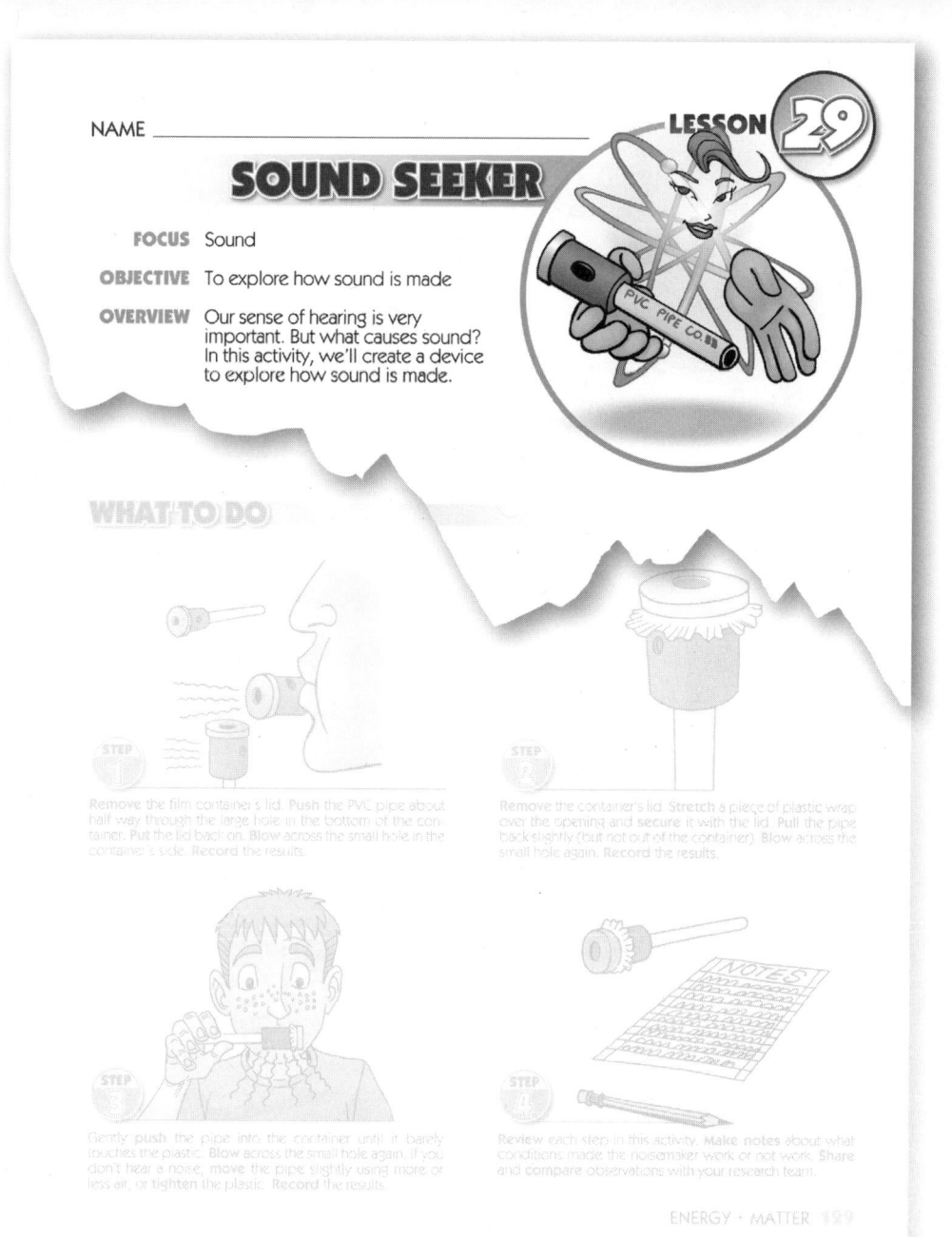

NAME _____

SOUND SEEKER

LESSON 29

FOCUS Sound

OBJECTIVE To explore how sound is made

OVERVIEW Our sense of hearing is very important. But what causes sound? In this activity, we'll create a device to explore how sound is made.

WHAT TO DO

STEP 1 Remove the film container's lid. Push the PVC pipe about half way through the large hole in the bottom of the container. Put the lid back on. Blow across the small hole in the container's side. Record the results.

STEP 2 Remove the container's lid. Stretch a piece of plastic wrap over the opening and secure it with the lid. Pull the pipe back slightly (but not out of the container). Blow across the small hole again. Record the results.

STEP 3 Gently push the pipe into the container until it barely touches the plastic. Blow across the small hole again. If you don't hear a noise, move the pipe slightly using more or less air, or tighten the plastic. Record the results.

STEP 4 Review each step in this activity. Make notes about what conditions made the noisemaker work or not work. Share and compare observations with your research team.

ENERGY · MATTER 129

Category
Physical Science
Energy/Matter

Focus
Sound

Objective
To explore how sound is made

National Standards
A1, A2, B1, B2, B3, E1, E2, F5, G1, G2

Materials Needed
film container
PVC pipe
plastic wrap

Safety Concerns
none

Additional Comments

You might want to warn the principal and other teachers before doing this activity — it has a tendency to be a bit loud! All materials (except the plastic wrap) can be reused. Wash with soap and water, dry, and store in a sealed plastic bag.

Overview

Read the overview aloud to your students. The goal is to create an atmosphere of curiosity and inquiry.

Lesson 29 · 129

WHAT TO DO

Monitor student research teams as they complete each step.

NAME _____

SOUND SEEKER

FOCUS Sound

OBJECTIVE To explore how sound is made

OVERVIEW Our sense of hearing is very important. But what causes sound? In this activity, we'll create a device to explore how sound is made.

WHAT TO DO

STEP 1
Remove the film container's lid. **Push** the PVC pipe about half way through the large hole in the bottom of the container. **Put** the lid back on. **Blow** across the small hole in the container's side. **Record** the results.

STEP 2
Remove the container's lid. **Stretch** a piece of plastic wrap over the opening and **secure** it with the lid. **Pull** the pipe back slightly (but not out of the container). **Blow** across the small hole again. **Record** the results.

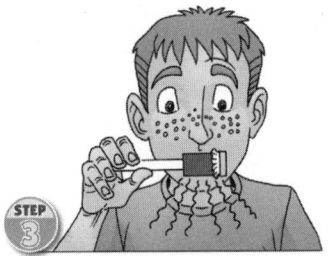

STEP 3
Gently **push** the pipe into the container until it barely touches the plastic. **Blow** across the small hole again. If you don't hear a noise, **move** the pipe slightly using more or less air, or **tighten** the plastic. **Record** the results.

STEP 4
Review each step in this activity. **Make** notes about what conditions made the noisemaker work or not work. **Share** and **compare** observations with your research team.

ENERGY • MATTER 129

Teacher to Teacher

Light, sound, heat, radio, television, cell phone signals — what do they all have in common? They're all forms of energy that travel in waves! Although each one has a different speed (velocity), length (wavelength), and vibration rate (frequency), they're all examples of energy being moved from one place to another.

WHAT HAPPENED?

Sound is produced by a sequence of events. It begins with some form of *energy*. The energy causes something to move causing *vibrations* (called waves). The *waves* make the air move, helping *transmit* the vibration to a device capable of detecting it.

In this activity, your lungs provided the energy to move air rapidly across the opening. This caused the plastic to vibrate, creating sound waves. The sound waves vibrated the air in the tube, *amplifying* the sound so your ears could detect it!

Notice that changing the length of the pipe changed the rate of vibration (also known as *frequency*). The adjustment in vibration rates changed the sound produced.

WHAT WE LEARNED

1. Describe what you heard in Step 1 and Step 2. How were the sounds similar? How were they different?

Answers will vary, but should reflect more sound in Step 2.

2. Describe what you heard in Step 3. How was it similar to sounds heard in the other steps? How was it different?

Answers will vary, but sound is usually more controlled in Step 3.

130 ENERGY • MATTER

3. Describe the steps necessary to produce sound.

Energy causes vibrations that make air move, which transmits the "sound" to a detection device.

4. Based on what you've learned, what are some factors that might affect how loud a sound is?

Amount of energy, rate of vibration, transfer medium (air, water, etc.) and so on.

5. Think about a band or orchestra you've heard. Choose three instruments. Based on what you've learned, explain why they produce different sounds.

Answers will vary, but should reflect differences in vibration produced.

ENERGY • MATTER 131

What Happened

Review the section with students. Emphasize bold-face words that identify key concepts and introduce new vocabulary.

Sound *is produced by a sequence of events. It begins with some form of* **energy**. *The energy causes something to move, causing* **vibrations** *(called waves). The* **waves** *make the air move, helping* **transmit** *the vibration to a device capable of detecting it.*

In this activity, your lungs provided the energy to move air rapidly across the opening. This caused the plastic to vibrate, creating sound waves. The sound waves vibrated the air in the tube, **amplifying** *the sound so your ears could detect it!*

Notice that changing the length of the pipe changed the rate of vibration (also known as **frequency**). *The adjustment in vibration rates changed the sound produced.*

What We Learned

Answers will vary. Suggested responses are shown at left.

Lesson 29 • **131**

Conclusion

Read this section aloud to the class to summarize the concepts learned in this activity.

Food for Thought

Read the Scripture aloud to the class. Talk about ways we can use our voices as an act of worship. Discuss other ways we can offer praise to God.

Journal

If time permits, have a general class discussion about notes and drawings various students added to their journal pages. Discuss correct and incorrect predictions, and remind students that this "trial and error" process is part of the scientific process.

CONCLUSION

To create sound, energy must produce vibration which leads to air movement. The rate of vibration is known as frequency. Frequency has an effect on a sound's pitch.

FOOD FOR THOUGHT

Psalm 95:1-2 In this activity, we discovered the ingredients of sound: energy, vibration, and air movement. The device you made put those all together to produce . . . well, not exactly music . . . but certainly a joyful noise!

Humans are certainly inclined to be noisy creatures, but the kind of noise we make is up to us. This Scripture talks about singing and making music to worship God. It's only one of many such verses in Scripture. Creating sounds of praise is a great way to exercise this part of our nature. Think of God's great love and make joyful, happy sounds for your creator!

JOURNAL — My Science Notes

132 ENERGY · MATTER

Extended Teaching

1. Repeat this activity using containers of different sizes. Compare the results with the original activity. How were they similar? How were they different?

2. Invite a band teacher to visit your classroom. Have him/her bring various instruments to show how sound is made. Have students write a paragraph about one thing they learn.

3. Challenge each team to make a list of energy forms that travel by waves. Have each team contribute materials (drawings, descriptions, etc.) for a classroom bulletin board on this topic.

4. Have teams discuss what life would be like if technology was unable to use energy waves (no radio, television, cell phones, etc.). Now challenge students to write a short story on this topic (either in groups or individually).

5. Take a field trip to a TV repair shop or science lab. Have a technician demonstrate the use of an oscilloscope. Find out how oscilloscopes are used. Have students write a paragraph about one thing they learn.

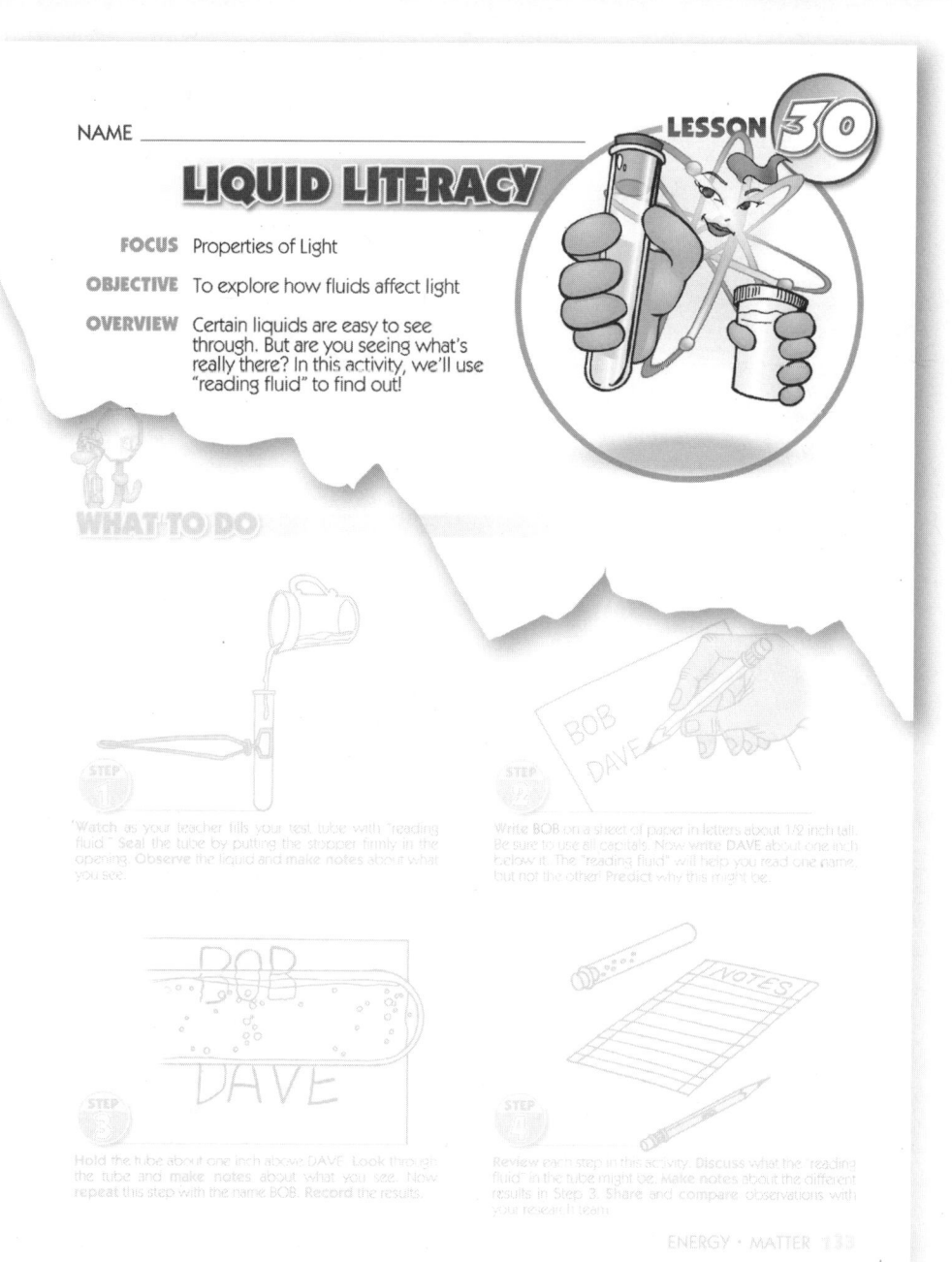

NAME _____

LIQUID LITERACY

LESSON 30

FOCUS Properties of Light

OBJECTIVE To explore how fluids affect light

OVERVIEW Certain liquids are easy to see through. But are you seeing what's really there? In this activity, we'll use "reading fluid" to find out!

WHAT TO DO

STEP 1 Watch as your teacher fills your test tube with "reading fluid." Seal the tube by putting the stopper firmly in the opening. Observe the liquid and make notes about what you see.

STEP 2 Write BOB on a sheet of paper in letters about 1/2 inch tall. Be sure to use all capitals. Now write DAVE about one inch below it. The "reading fluid" will help you read one name, but not the other. Predict why this might be.

STEP 3 Hold the tube about one inch above DAVE. Look through the tube and make notes about what you see. Now repeat this step with the name BOB. Record the results.

STEP 4 Review each step in this activity. Discuss what the "reading fluid" in the tube might be. Make notes about the different results in Step 3. Share and compare observations with your research team.

ENERGY · MATTER 133

Category
Physical Science
Energy/Matter

Focus
Properties of Light

Objective
To explore how fluids affect light

National Standards
A1, A2, B1, B2, B3, E1, E2, F5, G1, G2

Materials Needed
test tube
#6 solid stopper
reading fluid (water)
paper

Safety Concerns
4. Breakage
Remind students to exercise caution when handling the test tube.

Additional Comments

A great way to introduce this lesson is to tell students a special "reading fluid" will be used for this activity. When Step 4 is complete, reveal that this "reading fluid" is also called "water." This makes a great transition into the "What Happened" section.

Overview

Read the overview aloud to your students. The goal is to create an atmosphere of curiosity and inquiry.

Lesson 30 · **133**

WHAT TO DO

Monitor student research teams as they complete each step.

NAME _____

LIQUID LITERACY

LESSON 30

FOCUS Properties of Light

OBJECTIVE To explore how fluids affect light

OVERVIEW Certain liquids are easy to see through. But are you seeing what's really there? In this activity, we'll use "reading fluid" to find out!

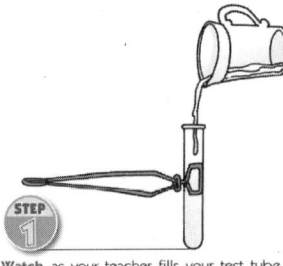

WHAT TO DO

STEP 1
Watch as your teacher fills your test tube with "reading fluid." **Seal** the tube by putting the stopper firmly in the opening. **Observe** the liquid and **make notes** about what you see.

STEP 2
Write **BOB** on a sheet of paper in letters about 1/2 inch tall. Be sure to use all capitals. Now **write DAVE** about one inch below it. The "reading fluid" will help you read one name, but not the other! **Predict** why this might be.

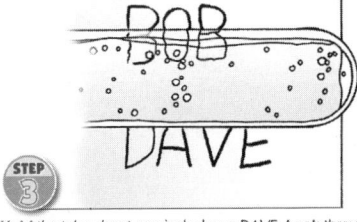

STEP 3
Hold the tube about one inch above DAVE. **Look** through the tube and **make notes** about what you see. Now **repeat** this step with the name BOB. **Record** the results.

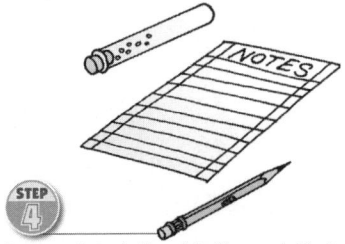

STEP 4
Review each step in this activity. **Discuss** what the "reading fluid" in the tube might be. **Make notes** about the different results in Step 3. **Share** and **compare** observations with your research team.

ENERGY · MATTER 133

Teacher to Teacher

The curved glass surface and dense layer of water caused the images to appear upside down. This phenomenon occurs with many lenses — even the ones in our eyes! Our brains must learn to compensate for this when we're infants. That's one reason babies "miss" as they first begin reaching for things.

WHAT HAPPENED?

The "reading fluid" we used for this activity was ordinary water. Clear water is easy to see through (*transparent*), but it also causes *light* to slow down. It's like running through a field of tall grass compared to running on the gym floor. The thick grass (high *density*) slows your movement.

When high density materials like water or glass slow light down, they cause the light to *refract* (bend). In Step 3, you used the tube like a *lens*. The light reaching your eyes from the *image* slowed down so much that it caused the image to *invert* (flip).

Now here's the trick. Since the capital letters O and B look the same right side up or upside down, you could read "BOB," but you couldn't read "DAVE" because the A and V were inverted!

WHAT WE LEARNED

1) Describe the liquid you put into the test tube in Step 1. What effect did this liquid have on light?

a) clear, flows easily, odorless, etc.

b) made light bend

2) What did you predict in Step 2? How did this prediction reflect what actually happened?

Answers will vary, but should reflect logical comparisons.

3) What is the process of bending light called? How is this process helpful in correcting eye problems?

a) refracting

b) allows us to change the amount light is bent to compensate for eye defects

4) Explain why one name was easy to read through the tube of water and the other wasn't.

Capital letters O and B look the same right side up or upside down.

5) Based on what you've learned, explain why Native Americans had to understand the relationship between water and light to hunt fish with a bow.

Because water bends light, a fish isn't where it appears to be . . . you must compensate for this to bow fish.

What Happened

Review the section with students. Emphasize bold-face words that identify key concepts and introduce new vocabulary.

*The "reading fluid" we used for this activity was ordinary water. Clear water is easy to see through (**transparent**), but it also causes **light** to slow down. It's like running through a field of tall grass compared to running on the gym floor. The thick grass (high **density**) slows your movement.*

*When high density materials like water or glass slow light down, they cause the light to **refract** (bend). In Step 3, you used the tube like a **lens**. The light reaching your eyes from the **image** slowed down so much that it caused the image to **invert** (flip).*

Now here's the trick. Since the capital letters O and B look the same right side up or upside down, you could read "BOB," but you couldn't read "DAVE" because the A and V were inverted!

What We Learned

Answers will vary. Suggested responses are shown at left.

Lesson 30 · 135

Conclusion

Read this section aloud to the class to summarize the concepts learned in this activity.

Food for Thought

Read the Scripture aloud to the class. Talk about how Hollywood can warp our thinking, and how outward appearances are often deceiving. Discuss what it takes to have a "beautiful" heart.

Journal

If time permits, have a general class discussion about notes and drawings various students added to their journal pages. Discuss correct and incorrect predictions, and remind students that this "trial and error" process is part of the scientific process.

CONCLUSION

Some materials can slow light, causing it to refract (bend). Lenses help control the degree of refraction. Certain kinds of lenses use refraction to produce an inverted image.

FOOD FOR THOUGHT

Proverbs 27:19 All vision is based on light reflecting off a surface to your eyes. But as we saw in this activity, there are times when things interfere with an accurate reflection. Often we need to know more in order to understand whether what we're seeing is the "real thing" or an illusion.

A good mirror shows you an accurate reflection of your face. However, this Scripture reminds us that outward appearance doesn't always show what's inside. The "real you" is shown by the kind of friends you choose and the way you treat others. When God is in your heart, his love can shine out for all to see!

JOURNAL — My Science Notes

136 ENERGY • MATTER

Extended Teaching

1. Repeat this activity, filling the test tube with different clear liquids (safe materials like glycerin, liquid soap, etc.). Compare the results to the original activity. How were they similar? How were they different?

2. Take a field trip to an optometrist's office. Ask him/her to demonstrate how lenses are used to help correct eye problems. Have students write a paragraph about one thing they learn.

3. Invite a professional photographer to visit your classroom. Ask him/her to show how lenses are used to achieve different effects. Have students write a paragraph about one thing they learn.

4. Using the Internet, have teams research "esotropia." What is it? How does it affect vision? How do doctors treat it? Challenge each team to create a poster about this or a similar vision problem.

5. Have teams research brain-related vision problems (amblyopia, dyslexia, etc.). Challenge each team to contribute material (drawings, descriptions) for a classroom bulletin board on this topic.

Category

Physical Science
Energy/Matter

Focus

Periodic Table

Objective

To explore the periodic table

National Standards

A1, A2, G1, G2

Materials Needed

Puzzle Pieces worksheet (student worktext, p.169)
Framework worksheet (student worktext, p.171)
Reference worksheet (Student Worktext, p.173)
scissors
glue

Safety Concerns

4. Sharp Objects
Remind students to exercise caution when using scissors.

Additional Comments

The focus of this lesson is the *concept* of organizing information scientifically. To avoid needless complexity, only a portion of the Periodic Table is used. (See "Teacher to Teacher" for more information.)

Overview

Read the overview aloud to your students. The goal is to create an atmosphere of curiosity and inquiry.

Lesson 31 · **137**

WHAT TO DO

Monitor student research teams as they complete each step.

NAME _____

PERIODIC PUZZLE

FOCUS Periodic Table

OBJECTIVE To explore the periodic table

OVERVIEW Everything around us is made of different elements. How do these elements relate to each other? In this activity, we'll explore how scientists organize this information.

WHAT TO DO

STEP 1
Remove the *Periodic Table Puzzle Pieces* page from the back of your worktext. **Cut out** every item. Carefully **examine** the elements with your research team. **Discuss** different ways you might sort and arrange them.

STEP 2
Remove the *Periodic Table Framework* page from the back of your worktext. **Place** it on your work surface and **arrange** the elements beside it in numeric order. (This will make them easy to locate.)

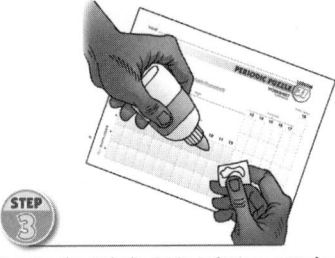

STEP 3
Remove the *Periodic Table Reference* page from the back of your worktext. Use this as a guide. Now **find** the *Puzzle Piece* from Step 1 that has the atomic number 1 (Hydrogen). **Glue** it in the correct spot on the *Framework* from Step 2.

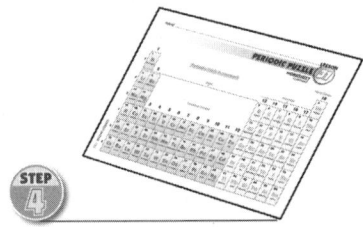

STEP 4
Attach atomic number 2 (Helium) to the *Framework*. **Continue** until all the elements are attached. **Compare** your table to the reference page. **Make notes** about similarities and differences. **Share** and **compare** observations with your research team.

ENERGY · MATTER 137

Teacher to Teacher

Like most scientific models, the periodic table continues to change over time. Although the concept of organizing elements began with Laviosier in the 1700s, our modern Periodic Table dates back to Mendeleyev in 1869. Harry Hubbard first published the familiar "standardized" Table in 1924. The newest version of the "Tables" is a 3-D model (created by Roy Alexander in the mid 1990s), which more clearly defines complex interrelationships between elements.

WHAT HAPPENED?

As early as 400 B.C., the Greeks referred to small particles of matter as elements. They believed there were four primary elements — earth, fire, air, and water. Over the centuries, understanding of elements increased greatly. Then in the 1800s, scientists began to notice that some elements behaved alike. Many scientists contributed to the organization of these elements into groups of various kinds based on different characteristics, eventually leading to what we know today as the Periodic Table.

The modern Periodic Table is based on an element's atomic number. Columns are called families or groups. They're numbered one to eighteen from left to right. Rows are called periods. They're numbered one to six from top to bottom. The periodic table we constructed doesn't include every element (there are 94 natural elements), but it does provide a good representation for study. The actual periodic table is much bigger, and even includes artificial elements engineered by man.

WHAT WE LEARNED

1. Describe the history of the word "element." What did the ancient Greeks believe? How does that compare to our understanding?

a) element = small particles of matter

b) four elements

c) modern Tables list over 100 elements

2. What are the columns on the Periodic Table called? How are they numbered and arranged?

a) families or groups

b) from one to eighteen, left to right

3. What are the rows on the Periodic Table called? How are they numbered and arranged?

a) periods

b) from one to six, top to bottom

4. On your table, what element is in period 4, column 2? What element is in period 6, column 11? What element is in period 2, column 14?

a) calcium

b) gold

c) carbon

5. Over the years, the Periodic Table has seen changes, additions, and improvements, including a three-dimensional version introduced in 1994. Why might a tool like this change over time?

As scientists discover new information, their models change to reflect that information.

What Happened

Review the section with students. Emphasize bold-face words that identify key concepts and introduce new vocabulary.

*As early as 400 B.C., the Greeks referred to small particles of **matter** as **elements**. They believed there were four primary elements — earth, fire, air, and water. Over the centuries, understanding of elements increased greatly. Then in the 1800s, scientists began to notice that some elements behaved alike. Many scientists contributed to the organization of these elements into groups of various kinds, based on different characteristics, eventually leading to what we know today as the **Periodic Table**.*

*The modern Periodic Table is based on an element's **atomic number**. Columns are called **families** or **groups**. They're numbered one to eighteen from left to right. Rows are called **periods**. They're numbered one to six from top to bottom. The periodic table we constructed doesn't include every element (there are 94 natural elements), but it does provide a good representation for study. The actual periodic table is much bigger, and even includes artificial elements engineered by man.*

What We Learned

Answers will vary. Suggested responses are shown at left.

Conclusion

Read this section aloud to the class to summarize the concepts learned in this activity.

Food for Thought

Read the Scripture aloud to the class. Talk about how God created each of us with "a mind and a soul." Discuss specific ways we should use these marvelous gifts.

Journal

If time permits, have a general class discussion about notes and drawings various students added to their journal pages. Discuss correct and incorrect predictions, and remind students that this "trial and error" process is part of the scientific process.

CONCLUSION

The elements that make up all matter have been organized into a chart called the Periodic Table. This chart organizes elements based on their atomic number and chemical properties.

FOOD FOR THOUGHT

Genesis 2:7 Science has shown us that the elements our bodies are made from are also found in rocks, water, plants, animals — virtually everything around us! The interactions between these different elements in all their various combinations is what science is all about.

But centuries before the first scientist figured out that elements are the basic building blocks of matter, Scripture talked about man being formed "from the dust of the ground." So what's the difference between you and a stone? You have a mind and a soul — put there by the Creator himself! How should you use this precious gift? Read Matthew 22:37 for the answer.

JOURNAL   My Science Notes

140   ENERGY • MATTER

Extended Teaching

1. Using the Internet, have teams research what radiation did to Madame Curie and her husband, Pierre. Have students compare this to scientific research today. How is it similar? How is it different?

2. Invite someone from a science lab to visit your classroom. Ask him/her to explain the difference between natural and artificial elements, and describe their uses. Have students write a paragraph about one thing they learn.

3. Arrange a field trip to a cancer treatment facility. Find out how radioactive isotopes are used in medicine to treat cancer. Have students write a paragraph about one thing they learn.

4. Have teams research the history of the Periodic Table. Find out about Laviosier, Mendeleyev, Hubbard, Alexander, and others. Have each team choose a scientist and contribute materials for a bulletin board on this topic.

5. Have teams visit www.periodictable.com — a website with a special section for students! Challenge teams to explore this site, then create a presentation on at least one interesting aspect of the Periodic Table.

140 · Lesson 31

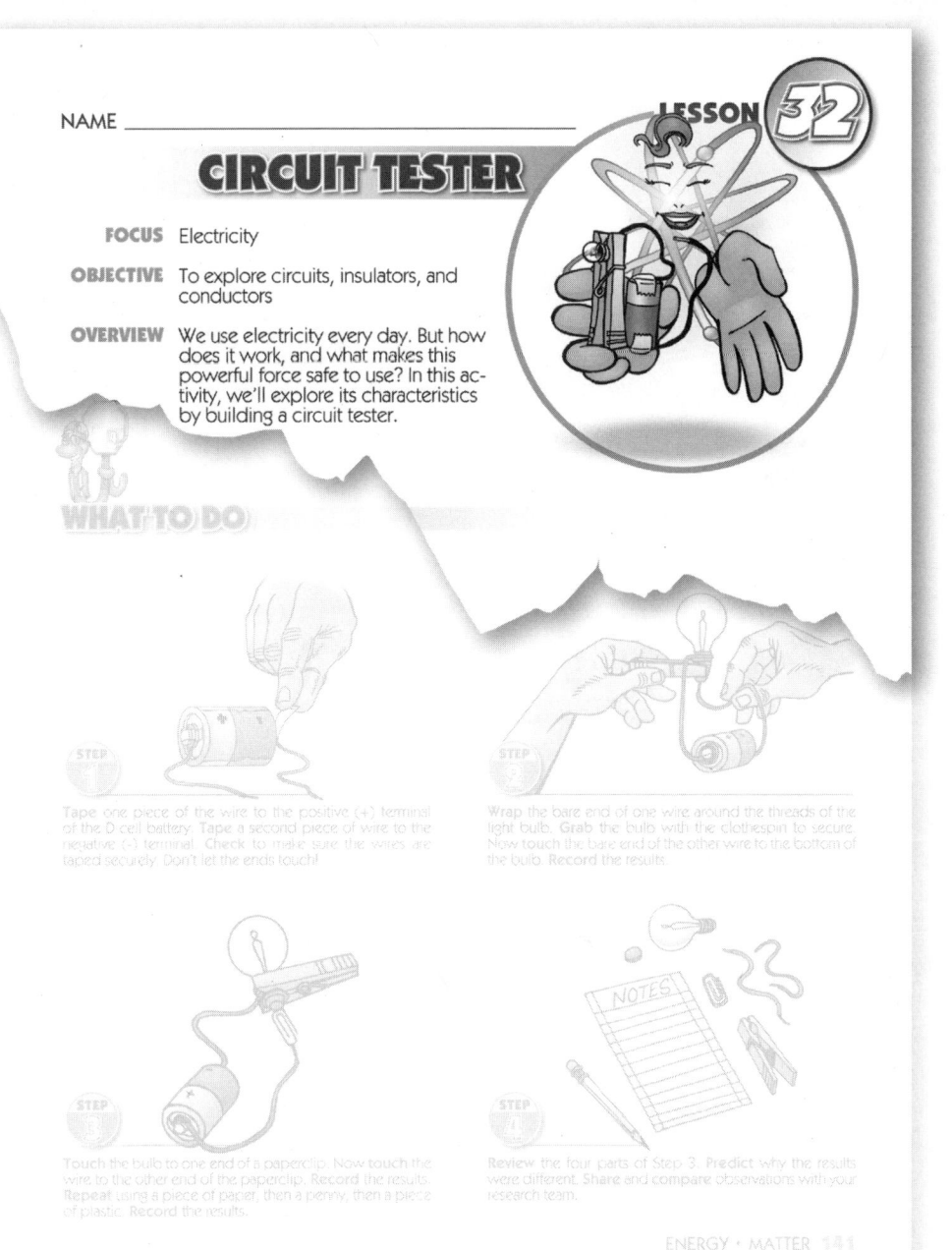

NAME _____

CIRCUIT TESTER

LESSON 32

FOCUS Electricity

OBJECTIVE To explore circuits, insulators, and conductors

OVERVIEW We use electricity every day. But how does it work, and what makes this powerful force safe to use? In this activity, we'll explore its characteristics by building a circuit tester.

WHAT TO DO

STEP 1
Tape one piece of the wire to the positive (+) terminal of the D cell battery. Tape a second piece of wire to the negative (–) terminal. Check to make sure the wires are taped securely. Don't let the ends touch!

STEP 2
Wrap the bare end of one wire around the threads of the light bulb. Grab the bulb with the clothespin to secure. Now touch the bare end of the other wire to the bottom of the bulb. Record the results.

STEP 3
Touch the bulb to one end of a paperclip. Now touch the wire to the other end of the paperclip. Record the results. Repeat using a piece of paper, then a penny, then a piece of plastic. Record the results.

STEP 4
Review the four parts of Step 3. Predict why the results were different. Share and compare observations with your research team.

ENERGY · MATTER 141

Category
Physical Science
Energy/Matter

Focus
Electricity

Objective
To explore circuits, insulators, and conductors

National Standards
A1, A2, B1, B2, B3, E1, E2, F5, G1, G2

Materials Needed
insulated wires - 2
battery
light bulb
pinching clothespin
paperclip
penny
plastic
tape

Safety Concerns
4. Breakage
Remind students to exercise caution when using the bulb.

Additional Comments
Remind students that the current used in this activity is minimal. Using household current for a science activity is extremely dangerous, and should never be attempted without adult direction and supervision!

Overview
Read the overview aloud to your students. The goal is to create an atmosphere of curiosity and inquiry.

Lesson 32 · **141**

WHAT TO DO

Monitor student research teams as they complete each step.

NAME _____

CIRCUIT TESTER

LESSON 32

FOCUS Electricity

OBJECTIVE To explore circuits, insulators, and conductors

OVERVIEW We use electricity every day. But how does it work, and what makes this powerful force safe to use? In this activity, we'll explore its characteristics by building a circuit tester.

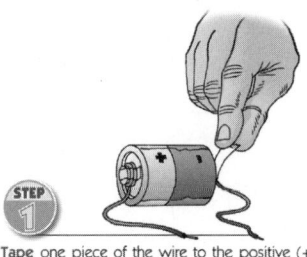

WHAT TO DO

STEP 1
Tape one piece of the wire to the positive (+) terminal of the D cell battery. Tape a second piece of wire to the negative (-) terminal. Check to make sure the wires are taped securely. Don't let the ends touch!

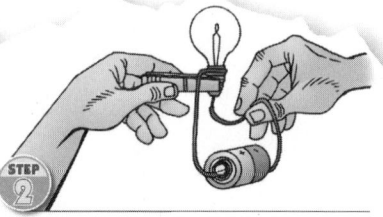

STEP 2
Wrap the bare end of one wire around the threads of the light bulb. Grab the bulb with the clothespin to secure. Now touch the bare end of the other wire to the bottom of the bulb. Record the results.

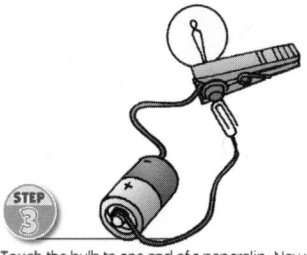

STEP 3
Touch the bulb to one end of a paperclip. Now touch the wire to the other end of the paperclip. Record the results. Repeat using a piece of paper, then a penny, then a piece of plastic. Record the results.

STEP 4
Review the four parts of Step 3. Predict why the results were different. Share and compare observations with your research team.

ENERGY • MATTER 141

Teacher to Teacher

When energy is transferred through the flow of electrons, we call it electricity. There are two primary forms: DC (direct current) and AC (alternating current). DC current flows in only one direction, from negative to positive. Batteries are a good example. AC current's flow is much more complicated. Household current is an example.

WHAT HAPPENED?

The **electricity** in your battery came from a **chemical reaction**. But the **electrons** couldn't get out of the battery to provide **energy** without a path to follow. When you touched the wire to the bulb, you created a path that allowed electrons to flow. This is called a **closed circuit**. Removing the wire broke the path, creating an **open circuit**.

Anything that allows electricity to flow from one place to another (like copper wire) is called a **conductor**. Anything that stops the flow of electricity, keeping it isolated (like the plastic coating on the wire) is called an **insulator**.

A **switch** controls electricity by **opening** or **closing** a circuit. You use a switch every time you turn out the lights. Most electrical devices have a switch of some sort.

WHAT WE LEARNED

1 Describe the difference between an open circuit and a closed circuit.

a) open circuit, electrons can't flow

b) closed circuit, creates a path that allows electrons to flow

2 Describe what happened in Step 2. What kind of circuit did this represent? What indicated it was working?

a) electricity made a complete path

b) closed circuit

c) the bulb lit up

142 ENERGY • MATTER

3 Explain what happened as you tested each item in Step 3. Which were conductors? Which were insulators?

a) the bulb lit up or it didn't

b) conductors: paperclip, penny; insulators: paper, plastic

4 What is the purpose of a switch in a circuit? Name three common devices that use switches.

a) controls electricity by opening or closing a circuit

b) answers will vary

5 What was the electricity source for this activity? How is this current different from household current? Why should you never experiment with household current?

a) a battery

b) lower voltage, flows one way only

c) it's very dangerous

ENERGY • MATTER 143

What Happened

Review the section with students. Emphasize bold-face words that identify key concepts and introduce new vocabulary.

*The **electricity** in your battery came from a **chemical reaction**. But the **electrons** couldn't get out of the battery to provide **energy** without a path to follow. When you touched the wire to the bulb, you created a path that allowed electrons to flow. This is called a **closed circuit**. Removing the wire broke the path, creating an **open circuit**.*

*Anything that allows electricity to flow from one place to another (like copper wire) is called a **conductor**. Anything that stops the flow of electricity, keeping it isolated (like the plastic coating on the wire) is called an **insulator**.*

*A **switch** controls electricity by **opening** or **closing** a circuit. You use a switch every time you turn out the lights. Most electrical devices have a switch of some sort.*

What We Learned

Answers will vary. Suggested responses are shown at left.

Lesson 32 • **143**

Conclusion

Read this section aloud to the class to summarize the concepts learned in this activity.

Food for Thought

Read the Scripture aloud to the class. Talk about the importance of staying connected to God's power. Discuss specific ways we can build a better relationship with God.

Journal

If time permits, have a general class discussion about notes and drawings various students added to their journal pages. Discuss correct and incorrect predictions, and remind students that this "trial and error" process is part of the scientific process.

CONCLUSION

A connected path for electricity is a closed circuit. A disconnected path is an open circuit. Materials that carry current are conductors. Materials that don't carry current are insulators. A switch can open and close circuits.

FOOD FOR THOUGHT

John 14:6 The bulb couldn't access the energy in the battery until it was connected. It didn't matter if the day was sunny or dark with clouds — as long as the bulb was firmly connected, it kept burning brightly. But when the connection was broken, the light faded away.

This Scripture reminds us there is only one way to connect to God's power — through Jesus! As long as we are connected to him, the life-giving power continues to flow. It doesn't matter if times are good, or our world is full of sorrow and pain. As long as we're connected to the Father, we'll continue to be filled with his light.

JOURNAL — My Science Notes

144 ENERGY · MATTER

Extended Teaching

1. Continue this activity by having teams test various classroom materials. Have them keep a list of which ones are conductors and which are insulators. Encourage them to share their findings with other teams.

2. Have teams collect pictures of electrical devices (both DC and AC) from magazines and newspapers. Challenge each team to contribute materials (pictures, descriptions, etc.) for a bulletin board on this topic.

3. Have students research "life before electricity" by interviewing elderly friends, relatives, and neighbors. Have them share stories with their team. Challenge each team to make a presentation based on the data gathered.

4. Take a field trip to a power plant. Ask a representative to explain how electricity is generated and the differences between DC and AC current. Have students write a paragraph about one thing they learn.

5. Invite an electrical lineman to visit your classroom. Ask him/her to talk about safety and interesting work experiences he/she has had. Have students write a paragraph about one thing they learn.

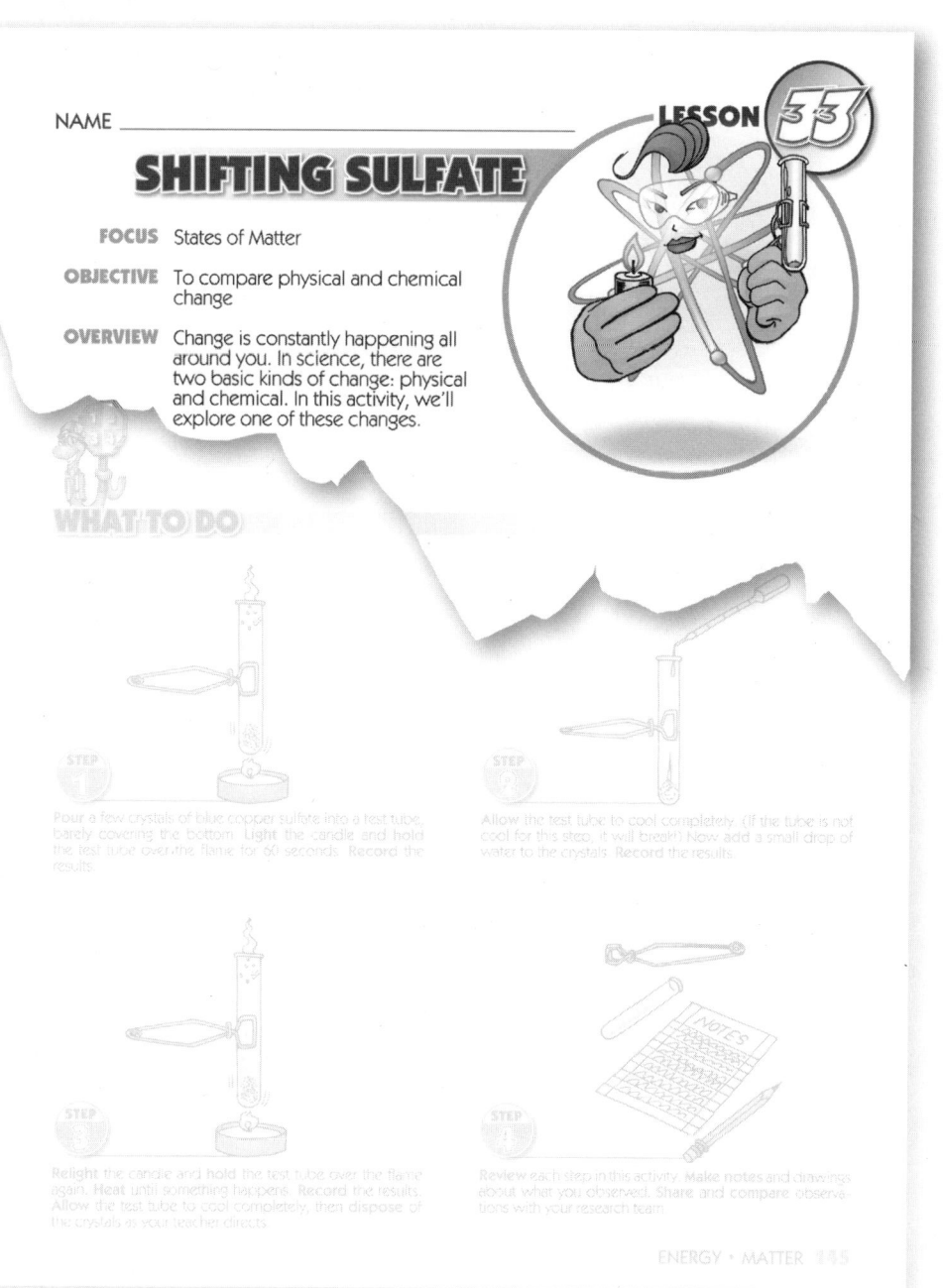

Shifting Sulfate

Category
Physical Science
Energy/Matter

Focus
States of Matter

Objective
To compare physical and chemical change

National Standards
A1, A2, B1, B2, B3, G1, G2

Materials Needed
copper sulfate
test tube
test tube holder
candle
matches
water

Safety Concerns

1. Goggles/Gloves
Always protect eyes when working with chemicals. Gloves are an added precaution.

2. Open Flame
Remind students to exercise extra caution when the candle is burning.

3. Skin Contact
Avoid direct skin contact with the copper sulfate.

4. Breakage
Remind students to exercise caution when handling the test tube.

Additional Comments

The focus for this activity should be whether the things students see are physical or chemical changes. In Step 2, remind students that test tubes can be hot even if they don't look like it! Copper sulfate can be reused if you let it dry completely.

Overview

Read the overview aloud to your students. The goal is to create an atmosphere of curiosity and inquiry.

Lesson 33 · 145

WHAT TO DO

Monitor student research teams as they complete each step.

NAME _____

SHIFTING SULFATE

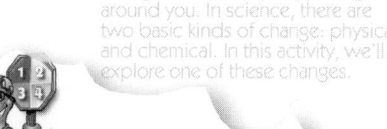

FOCUS States of Matter

OBJECTIVE To compare physical and chemical change

OVERVIEW Change is constantly happening all around you. In science, there are two basic kinds of change: physical and chemical. In this activity, we'll explore one of these changes.

WHAT TO DO

STEP 1
Pour a few crystals of blue copper sulfate into a test tube, barely covering the bottom. Light the candle and hold the test tube over the flame for 60 seconds. Record the results.

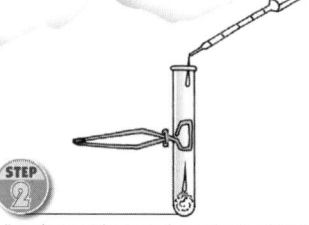

STEP 2
Allow the test tube to cool completely. (If the tube is not cool for this step, it will break!) Now add a small drop of water to the crystals. Record the results.

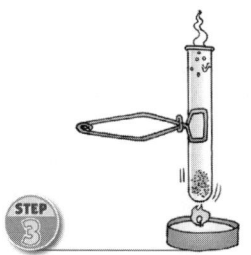

STEP 3
Relight the candle and hold the test tube over the flame again. Heat until something happens. Record the results. Allow the test tube to cool completely, then dispose of the crystals as your teacher directs.

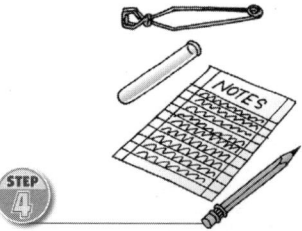

STEP 4
Review each step in this activity. Make notes and drawings about what you observed. Share and compare observations with your research team.

ENERGY • MATTER 145

Teacher to Teacher

Hydrates are chemicals with water inside. Some hydrates release water easily and take it back just as quickly. Others latch on tightly and refuse to let go. The chemical formula for Copper Sulfate is: $CuSO_4 \cdot 5H_2O$. The "dot" symbol lets chemists know this substance is a hydrate.

WHAT HAPPENED?

A **physical change** affects the **form** of a material, but it's still the same **substance** when you're through. (A good example is *freezing* water to make ice cubes. The form changes, but it's still water.) A *chemical change* creates a *different* substance from the one you started with. (A good example is *burning* a piece of wood. Once it's burned, it's no longer wood.)

The copper sulfate you used is a *hydrate*, which means it has water attached. The *heat energy* drove the water out, resulting in a color change. When you put water back in, there was another color change. But neither of these changes created a different substance. It was still copper sulfate when you were done.

WHAT WE LEARNED

1. Describe what happened to the crystals in Step 1. What color were they before heating? What color were they after heating?

a) they changed colors.

b) blue

c) white

2. Describe what happened to the crystals in Step 2. What color were they before adding water? What color were they after the water was added?

a) white

b) blue

3. Describe what happened in Step 3. Compare this with Step 1 and Step 2.

Answers should reflect the fact that water is released into the air, showing that the process is reversible.

4. Explain the difference between chemical change and physical change.

Chemical: creates a different substance; physical: affects form, but material is still the same substance.

5. Based on what you've learned, give an example of a chemical change and an example of a physical change. Explain your answers.

Chemical: burning a piece of wood, etc.; physical: freezing water to make ice cubes, etc.

What Happened

Review the section with students. Emphasize bold-face words that identify key concepts and introduce new vocabulary.

A **physical change** affects the form of a material, but it's still the same **substance** when you're through. (A good example is **freezing** water to make ice cubes. The form changes, but it's still water.) A **chemical change** creates a **different** substance from the one you started with. (A good example is **burning** a piece of wood. Once it's burned, it's no longer wood.)

The copper sulfate you used is a **hydrate**, which means it has water attached. The **heat energy** drove the water out, resulting in a color change. When you put water back in, there was another color change. But neither of these changes created a different substance. It was still copper sulfate when you were done.

What We Learned

Answers will vary. Suggested responses are shown at left.

Lesson 33 · 147

Conclusion

Read this section aloud to the class to summarize the concepts learned in this activity.

Food for Thought

Read the Scripture aloud to the class. Talk about the importance of renewing your relationship with God each day. Discuss specific ways to do this.

Journal

If time permits, have a general class discussion about notes and drawings various students added to their journal pages. Discuss correct and incorrect predictions, and remind students that this "trial and error" process is part of the scientific process.

CONCLUSION
A physical change affects the form of a material, but it's still the same substance. A chemical change results in a different substance from the one you started with. Both changes involve energy.

FOOD FOR THOUGHT
1 Samuel 10:6 This Scripture tells about the anointing of Saul by the prophet Samuel. Saul was changed by God's power, and he went on to become a great ruler of Israel. Unfortunately, as he grew older, Saul began to trust more and more in his own power. Eventually, this great king turned away from God.

You saw some significant changes inside that test tube, but they were only physical changes. No matter what form it took, the material was still copper sulfate. You can make great changes by allowing God's power in your life. But don't make Saul's mistake! Spend time every day renewing your contact with God and letting his power work through you.

JOURNAL — My Science Notes

148 ENERGY • MATTER

Extended Teaching

1. Have teams find pictures that show clear examples of chemical or physical change. Have them post these pictures on the correct half of a bulletin board labeled "Chemical and Physical Change."

2. Take a field trip to a pharmacy. Ask the pharmacist to talk about medicines that are hydrates and how they work. Have students write a paragraph about one thing they learn.

3. Invite someone to bring a dehydrator to class. Ask him/her to show how it works, and bring samples of dehydrated foods. Talk about how this slows spoilage. Have students write a paragraph about one thing they learn.

4. Find an Earth Science book which has chemical formulas for minerals. Have teams list the ones that are hydrates, then discuss similarities and differences. Challenge each team to create a poster about one hydrate.

5. Have each team place a different kind of dehydrated fruit in a sealable bag half full of water. Check the bags the next day. (Do not open bags!) How are the contents similar to yesterday? How are they different?

148 · Lesson 33

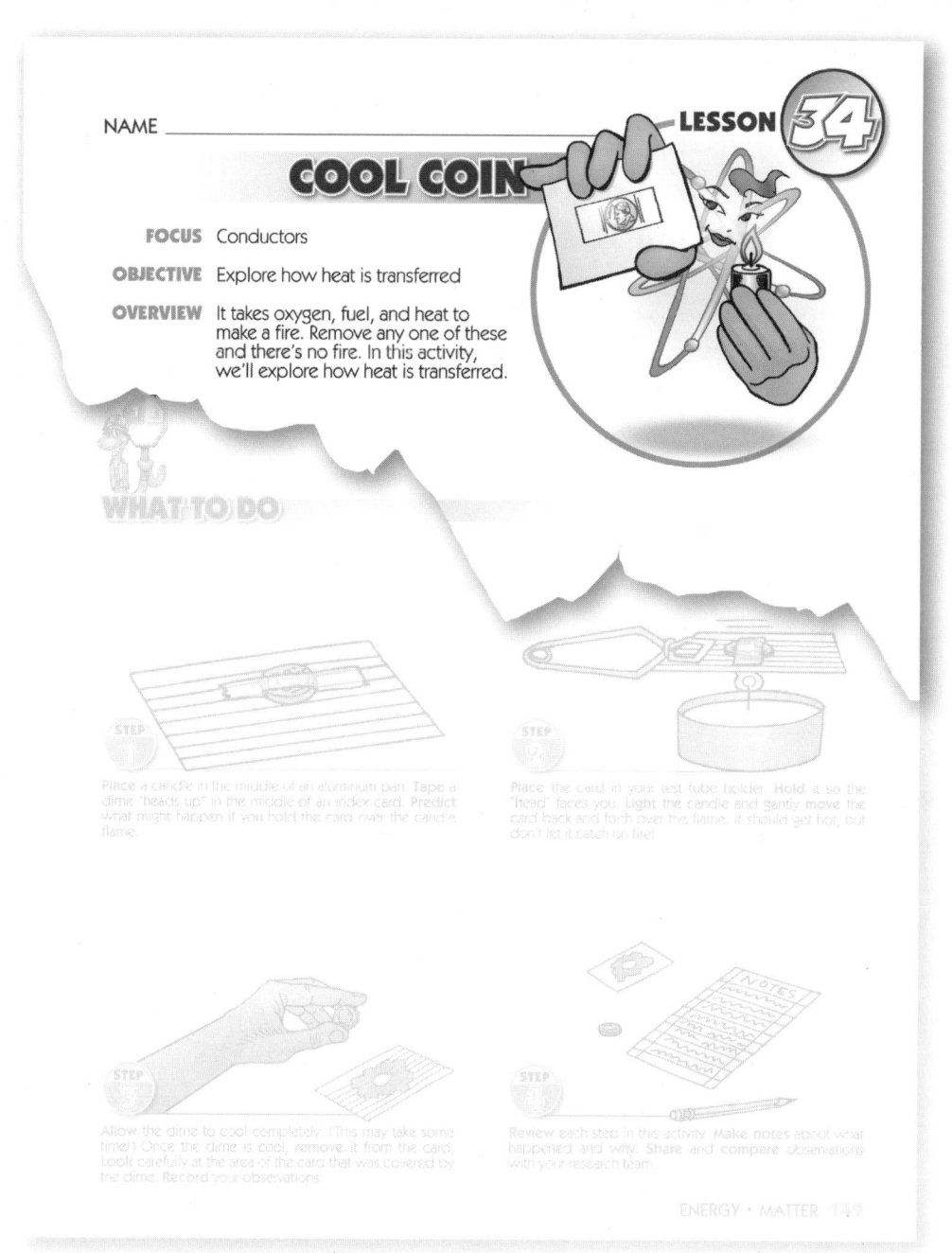

NAME _____

COOL COIN

LESSON 34

FOCUS Conductors

OBJECTIVE Explore how heat is transferred

OVERVIEW It takes oxygen, fuel, and heat to make a fire. Remove any one of these and there's no fire. In this activity, we'll explore how heat is transferred.

WHAT TO DO

STEP 1 Place a candle in the middle of an aluminum pan. Tape a dime "heads up" in the middle of an index card. Predict what might happen if you hold the card over the candle flame.

STEP 2 Place the card in your test tube holder. Hold it so the "head" faces you. Light the candle and gently move the card back and forth over the flame. It should get hot, but don't let it catch on fire!

STEP 3 Allow the dime to cool completely. (This may take some time!) Once the dime is cool, remove it from the card. Look carefully at the area of the card that was covered by the dime. Record your observations.

STEP 4 Review each step in this activity. Make notes about what happened and why. Share and compare observations with your research team.

ENERGY • MATTER 149

Category
Physical Science
Energy/Matter

Focus
Conductors

Objective
Explore how heat is transferred

National Standards
A1, A2, B1, B2, B3, G1, G2

Materials Needed
candle
index card
test tube holder
matches
aluminum pan
tape
dime

Safety Concerns

1. Gloves
Gloves are a reasonable precaution against burned fingers.

2. Open Flame
Remind students to exercise caution when the candle is burning.

Additional Comments

Make sure students understand the card is to be lightly scorched, not burned! Keep a pail of water beside each team so a burning card can be tossed in if necessary. If you have concerns about the maturity of your students, do this activity as a demonstration only.

Overview

Read the overview aloud to your students. The goal is to create an atmosphere of curiosity and inquiry.

Lesson 34 · **149**

WHAT TO DO

Monitor student research teams as they complete each step.

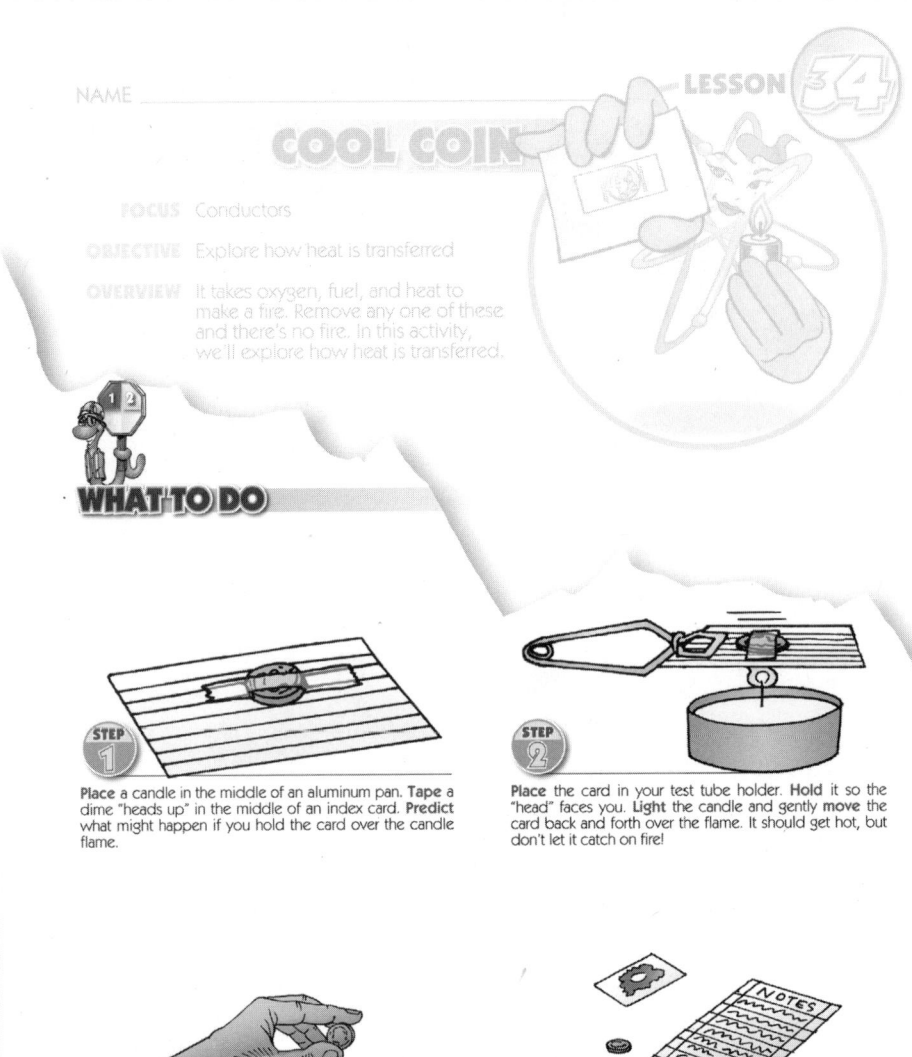

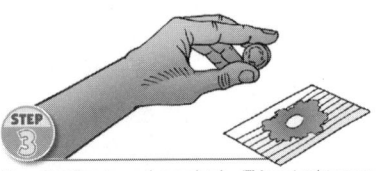

NAME _____

COOL COIN

FOCUS Conductors

OBJECTIVE Explore how heat is transferred

OVERVIEW It takes oxygen, fuel, and heat to make a fire. Remove any one of these and there's no fire. In this activity, we'll explore how heat is transferred.

WHAT TO DO

STEP 1
Place a candle in the middle of an aluminum pan. **Tape** a dime "heads up" in the middle of an index card. **Predict** what might happen if you hold the card over the candle flame.

STEP 2
Place the card in your test tube holder. **Hold** it so the "head" faces you. **Light** the candle and gently **move** the card back and forth over the flame. It should get hot, but don't let it catch on fire!

STEP 3
Allow the dime to cool completely. (This may take some time!) Once the dime is cool, **remove** it from the card. **Look** carefully at the area of the card that was covered by the dime. **Record** your observations.

STEP 4
Review each step in this activity. **Make** notes about what happened and why. **Share** and **compare** observations with your research team.

ENERGY • MATTER 149

Teacher to Teacher

Heat tends to flow from one place to another. Certain materials help regulate this flow. Insulation keeps heat out of our homes in summer and inside in winter. Some fabrics are great at conserving body heat in winter; others are perfect for keeping us cool in summer. Clothes and homes are just two examples of personal thermodynamics.

WHAT HAPPENED?

There are three sides to a fire triangle; oxygen, fuel, and heat. There was plenty of oxygen in the air, the paper provided the fuel, and a match has sufficient heat to start a fire. If all three parts of the fire triangle were balanced, the fire should have scorched the card evenly.

Yet when you removed the dime, you found an unburned area beneath it! This occurred because the metal in the dime is a great conductor of heat energy. It absorbed the heat, keeping it from burning the card.

Of course, this works both ways. Over time the dime could absorb so much heat that it might start a fire if you set it on a fresh card!

WHAT WE LEARNED

1. What are the three "sides" of a fire triangle? What does removing any one of these do?

a) oxygen, fuel, heat

b) puts out the fire

2. Describe what happened to the card in Step 2.

it turned brown, started to scorch, etc.

3. Why wasn't the area beneath the dime scorched? What did the metal do to the heat energy?

a) metal is a great conductor of heat energy

b) absorbed it

4. In this activity, the dime served as a conductor. Give at least three examples of metal conducting heat.

answers will vary

5. Based on what you've learned, would a metal wall provide good protection from a fire? Explain your answer.

Only a very thick one, and only for a short time (because it would absorb heat), but otherwise no protection.

What Happened

Review the section with students. Emphasize bold-face words that identify key concepts and introduce new vocabulary.

*There are three sides to a **fire triangle**; oxygen, fuel, and heat. There was plenty of **oxygen** in the air, the paper provided the **fuel**, and a match has sufficient **heat** to start a fire. If all three parts of the fire triangle were balanced, the fire should have scorched the card evenly.*

*Yet when you removed the dime, you found an unburned area beneath it! This occurred because the metal in the dime is a great **conductor** of **heat energy**. It **absorbed** the heat, keeping it from **burning** the card.*

Of course, this works both ways. Over time, the dime could absorb so much heat that it might start a fire if you set it on a fresh card!

What We Learned

Answers will vary. Suggested responses are shown at left.

Lesson 34 · 151

Conclusion

Read this section aloud to the class to summarize the concepts learned in this activity.

Food for Thought

Read the Scripture aloud to the class. Talk about how God can be our "shield" from evil, keeping our souls safe from harm. Discuss specific ways we can improve our relationship with God.

Journal

If time permits, have a general class discussion about notes and drawings various students added to their journal pages. Discuss correct and incorrect predictions, and remind students that this "trial and error" process is part of the scientific process.

CONCLUSION

Fire requires three things: oxygen, fuel, and heat. If any of these are removed, a fire can't occur. Heat energy can be absorbed and transferred by materials called conductors.

FOOD FOR THOUGHT

2 Samuel 22:31 You may have been surprised that the flame didn't scorch the entire index card. There was a dime-size area of safety. By absorbing the heat, the coin provided a shield for the paper, keeping it safe from harm.

This Scripture reminds us that God will shield those who stand behind him. This song of David is full of protective words like rock, refuge, fortress, and shield. Even though we're surrounded by a world full of evil, God keeps our souls safe from harm. Spend time learning to trust him better and let God be your shield!

JOURNAL — My Science Notes

Extended Teaching

1. Take a field trip to a fire station. Ask a firefighter to explain how the methods used to fight fires relate to the fire triangle. Have students write a paragraph about one thing they learn.

2. Have teams discuss and list ways that heat is added or removed from homes (air conditioner, furnace, coils on a refrigerator, etc.). Discuss the results, then compile the lists to create a classroom list.

3. Invite an electric company representative to visit your classroom. Ask him/her to explain how heat pumps work. Have students write a paragraph about one thing they learn.

4. Have teams research home fire safety. Challenge each team to contribute materials (drawings, pictures, descriptions) for a school bulletin board on this topic.

5. Have teams compile lists of insulators and conductors (both heat and electricity). Challenge each team to create a poster featuring at least one of these items.

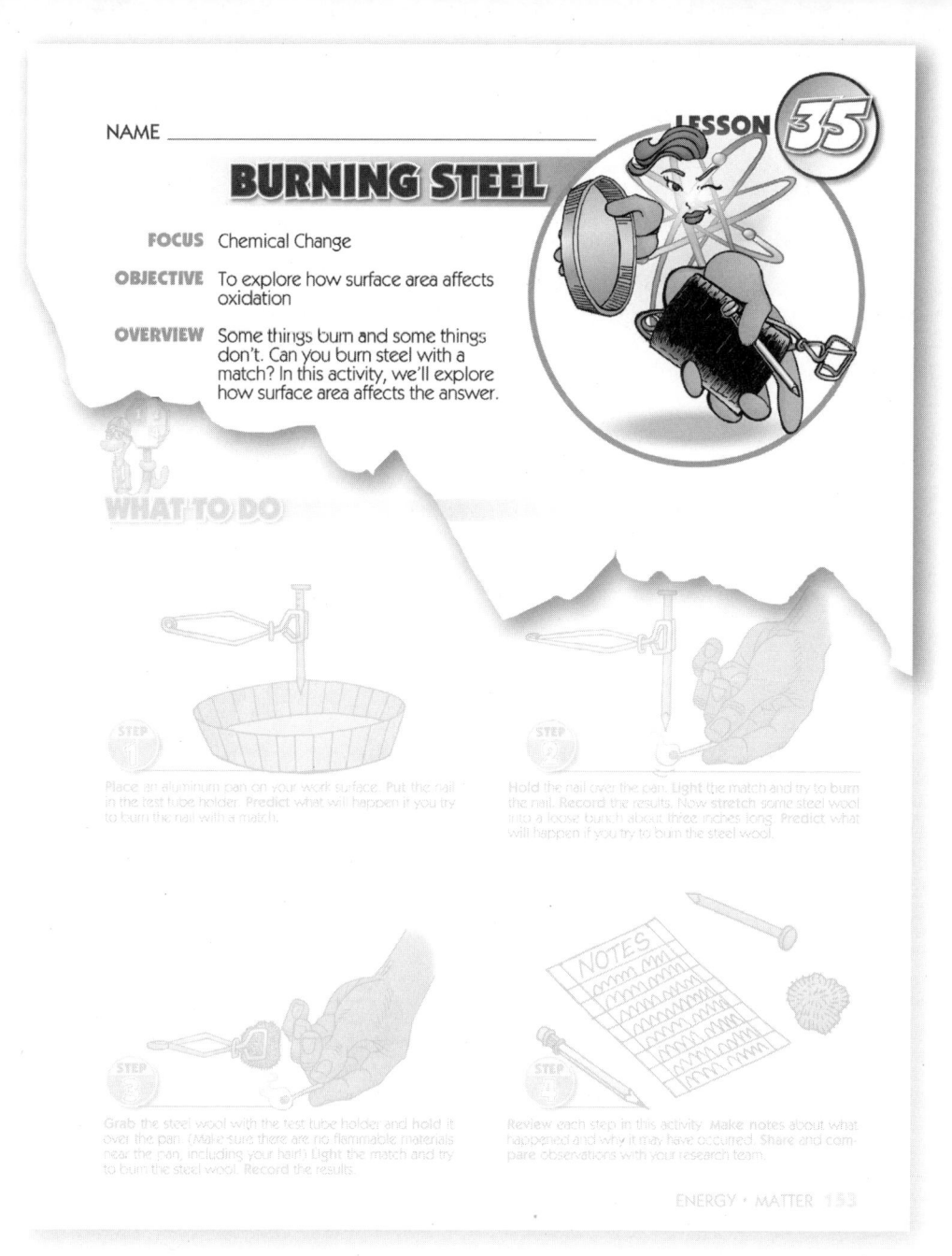

NAME _____

BURNING STEEL

LESSON 35

FOCUS Chemical Change

OBJECTIVE To explore how surface area affects oxidation

OVERVIEW Some things burn and some things don't. Can you burn steel with a match? In this activity, we'll explore how surface area affects the answer.

WHAT TO DO

STEP 1
Place an aluminum pan on your work surface. Put the nail in the test tube holder. Predict what will happen if you try to burn the nail with a match.

STEP 2
Hold the nail over the pan. Light the match and try to burn the nail. Record the results. Now stretch some steel wool into a loose bunch about three inches long. Predict what will happen if you try to burn the steel wool.

STEP 3
Grab the steel wool with the test tube holder and hold it over the pan. (Make sure there are no flammable materials near the pan, including your hair!) Light the match and try to burn the steel wool. Record the results.

STEP 4
Review each step in this activity. Make notes about what happened and why it may have occurred. Share and compare observations with your research team.

ENERGY • MATTER 153

Category
Physical Science
Energy/Matter

Focus
Chemical Change

Objective
To explore how surface area affects oxidation

National Standards
A1, A2, B1, B2, B3, G1, G2

Materials Needed
nail
test tube holder
steel wool
aluminum pan
match

Safety Concerns

1. Goggles/Gloves
Goggles and gloves are a reasonable precaution for this activity.

2. Open Flame
Remind students to exercise caution with open flame.

4. Sharp Objects
Remind students to be careful with the nail.

Additional Comments

To get a feel for how energetically steel wool burns, try Step 3 yourself in advance. Make sure the work surface is free of flammable materials and that students hold the steel wool just above the pan. Keep water or a fire extinquisher handy in case of emergencies.

Overview

Read the overview aloud to your students. The goal is to create an atmosphere of curiosity and inquiry.

Lesson 35 · 153

WHAT TO DO

Monitor student research teams as they complete each step.

NAME _____

BURNING STEEL

LESSON 35

FOCUS Chemical Change

OBJECTIVE To explore how surface area affects oxidation

OVERVIEW Some things burn and some things don't. Can you burn steel with a match? In this activity, we'll explore how surface area affects the answer.

WHAT TO DO

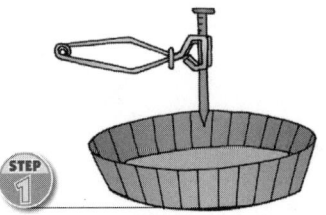

STEP 1
Place an aluminum pan on your work surface. Put the nail in the test tube holder. Predict what will happen if you try to burn the nail with a match.

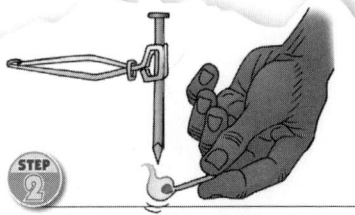

STEP 2
Hold the nail over the pan. Light the match and try to burn the nail. Record the results. Now stretch some steel wool into a loose bunch about three inches long. Predict what will happen if you try to burn the steel wool.

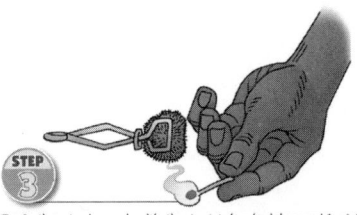

STEP 3
Grab the steel wool with the test tube holder and hold it over the pan. (Make sure there are no flammable materials near the pan, including your hair!) Light the match and try to burn the steel wool. Record the results.

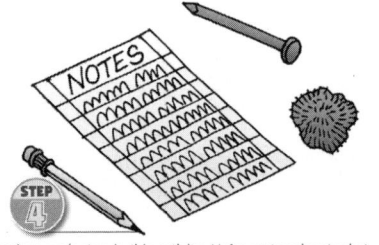

STEP 4
Review each step in this activity. Make notes about what happened and why it may have occurred. Share and compare observations with your research team.

ENERGY • MATTER 153

Teacher to Teacher

Increasing surface area often makes materials easier to burn. In power plants, for instance, coal is ground to a fine powder, then forced into burning chambers under enormous air pressure. Like "fuel injection" in automotive engines, this greatly increases the surface area of the fuel, making combustion more efficient.

154 • Lesson 35

What Happened

Review the section with students. Emphasize bold-face words that identify key concepts and introduce new vocabulary.

Burning is a **chemical change** (called **oxidation**). A chemical change results in a different **substance** than the substance you started with.

But why will steel wool burn, but not a nail? The answer has to do with **surface area** — the amount of a material directly exposed to oxygen (in the air). The nail is **dense** and compact, but the steel wool is thin and spread out. Steel wool exposes thousands of times more surface to the air.

For a fire to occur, iron **atoms** had to **combine** with oxygen atoms. The small surface area of the nail allowed only a limited number of iron atoms to touch the air. But the steel wool's surface area allowed thousands of times more iron atoms access to the oxygen. Add a **heat** source (the match), and the result is a flash fire!

What We Learned

Answers will vary. Suggested responses are shown at left.

WHAT HAPPENED?

Burning is a chemical change (called oxidation). A chemical change results in a different substance than the substance you started with.

But why will steel wool burn, but not a nail? The answer has to do with surface area — the amount of a material directly exposed to oxygen (in the air). The nail is dense and compact, but the steel wool is thin and spread out. Steel wool exposes thousands of times more surface to the air.

For a fire to occur, iron atoms had to combine with oxygen atoms. The small surface area of the nail allowed only a limited number of iron atoms to touch the air. But the steel wool's surface area allowed thousands of times more iron atoms access to the oxygen. Add a heat source (the match), and the result is a flash fire!

WHAT WE LEARNED

1. What did you predict in Step 1? How did this prediction reflect what actually happened?

Answers will vary, but should reflect logical comparisons.

2. What did you predict in Step 2? How did this prediction reflect what actually happened?

Answers will vary, but should reflect logical comparisons.

3. Describe what happened in Step 3.

The steel wool caught on fire and burned.

4. Explain why the steel in the nail didn't burn, but the steel in the steel wool did.

Steel wool has a much greater surface area than a nail.

5. If one piece of paper is smashed into a tight ball, and an identical piece of paper is shredded into tiny pieces, which paper would burn the easiest? Explain your answer.

a) the shredded paper.

b) it has a greater surface area.

Conclusion

Read this section aloud to the class to summarize the concepts learned in this activity.

Food for Thought

Read the Scripture aloud to the class. Ask, "What are some things that can keep us from spending daily time alone with God?" Discuss specific ways we can overcome these barriers.

Journal

If time permits, have a general class discussion about notes and drawings various students added to their journal pages. Discuss correct and incorrect predictions, and remind students that this "trial and error" process is part of the scientific process.

CONCLUSION

When a substance combines with oxygen, the change is called oxidation. Some oxidation is rapid (like burning) and some oxidation is slow (like rusting). However, both involve a chemical process.

FOOD FOR THOUGHT

Matthew 13:3-8 When you tried to burn the nail, nothing happened. You probably weren't surprised. When you tried to burn the steel wool, you got a completely different reaction! Preparing a material differently can significantly change its properties.

It's the same with our hearts. When we prepare with worship and prayer, God finds our hearts a great place to light the fire of love. But when we don't take time for God, our hearts can become hard and unreceptive. Why not spend some quality time with God this week? Let God's power set your heart on fire with heavenly love.

JOURNAL — My Science Notes

156 ENERGY • MATTER

Extended Teaching

1. Repeat this activity using different textures of steel wool (coarse, fine, etc.). Compare the results with the original activity. How are they similar? How are they different?

2. Take a field trip to a coal-fired power plant. Ask a representative to explain the process of burning coal for electricity. Have students write a paragraph about one thing they learn.

3. Invite a local car mechanic to visit your classroom. Ask him/her to explain how fuel injection works. How does this compare to a carburetor? Have students write a paragraph about one thing they learn.

4. Using the Internet, have teams research grain elevator explosions. What explodes (grain dust) and why? Challenge each team to make a poster showing how this occurs.

5. Have teams research how much coal is burned in the United States each year to make electricity. Since coal is a finite resource, challenge students to list ways we can save electricity to conserve coal reserves.

NAME _____

FLOWERS & FUMES

LESSON 36

FOCUS Indicators

OBJECTIVE To explore how indicators work

OVERVIEW Sometimes things aren't what they seem. There are many substances that our eyes can't detect. In this activity, we'll explore how an indicator can help us see what's really there!

WHAT TO DO

STEP 1 Pour about an inch of ammonium hydroxide into a paper cup. (Keep it away from eyes, noses, etc.) Carefully stretch a piece of plastic wrap over the cup and secure it with a rubber band.

STEP 2 Carefully cut a slit in the plastic. Dampen the flower by quickly dipping it in a cup of water. Shake off any excess. Now slip the flower through the plastic and hold it just above the liquid. Don't let it touch the liquid!

STEP 3 Observe what happens to the flower and record the results. Now remove the flower and blow on it gently. Record the results. Repeat until everyone has had a turn.

STEP 4 Review each step in this activity. Make notes and drawings about what happened. Share and compare observations with your research team.

ENERGY • MATTER 157

Additional Comments

Make sure students don't try to smell the contents of the cup. After the activity is completed, pour all liquids down the drain, then flush thoroughly with water. Students should also wash their hands with soap and water.

Overview

Read the overview aloud to your students. The goal is to create an atmosphere of curiosity and inquiry.

Category
Physical Science
Energy/Matter

Focus
Indicators

Objective
To explore how indicators work

National Standards
A1, A2, B1, B2, B3, G1, G2

Materials Needed
**ammonium hydroxide
paper cup
rubber band
flower cluster**
plastic wrap
scissors
water

Safety Concerns

1. Goggles/Gloves
Always protect eyes when working with chemicals. Gloves are an added precaution.

2. Corrosion
Prolonged contact with Ammonium Hydroxide can burn skin.

3. Skin Contact
Remind students to avoid skin contact with Ammonium Hydroxide solution.

4. Slipping
There is a potential for spills with this activity. Remind students to exercise caution.

4. Sharp Objects
Remind students to be careful when using scissors.

Lesson 36 • **157**

WHAT TO DO

Monitor student research teams as they complete each step.

NAME _____

FLOWERS & FUMES

FOCUS Indicators

OBJECTIVE To explore how indicators work

OVERVIEW Sometimes things aren't what they seem. There are many substances that our eyes can't detect. In this activity, we'll explore how an indicator can help us see what's really there!

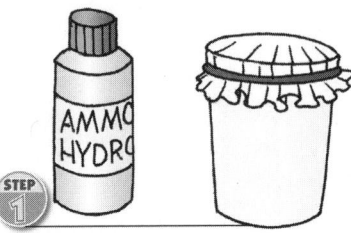

WHAT TO DO

STEP 1 Pour about an inch of ammonium hydroxide into a paper cup. (Keep it away from eyes, noses, etc.) Carefully **stretch** a piece of plastic wrap over the cup and **secure** it with a rubber band.

STEP 2 Carefully **cut** a slit in the plastic. **Dampen** the flower by quickly dipping it in a cup of water. **Shake** off any excess. Now **slip** the flower through the plastic and **hold** it just above the liquid. Don't let it touch the liquid!

STEP 3 **Observe** what happens to the flower and **record** the results. Now **remove** the flower and **blow** on it gently. **Record** the results. **Repeat** until everyone has had a turn.

STEP 4 **Review** each step in this activity. **Make notes** and drawings about what happened. **Share** and **compare** observations with your research team.

ENERGY • MATTER 157

Teacher to Teacher

Ammonium hydroxide is the active ingredient in most "ammonia" cleansers. Bleach is another common cleaner. While both of these simple household chemicals are relatively safe, mixing them together can create chlorine gas, a substance so deadly it was used as a chemical weapon in World War I!

WHAT HAPPENED?

Even though it looked clean, your flower had been soaked in phenolphthalein. Phenolphthalein is a chemical called an indicator. It doesn't change colors when there's an acid around, but it turns pink when a base is near. The ammonium hydroxide in your cup was giving off fumes (gas). Since these fumes contained a base (ammonia), the flower turned pink when the fumes touched it!

Then in Step 3, you began to blow on the flower. The ammonia began to evaporate. In addition, your breath contains carbon dioxide, and this reacted with the water to create a mild acid. With no more base present, and the addition of the acid from your breath, the flower changed back to white.

WHAT WE LEARNED

1. What was the purpose of the plastic cover on the cup in Step 1? What were you trying to contain?

a) to seal the cup

b) the ammonia fumes

2. Describe what the flower looked like in Step 1. How did its appearance change in Step 2?

a) white, petals, soft, etc.

b) it turned pink when it got exposed to the ammonia fumes

3. Describe what happened to the flower in Step 3. How did its appearance change?

a) blew it dry

b) it turned white again

4. Why did the flower change colors? Describe each step in the process.

a) it was treated with an indicator

b) answers will vary, but should reflect the "What Happened" section.

5. How might the results have been affected if the ammonium hydroxide had been sitting in an uncovered cup for a week. Explain your answer.

a) there would have been no reaction

b) the ammonium hydroxide would have all evaporated

What Happened

Review the section with students. Emphasize bold-face words that identify key concepts and introduce new vocabulary.

*Even though it looked clean, your flower had been soaked in **phenolphthalein**. Phenolphthalein is a chemical called an **indicator**. It doesn't change colors when there's an **acid** around, but it turns pink when a **base** is near. The **ammonium hydroxide** in your cup was giving off **fumes** (gas). Since these fumes contained a base (ammonia), the flower turned pink when the fumes touched it!*

*Then in Step 3, you began to blow on the flower. The ammonia began to **evaporate**. In addition, your breath contains **carbon dioxide**, and this **reacted** with the water to create a mild acid. With no more base present, and the addition of the acid from your breath, the flower changed back to white.*

What We Learned

Answers will vary. Suggested responses are shown at left.

Lesson 36 · **159**

Conclusion

Read this section aloud to the class to summarize the concepts learned in this activity.

Food for Thought

Read the Scripture aloud to the class. Talk about how spending time with God has an affect on our souls. Discuss how being filled with God's love makes us more alive!

Journal

If time permits, have a general class discussion about notes and drawings various students added to their journal pages. Discuss correct and incorrect predictions, and remind students that this "trial and error" process is part of the scientific process.

CONCLUSION

Indicators can be used to detect the presence of an acid or a base. Different kinds of indicators are used for different purposes.

FOOD FOR THOUGHT

Genesis 2:7 In this activity, you saw an amazing change. The ammonia fumes made the flower's colors suddenly come alive! Everything that was dull before was instantly bright with color.

This Scripture tells how God gathered materials from the Earth, formed a body, and breathed into it the breath of life. In one amazing moment, man became a living creature. Spending time with our creator God has a similar effect on our souls. The more we're filled with God's love, the more alive we become!

JOURNAL — My Science Notes

160 ENERGY · MATTER

Extended Teaching

1. Repeat this activity, but this time refrigerate the ammonium hydroxide first. Compare the results of the cold solution with the original room temperature one. How were they similar? How were they different?

2. Using the Internet, have teams research a material called "anhydrous ammonia". Find out how it's used, why it's dangerous, etc. Challenge each team to contribute materials on this topic for a classroom bulletin board.

3. Invite an agricultural extension agent to visit your classroom. Have him/her discuss soil testing (especially indicators used) and the kind of soils in your area. Have students write a paragraph about one thing they learn.

4. Using indicator paper, have teams test various household liquids to find out if they are an acid, base, or neutral. Challenge each team to create a poster showing each item in the correct category.

5. Take a field trip to a municipal swimming pool. Ask a lifeguard to demonstrate how the water is tested daily for proper pH levels. Find out why this is important. Have students write a paragraph about one thing they learn.

ASSESSMENT

NAME_____ DATE_____

SURVIVOR SEEDS

LESSON 1

True/False (Circle T for true, F for false.)

T F **1.** Seeds do not use oxygen as they begin growing into plants.

T F **2.** Plants produce the oxygen we breathe.

T F **3.** The chemical that makes plants look green is called chlorophyll.

T F **4.** Once young plants begin photosynthesis, they produce more oxygen than they use.

T F **5.** Another name for a baby plant is an embryo.

Multiple Choice (Fill in the circle beside the best answer.)

6. The scientific term for sprouting is . . .
- **a.** embryo
- **b.** photosynthesis
- **c.** germinatation
- **d.** reproduction

7. In this activity, water began to rise up the tube because . . .
- **a.** pressure inside the tube was less than the air pressure outside.
- **b.** pressure inside the tube was greater than the air pressure outside.
- **c.** pressure inside and outside the tube were exactly equal.
- **d.** pressure inside the tube disappeared completely.

8. What gas do plants take from the air during photosynthesis?
- **a.** oxygen
- **b.** nitrogen
- **c.** gasoline
- **d.** carbon dioxide

9. What two things are stored inside every seed?
- **a.** oxygen and food
- **b.** food and water
- **c.** an embryo and water
- **d.** an embryo and food

10. In this activity, the seeds . . .
- **a.** produced oxygen through photosynthesis.
- **b.** produced oxygen through germination.
- **c.** consumed oxygen, lowering pressure inside the tube.
- **d.** produced oxygen, raising pressure inside the tube.

Copyright ©2003 The Concerned Group, Inc.

NAME_____ DATE_____

LESSON 2
APPLE EMBRYO

True/False (Circle T for true, F for false.)

T F **1.** Many plants reproduce by making seeds.

T F **2.** Lemon juice speeds up the decomposition process in an apple.

T F **3.** Pollen is made by the male part of the flower.

T F **4.** Flowers that have both male and female parts can self-pollinate.

T F **5.** Wind usually has a negative affect on the pollination of all flowers.

Multiple Choice (Fill in the circle beside the best answer.)

6. Dipping the cut face of an apple in lemon juice will cause it to . . .
- a. decompose more rapidly.
- b. decompose less rapidly.
- c. completely stop decomposing.
- d. decompose more completely.

7. When flowers from different plants pollinate each other, it is called . . .
- a. self-pollination
- b. self-propagation
- c. cross-pollination
- d. cross-propagation

8. The major part of an apple is . . .
- a. food
- b. seeds
- c. pollen
- d. skin

9. Scientists call the "baby plant" found inside every seed . . .
- a. a pollinate
- b. a seed pod
- c. a propagate
- d. an embryo

10. When animals eat apples, how does this affect the apple tree?
- a. It causes damage to the tree's root system.
- b. It helps scatter the seeds produced by the tree.
- c. It destroys embryos needed for the tree's survival.
- d. It helps produce new varieties of apple trees.

Copyright ©2003 The Concerned Group, Inc.

NAME _____ DATE _____

PYRIC PEANUT

LESSON 3

True/False (Circle T for true, F for false.)

T   F   **1.** Most food contains some form of energy.

T   F   **2.** The human body needs food energy in order to stay alive.

T   F   **3.** Peanuts burn because they contain small amounts of gasoline.

T   F   **4.** Food energy is measured in calories.

T   F   **5.** Kinetic energy is also called stored (or potential) energy.

Multiple Choice (Fill in the circle beside the best answer.)

6. The scientific term for burning is . . .
- a. pollination
- b. potential energy
- c. heat energy
- d. combustion

7. Peanuts burn because they have a high content of . . .
- a. sugar
- b. gasoline
- c. oil (fat)
- d. heat

8. Your body can use food energy to produce all of the following except . . .
- a. light energy
- b. heat energy
- c. electrical energy
- d. mechanical energy

9. When something burns, it changes from _____ energy into some form of kinetic energy.
- a. heat
- b. potential
- c. light
- d. electrical

10. Which of the following is not a form of kinetic energy?
- a. food
- b. light
- c. heat
- d. electricity

Copyright ©2003 The Concerned Group, Inc

NAME _____ DATE _____

STARCH SEARCH
LESSON 4

True/False (Circle T for true, F for false.)

T F **1.** Most foods do not contain nutrients.

T F **2.** Corn is a kind of starch.

T F **3.** Corn-based solutions react with starch to produce a dark-colored material.

T F **4.** A renewable resource is one that can't be replaced.

T F **5.** An iodine solution can help determine if a food contains starch.

Multiple Choice (Fill in the circle beside the best answer.)

6. Carbohydrate is a compound word combining what two terms?
- ○ **a.** oxygen and water
- ○ **b.** oxygen and carbon
- ○ **c.** carbon and water
- ○ **d.** carbon and hydrogen

7. Adding an iodine solution to a starch will . . .
- ○ **a.** prove that starch contains sugar.
- ○ **b.** result in a positive test (color change).
- ○ **c.** result in a negative test (no color change).
- ○ **d.** give a result that is inconclusive.

8. Which of the following is not a nutrient the human body needs?
- ○ **a.** proteins
- ○ **b.** fats
- ○ **c.** sugars
- ○ **d.** carbon dioxide

9. Sugars and starches belong to which of the following nutrient groups?
- ○ **a.** proteins
- ○ **b.** fats
- ○ **c.** carbohydrates
- ○ **d.** vitamins

10. Something that can be grown, used, and recycled is called . . .
- ○ **a.** a non-renewable resource.
- ○ **b.** a non-mineral resource.
- ○ **c.** a renewable resource.
- ○ **d.** a mineral resource.

Copyright ©2003 The Concerned Group, Inc

NAME _____ DATE _____

LESSON 5
SEALED CELL

True/False (Circle T for true, F for false.)

T F **1.** Only one kind of material can pass through a cell membrane.

T F **2.** The diffusion process makes cells weak.

T F **3.** Iodine particles are smaller than starch particles.

T F **4.** The larger the particle, the easier it can pass through a membrane.

T F **5.** Diffusion lets some things into a cell and some things out.

Multiple Choice (Fill in the circle beside the best answer.)

6. What do scientists call the process of materials entering and leaving a cell?
- a. confusion
- b. diversion
- c. combustion
- d. diffusion

7. Starch is a huge molecule made from many small ____ molecules hooked together.
- a. water
- b. chlorophyll
- c. starch
- d. sugar

8. What kind of reaction happens between iodine and starch?
- a. physical
- b. chemical
- c. both chemical and physical
- d. neither chemical nor physical

9. The diffusion process . . .
- a. helps control the flow of materials in and out of a cell.
- b. lets materials into a cell, but not out of it.
- c. lets materials out of a cell, but not into it.
- d. lets water into a cell, and other materials out of it.

10. In order for a cell to be healthy, materials must . . .
- a. be kept from passing through the cell membrane.
- b. must be allowed to pass into the cell, but not out.
- c. must be allowed to pass out of the cell, but not in.
- d. none of the above.

Copyright ©2003 The Concerned Group, Inc.

NAME _____ DATE _____

LESSON 6
BEADS OF BLOOD

True/False (Circle T for true, F for false.)

T F **1.** The major portion of your blood is liquid, primarily water.

T F **2.** The liquid part of your blood is called plasma.

T F **3.** Dissolved nutrients are carried in the platelets.

T F **4.** Your blood can only carry liquids, not gasses.

T F **5.** Plasma can help warm or cool various parts of your body.

Multiple Choice (Fill in the circle beside the best answer.)

6. Scientists call the red blood cells that carry oxygen in the blood . . .
- **a.** erythrocytes
- **b.** leukocytes
- **c.** platelets
- **d.** hormones

7. Scientists call the white blood cells whose purpose is to fight disease . . .
- **a.** erythrocytes
- **b.** leukocytes
- **c.** platelets
- **d.** hormones

8. Scientists call the special cells which help clot your blood when you're cut . . .
- **a.** erythrocytes
- **b.** leukocytes
- **c.** platelets
- **d.** hormones

9. Which of the following is not a function of blood?
- **a.** to carry away waste products
- **b.** to help fight disease
- **c.** to transport gasses like oxygen and carbon dioxide
- **d.** to digest food

10. Scientists call the disease fighting chemicals in blood . . .
- **a.** hormones
- **b.** antibodies
- **c.** erythrocytes
- **d.** leukocytes

a reason for Science

Copyright ©2003 The Concerned Group, Inc

NAME _____ DATE _____

PREDATOR OR PREY

LESSON 7

True/False (Circle T for true, F for false.)

T F **1.** Predators' eyes are high on the sides of their heads so they can watch large areas.

T F **2.** Prey animals have eyes close together in the front so they can spot food easily.

T F **3.** A rabbit could be either a predator or prey.

T F **4.** A lion is a good example of a predator.

T F **5.** An animal is always either a predator or prey.

Multiple Choice (Fill in the circle beside the best answer.)

6. Which of the following is a common characteristic of predators?
- a. long legs to run away rapidly
- b. long ears to hear other predators coming
- c. sharp teeth and claws
- d. blunt teeth made for grazing

7. Which of the following is a common characteristic of prey?
- a. long legs to run away rapidly
- b. eyes in the front to spot food easily
- c. sharp teeth and claws
- d. talons and sharp beaks

8. Deer, turkey, and elk would best fit which of the following categories?
- a. predators
- b. prey
- c. carnivores
- d. decomposers

9. Bears, eagles, and lions would best fit which of the following categories?
- a. predators
- b. prey
- c. herbivores
- d. decomposers

10. Dividing animals into groups based on their characteristics is called . . .
- a. topography
- b. taxation
- c. kingdomization
- d. classification

NAME_____ DATE_____

LESSON 8
SPINDLY SPINE

True/False (Circle T for true, F for false.)

T F **1.** In the model you made, the cardboard tubes represent vertebrae.

T F **2.** In the model you made, the pipe cleaners represent the spinal cord.

T F **3.** In the model you made, the rubber bands represent nerves attached to the spine.

T F **4.** In the model you made, the foam rubber represents cartilage between bones.

T F **5.** A severly damaged spinal cord can result in paralysis or death.

Multiple Choice (Fill in the circle beside the best answer.)

6. Another name for the spine is the . . .
   ○ **a.** backbone
   ○ **b.** cranium
   ○ **c.** vertebrae
   ○ **d.** cartilage

7. The individual bones that compose your spine are called . . .
   ○ **a.** backbone
   ○ **b.** cranium
   ○ **c.** vertebrae
   ○ **d.** cartilage

8. Which of the following is not a function of the spine?
   ○ **a.** protecting the spinal cord
   ○ **b.** making antibodies to fight disease
   ○ **c.** supporting the structure of the body
   ○ **d.** allowing flexibility of movement

9. The human spine contains how many bones?
   ○ **a.** 206
   ○ **b.** 13
   ○ **c.** 33
   ○ **d.** 113

10. What is the purpose of the cartilage in your spine?
   ○ **a.** to carry information to various parts of the body
   ○ **b.** to enhance the circulation of blood through the spine
   ○ **c.** to fight disease and create antibodies
   ○ **d.** to provide padding between the bones

Copyright ©2003 The Concerned Group, Inc.

NAME_____ DATE_____

EXPERIMENTAL EPIDEMIC

LESSON 9

True/False (Circle T for true, F for false.)

T F **1.** Scientists use the word "epidemic" to describe a fast-spreading disease.

T F **2.** The individual who gets the sickest in an epidemic is called the index case.

T F **3.** To "contract" a disease means you are immune from that particular disease.

T F **4.** Medical tests often use an indicator to determine if a person has a disease.

T F **5.** To get a disease, you must come in direct contact with the person who is the index case.

Multiple Choice (Fill in the circle beside the best answer.)

6. Scientists refer to any sickness as . . .
- a. a curse
- b. an index case
- c. an epidemic
- d. a disease

7. During the rapid spread of disease, the first person to get it is called . . .
- a. the primary donor
- b. the epicenter
- c. the index case
- d. the experimental

8. An indicator . . .
- a. changes colors when it is warmed.
- b. changes colors when it cools.
- c. changes colors when it contacts specific chemicals.
- d. stays the same regardless of circumstances.

9. The indicator we used in this activity was . . .
- a. phenolphthalein
- b. sodium hydroxide
- c. potassium cyanide
- d. tap water

10. All of the following terms are related to a disease that spreads except . . .
- a. contagious
- b. frivolous
- c. infectious
- d. communicable

Copyright ©2003 The Concerned Group, Inc.

NAME _____ DATE _____

MAGNET MOTIONS

LESSON 10

True/False (Circle T for true, F for false.)

T F **1.** Magnetism is one of the basic forces on Earth.

T F **2.** Some materials are magnetic and some are not.

T F **3.** Magnets can be either permanent or temporary.

T F **4.** Like poles on a magnet attract each other.

T F **5.** A magnet must touch something to affect it.

Multiple Choice (Fill in the circle beside the best answer.)

6. Materials that are attracted by a magnet are . . .
  ○ **a.** non-magnetic.
  ○ **b.** ferromagnetic.
  ○ **c.** silicate based.
  ○ **d.** none of the above

7. All of the following might be attracted by a magnet except . . .
  ○ **a.** an iron nail.
  ○ **b.** another magnet.
  ○ **c.** a soft drink bottle.
  ○ **d.** a steel paperclip.

8. If the north poles of two magnets are placed together, they will . . .
  ○ **a.** repel each other.
  ○ **b.** attract each other.
  ○ **c.** point south.
  ○ **d.** explode.

9. A temporary magnet can be made from a nail by . . .
  ○ **a.** wrapping it with uninsulated wire and applying AC current.
  ○ **b.** wrapping it with uninsulated wire and applying DC current.
  ○ **c.** wrapping it with insulated wire and applying AC current.
  ○ **d.** wrapping it with insulated wire and applying DC current.

10. Magnets are useful . . .
  ○ **a.** for simple tasks like holding messages on a refrigerator.
  ○ **b.** in complex devices like appliances and tools.
  ○ **c.** in huge equipment like electrical generators.
  ○ **d.** all of the above

Copyright ©2003 The Concerned Group, Inc.

NAME _____ DATE _____

PEANUT PASTE
LESSON 11

True/False (Circle T for true, F for false.)

T F **1.** Adhesives are designed to hold things together.

T F **2.** All adhesives have approximately the same strength.

T F **3.** Scientific experiments require careful measurements.

T F **4.** A variable is the thing that changes in an experiment.

T F **5.** Only two variables should be changed for each experiment.

Multiple Choice (Fill in the circle beside the best answer.)

6. Writing down what happens in an experiment is called . . .
- a. measuring
- b. varying
- c. approximating
- d. recording.

7. Another term for "ideal" or "best" is . . .
- a. test
- b. optimum
- c. model
- d. minimum

8. Good science experiments require accurate . . .
- a. control
- b. observation
- c. recording
- d. all of the above

9. All adhesives have what in common?
- a. They hold things together.
- b. They are based on starch.
- c. They require water.
- d. all of the above

10. Scientists repeat experiments because . . .
- a. results are often sloppy and inaccurate.
- b. multiple results help verify accuracy.
- c. it takes one experiment each to measure, observe, and record.
- d. all of the above

Copyright ©2003 The Concerned Group, Inc.

NAME _____ DATE _____

BALANCING NAILS

LESSON 12

True/False (Circle T for true, F for false.)

T F **1.** Logical science principles can lead to seemingly impossible results.

T F **2.** All objects have a center of gravity.

T F **3.** An object's balance point is always its exact center.

T F **4.** The shape of an object has no affect on its balance point.

T F **5.** Center of gravity is based on the mid-point of the object's mass.

Multiple Choice (Fill in the circle beside the best answer.)

6. Scientists refer to an object's "balance point" as its . . .
  ○ **a.** center of mass.
  ○ **b.** center of gravity.
  ○ **c.** gravitational force.
  ○ **d.** logical mass.

7. A term that is very similar to mass is . . .
  ○ **a.** gravity
  ○ **b.** balance
  ○ **c.** weight
  ○ **d.** equilibrium

8. The center of gravity for an object of uniform shape and balance is . . .
  ○ **a.** its exact center.
  ○ **b.** near one end.
  ○ **c.** impossible to determine.
  ○ **d.** none of the above

9. Scientists refer to a balancing of forces as . . .
  ○ **a.** gravity
  ○ **b.** distribution
  ○ **c.** weight
  ○ **d.** equilibrium

10. The center of gravity on a hammer would probably be . . .
  ○ **a.** in the exact middle of the handle.
  ○ **b.** closer to the end of the handle.
  ○ **c.** closer to the hammer's head.
  ○ **d.** wherever you hold the handle.

Copyright ©2003 The Concerned Group, Inc.

NAME _____ DATE _____

LESSON 13
CORKS & FORKS

True/False (Circle T for true, F for false.)

T F **1.** When forces are balanced, scientists call this "equilibrium."

T F **2.** Torque is a kind of twisting force.

T F **3.** Equal torque can lead to equilibrium.

T F **4.** Any action that requires a circular motion creates equilibrium.

T F **5.** Shifting weight between points may create equilibrium.

Multiple Choice (Fill in the circle beside the best answer.)

6. The term closest to "balance point" is . . .
- a. torque
- b. center of gravity
- c. equilibrium
- d. mass

7. The term closest to "balanced forces" is . . .
- a. torque
- b. center of gravity
- c. equilibrium
- d. mass

8. The term closest to "twisting force" is . . .
- a. torque
- b. center of gravity
- c. equilibrium
- d. mass

9. All of these are examples of torque except . . .
- a. driving a nail with a hammer.
- b. pitching a softball to a friend.
- c. feeling sunshine on your shoulders.
- d. opening a door for your teacher.

10. Making a teeter-totter work properly requires . . .
- a. mass
- b. center of gravity
- c. torque
- d. all of the above

Copyright ©2003 The Concerned Group, Inc.

NAME_____ DATE_____

LESSON 14
EGG AIRBAG

True/False (Circle T for true, F for false.)

T F **1.** Scientists refer to moving energy as "kinetic" energy.

T F **2.** Kinetic energy contains no force.

T F **3.** Potential energy can be converted to kinetic energy.

T F **4.** Kinetic energy cannot be absorbed.

T F **5.** Gravity can be involved in both storing and releasing energy.

Multiple Choice (Fill in the circle beside the best answer.)

6. Holding an egg over the edge of a cliff gives the egg . . .
   ○ **a.** gravitational force.
   ○ **b.** potential energy.
   ○ **c.** kinetic energy.
   ○ **d.** magnetic force.

7. When energy is moving, it is said to be . . .
   ○ **a.** gravity
   ○ **b.** potential
   ○ **c.** kinetic
   ○ **d.** magnetic

8. A force in the opposite direction of the original force is . . .
   ○ **a.** a potential force.
   ○ **b.** an opposing force.
   ○ **c.** never as strong as the original force.
   ○ **d.** always completely absorbed.

9. The force that stored and released energy in this activity was . . .
   ○ **a.** magnetism
   ○ **b.** kineticism
   ○ **c.** gravity
   ○ **d.** all of the above

10. A passenger can be injured if a car's air bag . . .
   ○ **a.** provides too little opposing force.
   ○ **b.** provides too much opposing force.
   ○ **c.** fails to inflate.
   ○ **d.** all of the above

Copyright ©2003 The Concerned Group, Inc.

NAME _____ DATE _____

BUOYANT BALL

LESSON 15

True/False (Circle T for true, F for false.)

T F **1.** All matter on Earth is pulled downward by gravity.

T F **2.** Buoyancy is a force that opposes gravity.

T F **3.** An object's buoyancy is related to its density.

T F **4.** The more dense an object is, the more likely it is to float.

T F **5.** The amount of liquid an object displaces can affect buoyancy.

Multiple Choice (Fill in the circle beside the best answer.)

6. Water is . . .
- **a.** more dense than steel.
- **b.** less dense than steel.
- **c.** the same density as steel.
- **d.** has no density because it's a liquid.

7. The density of steel causes it to . . .
- **a.** always sink in water.
- **b.** never sink in water.
- **c.** sink unless its shape displaces water with air.
- **d.** none of the above

8. The structure of Styrofoam® causes it to . . .
- **a.** sink in water.
- **b.** float in water.
- **c.** float only if it's shaped like a boat.
- **d.** none of the above

9. Buoyancy is a force that . . .
- **a.** works to support gravity.
- **b.** opposes gravity.
- **c.** is the same as gravity.
- **d.** has no relationship to gravity.

10. If a steel ship springs a leak, it can sink because . . .
- **a.** it becomes much more buoyant.
- **b.** water begins to displace the air inside.
- **c.** its buoyancy becomes greater than gravity.
- **d.** air begins to replace the water inside.

Copyright ©2003 The Concerned Group, Inc.

NAME _____ DATE _____

PAPER PYRAMID

LESSON 16

True/False (Circle T for true, F for false.)

T F **1.** Forces cannot be transferred from one place to another.

T F **2.** Materials are often much stronger in layers.

T F **3.** Layered materials can transfer forces within a structure.

T F **4.** The structure of an object has an affect on its strength.

T F **5.** Most paper is made from wood fibers.

Multiple Choice (Fill in the circle beside the best answer.)

6. Trees are strong because their wood fibers are . . .
- a. all connected together.
- b. separated and smoothed into sheets.
- c. rolled into very thin layers.
- d. none of the above

7. Good buildings are designed to transfer . . .
- a. weight
- b. force
- c. load
- d. all of the above

8. Materials are most likely to gain strength when placed . . .
- a. in piles.
- b. in layers.
- c. end to end.
- d. side by side.

9. The strength of a structure is based primarily on its . . .
- a. weight
- b. height
- c. structure
- d. size

10. Which of the following is an example of a structure transferring forces?
- a. the framework of a building
- b. the human skeleton
- c. a huge oak tree
- d. all of the above

Copyright ©2003 The Concerned Group, Inc.

NAME _____ DATE _____

PAPER PILLAR
LESSON 17

True/False (Circle T for true, F for false.)

T F **1.** A material's shape can affect its overall strength.

T F **2.** Shape does not affect a material's ability to transfer force.

T F **3.** Generally the more material used, the stronger the structure.

T F **4.** More material creates greater weight, often driving up costs.

T F **5.** Lighter materials always make a structure stronger.

Multiple Choice (Fill in the circle beside the best answer.)

6. When engineers design a structure, they look for . . .
- a. lighter and less expensive materials.
- b. materials that offer great strength.
- c. shapes that offer great strength.
- d. all of the above

7. Engineers primarily use columns for support because . . .
- a. columns are pleasing to look at.
- b. the circular shape supports greater loads.
- c. they can be folded easily.
- d. all of the above

8. Adding material to a structure usually . . .
- a. increases strength and increases costs.
- b. decreases strength and decreases costs.
- c. increases strength and decreases costs.
- d. decreases strength and increases costs.

9. In general, which of the following shapes would support the most weight?
- a. a hollow square
- b. a reinforced tube
- c. a flat sheet of paper
- d. none of the above

10. The more efficient the shape of a structure . . .
- a. the more likely the structure is to collapse.
- b. the better the transfer of forces.
- c. the weaker the overall strength of the structure.
- d. the more expensive it is to build.

Copyright ©2003 The Concerned Group, Inc.

NAME _____ DATE _____

FOAM FLYER
LESSON 18

True/False (Circle T for true, F for false.)

T F **1.** Fast moving air creates higher air pressure.

T F **2.** The curved surface of a wing can create lift.

T F **3.** Lift is a force that opposes gravity.

T F **4.** Air pressure has little affect on the process of flight.

T F **5.** Flight is based on an application of the "Bernoulli Principle."

Multiple Choice (Fill in the circle beside the best answer.)

6. The upward force that results in flight is called . . .
- a. shape
- b. lift
- c. drag
- d. thrust

7. Faster moving air creates . . .
- a. higher air pressure.
- b. lower air pressure.
- c. gravitational pull.
- d. none of the above

8. The phenomenon that creates lift is known as . . .
- a. the Bernoulli Principle.
- b. the Barnouchi Principle.
- c. the Barnicle Principal.
- d. the Bernoulli Principal.

9. What force allows planes to take off?
- a. the push of gravity
- b. the lift of gravity
- c. the thrust of an engine
- d. the drag of an engine

10. Which characteristic most greatly affects a plane's ability to fly.
- a. the shape of its wings
- b. the number of its wings
- c. the color of its wings
- d. none of the above

Copyright ©2003 The Concerned Group, Inc.

NAME _____ DATE _____

LESSON 19
OCEAN OF AIR

True/False (Circle T for true, F for false.)

T F **1.** Air is not matter so it has no weight.

T F **2.** Air pressure is constantly pushing against our bodies.

T F **3.** Air pressure is a kind of force.

T F **4.** Air resistance is not a force that can be transferred.

T F **5.** Larger surface areas are affected less by air than smaller ones.

Multiple Choice (Fill in the circle beside the best answer.)

6. In general, the faster an object moves . . .
- a. the less air resistance it has to overcome.
- b. the more air resistance it has to overcome.
- c. the less gravity it has to overcome.
- d. none of the above

7. Larger surface area usually means the object has . . .
- a. less air resistance.
- b. more air resistance.
- c. less gravity.
- d. none of the above

8. Atmospheric pressure is most similar to . . .
- a. the weight of air pushing down.
- b. the size of cloud formations.
- c. the shape of ocean waves.
- d. none of the above

9. Air resistance is a type of . . .
- a. gravity
- b. lift
- c. force
- d. movement

10. A car is speeding down the road. The opposing force is . . .
- a. friction
- b. air resistance
- c. gravity
- d. all of the above

Copyright ©2003 The Concerned Group, Inc.

NAME_____ DATE_____

LESSON 20
CLASSIFIED CLOUDS

True/False (Circle T for true, F for false.)

T F **1.** Meteorologists can use clouds to predict the weather.

T F **2.** Clouds can be classified according to their characteristics.

T F **3.** Clouds are found only at one specific altitude.

T F **4.** Weather changes help distribute moisture around the globe.

T F **5.** All clouds are essentially the same shape and size.

Multiple Choice (Fill in the circle beside the best answer.)

6. A cloud can contain . . .
 ○ **a.** solids
 ○ **b.** liquids
 ○ **c.** gasses
 ○ **d.** all of the above

7. The energy that creates the weather comes from . . .
 ○ **a.** clouds
 ○ **b.** gravity
 ○ **c.** the sun
 ○ **d.** water vapor

8. The amount of solar energy varies depending on . . .
 ○ **a.** location and season.
 ○ **b.** gravity and water vapor.
 ○ **c.** water vapor and gas.
 ○ **d.** national energy prices.

9. One important role of weather is . . .
 ○ **a.** keeping the atmosphere near Earth's surface.
 ○ **b.** constantly increasing all global temperatures.
 ○ **c.** distributing atmospheric energy around the planet.
 ○ **d.** removing moisture from Earth's core.

10. Ice crystals high in cirrus clouds prove that . . .
 ○ **a.** gravity increases with altitude.
 ○ **b.** clouds are always a liquid.
 ○ **c.** clouds are always a gas.
 ○ **d.** clouds can contain solid forms.

Copyright ©2003 The Concerned Group, Inc.

NAME _____ DATE _____

MARVELOUS MAPPING

LESSON 21

True/False (Circle T for true, F for false.)

T F **1.** Remote sensing provides a way to map places humans can't go.

T F **2.** Maps made remotely are interesting, but of little practical use.

T F **3.** Inaccuracy of scale results from wide-spread data points.

T F **4.** Maps are usually more accurate than first-hand exploration.

T F **5.** Increasing the number of data points usually decreases accuracy.

Multiple Choice (Fill in the circle beside the best answer.)

6. Remote sensing technology was originally developed by . . .
 ○ **a.** NBC
 ○ **b.** NASCAR
 ○ **c.** NASA
 ○ **d.** none of the above

7. Which of the following energy beams might be used as a probe?
 ○ **a.** radar
 ○ **b.** sonar
 ○ **c.** laser
 ○ **d.** all of the above

8. Remote sensing is usually used . . .
 ○ **a.** when a location is easily accessible for humans.
 ○ **b.** for locations where humans cannot go.
 ○ **c.** when human operators are busy with more important tasks.
 ○ **d.** only when the location is underwater.

9. The spots where measurements are made are called . . .
 ○ **a.** data points.
 ○ **b.** ocean points.
 ○ **c.** data spots.
 ○ **d.** spot points.

10. In general, a map with more data points is . . .
 ○ **a.** less accurate.
 ○ **b.** more accurate.
 ○ **c.** inaccurate.
 ○ **d.** Data points do not affect accuracy.

Copyright ©2003 The Concerned Group, Inc.

NAME _____ DATE _____

LESSON 22
COOKED COAL

True/False (Circle T for true, F for false.)

T F **1.** All rocks have the same properties.

T F **2.** Coal is an important form of energy.

T F **3.** The chemicals in coal are released by freezing.

T F **4.** Coal gas was once used for lighting homes.

T F **5.** The residue from heating coal is called coke.

Multiple Choice (Fill in the circle beside the best answer.)

6. The physical state of coal can be . . .
- a. solid
- b. liquid
- c. gas
- d. all of the above

7. When coal is heated, the result is a . . .
- a. physical change.
- b. chemical change.
- c. both physical and chemical change.
- d. none of the above

8. As coal cools after extended heating, it leaves behind a solid residue called . . .
- a. coal tar
- b. coal gas
- c. coal stew
- d. coke

9. Coal tar can be . . .
- a. used to produce medicine.
- b. used to produce plastic.
- c. a complex stew of chemicals.
- d. all of the above

10. Coke is used to make . . .
- a. iron and steel.
- b. medicines and plastic.
- c. soft drinks.
- d. coal stew.

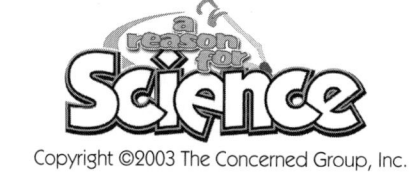

Copyright ©2003 The Concerned Group, Inc.

NAME _____ DATE _____

SPACIOUS SPACE

LESSON 23

True/False (Circle T for true, F for false.)

T F **1.** A group of planets orbiting a star is called a solar system.

T F **2.** A group of solar systems is called a galaxy.

T F **3.** A planet's size determines the amount of energy it receives.

T F **4.** Planets in our solar system are all the same distance from the Sun.

T F **5.** Planets in our solar system always orbit in exact circles.

Multiple Choice (Fill in the circle beside the best answer.)

6. According to scientists, the outermost planet in our solar system is . . .
- **a.** Pluto.
- **b.** Neptune.
- **c.** sometimes Pluto, sometimes Neptune.
- **d.** neither Pluto nor Neptune.

7. The galaxy our solar system belongs to is called the . . .
- **a.** Orion Nebula.
- **b.** Milky Way.
- **c.** Solarian Universe.
- **d.** none of the above

8. The heavenly body we call "the Sun" is also . . .
- **a.** a star.
- **b.** a planet.
- **c.** a solar system.
- **d.** a galaxy.

9. Scientists estimate our galaxy contains . . .
- **a.** millions of solar systems.
- **b.** hundreds of galaxies.
- **c.** billions of solar systems.
- **d.** millions of galaxies.

10. The two planets closest to Earth are . . .
- **a.** Venus and Mercury.
- **b.** Mercury and Mars.
- **c.** Venus and Mars.
- **d.** none of the above

Copyright ©2003 The Concerned Group, Inc.

PLANET PERSPECTIVE

LESSON 24

True/False (Circle T for true, F for false.)

T F **1.** Planets vary significantly in size and other characteristics.

T F **2.** Scale models help scientists study relationships between objects.

T F **3.** The Sun is the largest object in our solar system.

T F **4.** Planets decrease in size the farther you get from the Sun.

T F **5.** Venus and Earth have very similar atmospheres.

Multiple Choice (Fill in the circle beside the best answer.)

6. The two largest planets in our solar system are . . .
- a. Jupiter and Neptune.
- b. Neptune and Saturn.
- c. Saturn and Jupiter.
- d. none of the above

7. The two smallest planets in our solar system are . . .
- a. Mercury and Mars.
- b. Mercury and Pluto.
- c. Pluto and Mars.
- d. none of the above

8. Planets can vary significantly in . . .
- a. composition
- b. temperature
- c. atmosphere
- d. all of the above

9. If Earth were farther from the Sun, it would probably be . . .
- a. hotter
- b. colder
- c. drier
- d. smaller

10. Scientists make models to help them . . .
- a. teach.
- b. test ideas.
- c. enhance understanding.
- d. all of the above

Copyright ©2003 The Concerned Group, Inc.

NAME_____ DATE_____

LESSON 25
STAR STRUCTURES

True/False (Circle T for true, F for false.)

T F **1.** When viewed from Earth, some groups of stars seem to form patterns.

T F **2.** Star patterns are the same from anywhere in the Universe.

T F **3.** Every star is part of a constellation.

T F **4.** All the stars in a constellation are roughly the same size.

T F **5.** Most constellations were named by ancient peoples.

Multiple Choice (Fill in the circle beside the best answer.)

6. From outside our galaxy, most constellations would look . . .
- **a.** larger
- **b.** smaller
- **c.** the same
- **d.** different

7. A constellation is . . .
- **a.** a group of planets in a recognizable pattern.
- **b.** a group of planets with no recognizable pattern.
- **c.** a group of stars in a recognizable pattern.
- **d.** none of the above

8. The Milky Way . . .
- **a.** is a large, heavy band of stars.
- **b.** is a huge disk of stars.
- **c.** is a twisting spiral of stars.
- **d.** all of the above

9. The arrangement of stars in a constellation . . .
- **a.** never changes.
- **b.** can change very rapidly.
- **c.** may change if viewed from another part of the galaxy.
- **d.** none of the above

10. Which of the following would be most helpful in scientifically studying stars?
- **a.** a telescope
- **b.** a microscope
- **c.** a laser tape
- **d.** a horoscope

Copyright ©2003 The Concerned Group, Inc.

NAME _____ DATE _____

LESSON 26
GRAVITY GRABBER

True/False (Circle T for true, F for false.)

T   F   **1.** The greater an object's mass, the greater its gravitational field.

T   F   **2.** A star's gravitational field can affect objects far off in space.

T   F   **3.** Planets are too small to have gravitational fields.

T   F   **4.** NASA uses gravitational fields to extend the range of some satellites.

T   F   **5.** A gravitational field can affect the path of passing objects.

Multiple Choice (Fill in the circle beside the best answer.)

6. The larger the mass . . .
- a. the smaller the gravitational field.
- b. the larger the gravitational field.
- c. the weaker the gravitational field.
- d. There is no relationship between mass and gravity.

7. A gravitational field may have less effect on an object that is . . .
- a. sitting motionless.
- b. moving very slowly.
- c. moving very rapidly.
- d. oscillating back and forth.

8. A gravitational field may have little effect on an object that is . . .
- a. very close.
- b. far away.
- c. made of metal.
- d. made of plastic.

9. If a small meteor passes close to a large planet, it probably would . . .
- a. speed away more rapidly.
- b. enter a geosynchronous orbit.
- c. be caught in the planet's gravitational field.
- d. not be affected at all.

10. The closer an object gets to a planet's gravitational field . . .
- a. the more the object is repelled.
- b. the more the object is attracted.
- c. the greater the object's mass.
- d. the less the object's mass.

Copyright ©2003 The Concerned Group, Inc.

NAME _____ DATE _____

PERSONAL PLANET

LESSON 27

True/False (Circle T for true, F for false.)

T F **1.** The Earth is composed of 17 distinct layers.

T F **2.** Earth's layers are very similar to each other.

T F **3.** The crust of the Earth is relatively solid.

T F **4.** Scientists believe Earth's core is mostly iron and nickel.

T F **5.** The thickest of Earth's layers is the crust.

Multiple Choice (Fill in the circle beside the best answer.)

6. Earth's major layers are known as the . . .
- **a.** endo, messo, and exto.
- **b.** inner, mid, and outer.
- **c.** core, mantle, and crust.
- **d.** igneous, magma, and crust.

7. Scientists call Earth's middle layer the . . .
- **a.** messo
- **b.** magma
- **c.** mid
- **d.** mantle

8. The composition of Earth's middle layer is . . .
- **a.** completely solid.
- **b.** completely liquid.
- **c.** between liquid and solid.
- **d.** none of the above

9. Scientists call Earth's center the . . .
- **a.** endo
- **b.** inner
- **c.** core
- **d.** igneous

10. The composition of Earth's outer layer is . . .
- **a.** mostly rock, soil, and similar materials.
- **b.** mostly magma and igneous rock.
- **c.** mostly molten iron and nickle.
- **d.** It is impossible to know for sure.

Copyright ©2003 The Concerned Group, Inc

NAME _____ DATE _____

LESSON 28
BAFFLING BEADS

True/False (Circle T for true, F for false.)

T F **1.** Only a small portion of the light spectrum is visible to human eyes.

T F **2.** Ultraviolet light is one form of light that is easy to see.

T F **3.** Light energy can be absorbed and released.

T F **4.** The light in most classrooms is identical to sunlight.

T F **5.** A rainbow can show all the colors of visible light.

Multiple Choice (Fill in the circle beside the best answer.)

6. The speed at which a light wave vibrates is called its . . .
   - a. wavelength.
   - b. frequency.
   - c. amplitude.
   - d. ultra rate.

7. The prefix "ultra" means . . .
   - a. less than.
   - b. greater than.
   - c. shinier than.
   - d. none of the above

8. Ultraviolet light is . . .
   - a. higher in frequency than violet light.
   - b. lower in wavelength than violet light.
   - c. identical to violet light.
   - d. a form of x-ray energy.

9. Ultraviolet light can be detected by . . .
   - a. radio waves.
   - b. x-rays.
   - c. humans with good eyesight.
   - d. special materials or equipment.

10. The opposite of "absorb" is . . .
   - a. vibrate.
   - b. immigrate.
   - c. radiate.
   - d. imitate.

Copyright ©2003 The Concerned Group, Inc.

NAME _____ DATE _____

SOUND SEEKER

LESSON 29

True/False (Circle T for true, F for false.)

T F **1.** To create sound, energy must produce vibration.

T F **2.** Scientists refer to the rate of vibration as "frequency".

T F **3.** Frequency has an effect on a sound's pitch.

T F **4.** Sound travels more rapidly in space since there is no air.

T F **5.** Amplifying a sound makes it softer and quieter.

Multiple Choice (Fill in the circle beside the best answer.)

6. Scientists refer to vibrations as . . .
- ○ **a.** frequency
- ○ **b.** waves
- ○ **c.** amplification
- ○ **d.** wavelengths

7. The correct sequence of events for creating sound is . . .
- ○ **a.** energy, vibration, air movement, detection.
- ○ **b.** air movement, energy, vibration, detection.
- ○ **c.** vibration, air movement, energy, detection.
- ○ **d.** detection, air movement, energy, vibration.

8. Which of the following can change a sound?
- ○ **a.** vibration rate
- ○ **b.** pitch
- ○ **c.** amplification
- ○ **d.** all of the above

9. Adjusting the "vibration rate" is changing a sound's . . .
- ○ **a.** amplification
- ○ **b.** transmission
- ○ **c.** frequency
- ○ **d.** all of the above

10. Sound waves are a form of . . .
- ○ **a.** energy
- ○ **b.** amplification
- ○ **c.** detection
- ○ **d.** none of the above

Copyright ©2003 The Concerned Group, Inc

NAME _____ DATE _____

LESSON 30
LIQUID LITERACY

True/False (Circle T for true, F for false.)

T F **1.** Some materials can cause light to bend.

T F **2.** Reflection and refraction mean the same thing.

T F **3.** Lenses help control the degree of refraction.

T F **4.** Certain kinds of lenses produce an inverted image.

T F **5.** When light goes through water, it speeds up rapidly.

Multiple Choice (Fill in the circle beside the best answer.)

6. When a material is easy to see through, we call it . . .
   ○ **a.** transmitting
   ○ **b.** translucent
   ○ **c.** transparent
   ○ **d.** transient

7. When light from an image slows down, it can . . .
   ○ **a.** refract
   ○ **b.** bend
   ○ **c.** invert
   ○ **d.** all of the above

8. Which of the following is most likely to cause refraction?
   ○ **a.** a small hand mirror
   ○ **b.** a goldfish bowl full of water
   ○ **c.** a very shiny chrome plate
   ○ **d.** a large, blue plastic cup

9. High density transparent materials . . .
   ○ **a.** stop the movement of light.
   ○ **b.** slow the movement of light.
   ○ **c.** speed up light movement.
   ○ **d.** improve the reflection ratio.

10. A person who "fishes" with a bow and arrow must . . .
   ○ **a.** aim directly at the fish.
   ○ **b.** learn to allow for refraction.
   ○ **c.** wear special contact lens.
   ○ **d.** none of the above

Copyright ©2003 The Concerned Group, Inc.

NAME _____ DATE _____

PERIODIC PUZZLE

LESSON 31

True/False (Circle T for true, F for false.)

T F **1.** Everything around us is made from different elements.

T F **2.** The concept of "elements" began in the early 1900s.

T F **3.** The Periodic Table is a chart that organizes the elements for study.

T F **4.** Elements can be organized by their atomic number.

T F **5.** Elements can be organized by their chemical properties.

Multiple Choice (Fill in the circle beside the best answer.)

6. The ancient Greeks called small particles of matter . . .
- ○ **a.** primaries
- ○ **b.** properties
- ○ **c.** elements
- ○ **d.** none of the above

7. The modern periodic table is organized by . . .
- ○ **a.** atomic number.
- ○ **b.** chemical properties.
- ○ **c.** relationships between elements.
- ○ **d.** all of the above

8. Columns on the periodic table are also called . . .
- ○ **a.** rows
- ○ **b.** properties
- ○ **c.** periods
- ○ **d.** families

9. Rows on the periodic table are also called . . .
- ○ **a.** rows
- ○ **b.** properties
- ○ **c.** periods
- ○ **d.** families

10. There are ____ naturally occuring elements.
- ○ **a.** less than 10
- ○ **b.** more than 80
- ○ **c.** about 24
- ○ **d.** thousands of

Copyright ©2003 The Concerned Group, Inc

NAME _____ DATE _____

CIRCUIT TESTER

LESSON 32

True/False (Circle T for true, F for false.)

T F **1.** A connected path for electricity is called a closed circuit.

T F **2.** Materials that carry electricity are called insulators.

T F **3.** Materials that don't carry electricity are called conductors.

T F **4.** A "switch" is one device that can open and close circuits.

T F **5.** Electricity can trasmit energy from one place to another.

Multiple Choice (Fill in the circle beside the best answer.)

6. The electricity in a battery comes from . . .
- a. a chemical reaction.
- b. an open circuit.
- c. an insulator.
- d. none of the above

7. Electricity involves the flow of . . .
- a. electrons
- b. energy
- c. power
- d. all of the above

8. Turning off the light in a room creates . . .
- a. an open circuit.
- b. a closed circuit.
- c. a neutral circuit.
- d. none of the above

9. A material that stops the flow of electricity is called . . .
- a. a conductor.
- b. an insulator.
- c. a circuit.
- d. an electron.

10. Most common household appliances have . . .
- a. a switch.
- b. a conductor.
- c. an insulator.
- d. all of the above

Copyright ©2003 The Concerned Group, Inc

NAME _____ DATE _____

SHIFTING SULFATE

LESSON 33

True/False (Circle T for true, F for false.)

T F **1.** Matter can change states.

T F **2.** There are two basic kinds of change: physical and chemical.

T F **3.** Physical changes do not affect the form of a material.

T F **4.** Chemical changes result in a different substance.

T F **5.** Chemical changes involve energy; physical changes do not.

Multiple Choice (Fill in the circle beside the best answer.)

6. Burning a piece of wood is an example of . . .
- **a.** a physical change.
- **b.** a chemical change.
- **c.** hydration.
- **d.** none of the above

7. Which of the following is a chemical change?
- **a.** burning
- **b.** freezing
- **c.** chopping
- **d.** none of the above

8. Which of the following is a physical change?
- **a.** freezing
- **b.** chopping
- **c.** grinding
- **d.** all of the above

9. A "hydrate" is a material with attached . . .
- **a.** water
- **b.** heat
- **c.** color
- **d.** change

10. The color of copper sulfate . . .
- **a.** is a reddish gold.
- **b.** is a deep blue.
- **c.** is impossible to determine.
- **d.** can change when water is added.

Copyright ©2003 The Concerned Group, Inc

NAME _____ DATE _____

COOL COIN

LESSON 34

True/False (Circle T for true, F for false.)

T F **1.** It takes oxygen, fuel, and heat to make a fire.

T F **2.** Heat energy can be absorbed by a conductor.

T F **3.** "Fire triangle" refers to the usual shape of flames.

T F **4.** Paper is a good material for transferring heat.

T F **5.** Oxygen for combustion usually comes from the air.

Multiple Choice (Fill in the circle beside the best answer.)

6. The three sides of the fire triangle are . . .
- a. fuel, food, heat.
- b. oxygen, fuel, heat.
- c. oxygen, heat, food.
- d. none of the above

7. A dime is a good example of . . .
- a. an oxygen source.
- b. a fuel source.
- c. a food source.
- d. a conductor.

8. A sheet of newspaper is an example of . . .
- a. an oxygen source.
- b. a fuel source.
- c. a food source.
- d. a conductor.

9. A conductor can . . .
- a. absorb heat, protecting the area beneath it.
- b. transfer absorbed heat, starting a fire.
- c. both of the above
- d. neither of the above

10. Removing a hot pan from the oven requires using . . .
- a. a conductor to protect your hands.
- b. an insulator to protect your hands.
- c. an oxygen source to protect your hands.
- d. all of the above

Copyright ©2003 The Concerned Group, Inc

NAME _____ DATE _____

BURNING STEEL
LESSON 35

True/False (Circle T for true, F for false.)

T F **1.** Oxidation can occur when a substance combines with oxygen.

T F **2.** Scientists consider oxidation a physical process.

T F **3.** Oxidation is always a very slow process, like rusting.

T F **4.** A pile of burning brush is a form of oxidation.

T F **5.** More surface area usually means slower burning.

Multiple Choice (Fill in the circle beside the best answer.)

6. Burning . . .
- a. is also called oxidation.
- b. is a chemical change.
- c. results in a different substance.
- d. all of the above

7. In order for steel wool to burn . . .
- a. iron atoms must combine with oxygen atoms.
- b. a physical change must occur.
- c. only one part of the "fire triangle" must be present.
- d. all of the above

8. Steel wool burns primarily because it . . .
- a. is made of iron.
- b. has a huge surface area.
- c. is made of oxygen.
- d. none of the above

9. A material is more likely to burn if it is . . .
- a. dense and compact.
- b. thin and spread out.
- c. protected from oxygen.
- d. heavily oxidized.

10. Which of the following would be easiest to burn?
- a. a large pine log
- b. a sheet of thick cardboard
- c. a city phone book
- d. a sheet of newspaper

Copyright ©2003 The Concerned Group, Inc.

NAME _____ DATE _____

FLOWERS & FUMES

LESSON 36

True/False (Circle T for true, F for false.)

T F **1.** Indicators may be used to detect an acid or a base.

T F **2.** All indicators are made of phenolphthalein.

T F **3.** Indicators can change colors.

T F **4.** Breathing on water can create a mild acid.

T F **5.** Ammonium hydroxide is always a gas.

Multiple Choice (Fill in the circle beside the best answer.)

6. An indicator is a special kind of . . .
- **a.** acid
- **b.** hydrate
- **c.** chemical
- **d.** base

7. Phenolphthalein changes colors in the presence of . . .
- **a.** an acid.
- **b.** a base.
- **c.** an indicator.
- **d.** none of the above.

8. Blowing carbon dioxide onto water can produce . . .
- **a.** a strong acid.
- **b.** a strong base.
- **c.** a weak base.
- **d.** none of the above

9. Ammonium hydroxide is . . .
- **a.** an acid.
- **b.** a base.
- **c.** an indicator.
- **d.** none of the above

10. Phenolphthalein is . . .
- **a.** an acid.
- **b.** a base.
- **c.** an indicator.
- **d.** none of the above

Copyright ©2003 The Concerned Group, Inc.

Assessment Answer Key
LIFE

Lesson 1
Survivor Seeds

1. F
2. T
3. T
4. T
5. T
6. c
7. a
8. d
9. d
10. c

Lesson 2
Apple Embryo

1. T
2. F
3. T
4. T
5. F
6. b
7. c
8. a
9. d
10. b

Lesson 3
Pyric Peanut

1. T
2. T
3. F
4. T
5. F
6. d
7. c
8. a
9. b
10. a

Lesson 4
Starch Search

1. F
2. T
3. F
4. F
5. T
6. c
7. b
8. d
9. c
10. c

Lesson 5
Sealed Cell

1. F
2. F
3. T
4. F
5. T
6. d
7. d
8. b
9. a
10. d

Lesson 6
Beads of Blood

1. T
2. T
3. F
4. F
5. T
6. a
7. b
8. c
9. d
10. b

Lesson 7
Predator or Prey

1. F
2. F
3. F
4. T
5. F
6. c
7. a
8. b
9. a
10. d

Lesson 8
Spindly Spine

1. T
2. F
3. F
4. T
5. T
6. a
7. c
8. b
9. c
10. d

Lesson 9
Experimental Epidemic

1. T
2. F
3. F
4. T
5. F
6. d
7. c
8. c
9. a
10. b

Assessment Answer Key
FORCES

Lesson 10
Magnet Motions

1. T
2. T
3. T
4. F
5. F
6. b
7. c
8. a
9. d
10. d

Lesson 11
Peanut Paste

1. T
2. F
3. T
4. T
5. F
6. d
7. b
8. d
9. a
10. b

Lesson 12
Balancing Nails

1. T
2. T
3. F
4. F
5. T
6. b
7. c
8. a
9. d
10. c

Lesson 13
Corks & Forks

1. T
2. T
3. T
4. F
5. T
6. b
7. c
8. a
9. c
10. d

Lesson 14
Egg Airbag

1. T
2. F
3. T
4. F
5. T
6. b
7. c
8. b
9. c
10. d

Lesson 15
Buoyant Ball

1. T
2. T
3. T
4. F
5. T
6. b
7. c
8. b
9. b
10. b

Lesson 16
Paper Pyramid

1. F
2. T
3. T
4. T
5. T
6. a
7. d
8. b
9. c
10. d

Lesson 17
Paper Pillar

1. T
2. F
3. T
4. T
5. F
6. d
7. b
8. a
9. b
10. b

Lesson 18
Foam Flyer

1. F
2. T
3. T
4. F
5. T
6. b
7. b
8. a
9. c
10. a

Assessment Answer Key
EARTH

Lesson 19
Ocean of Air

1. F
2. T
3. T
4. F
5. F
6. b
7. b
8. a
9. c
10. d

Lesson 20
Classified Clouds

1. T
2. T
3. F
4. T
5. F
6. d
7. c
8. a
9. c
10. d

Lesson 21
Marvelous Mapping

1. T
2. F
3. T
4. F
5. F
6. c
7. d
8. b
9. a
10. b

Lesson 22
Cooked Coal

1. F
2. T
3. F
4. T
5. T
6. d
7. c
8. d
9. d
10. a

Lesson 23
Spacious Space

1. T
2. T
3. F
4. F
5. F
6. c
7. b
8. a
9. c
10. c

Lesson 24
Planet Perspective

1. T
2. T
3. T
4. F
5. F
6. c
7. b
8. d
9. b
10. d

Lesson 25
Star Structures

1. T
2. F
3. F
4. F
5. T
6. d
7. c
8. d
9. c
10. a

Lesson 26
Gravity Grabber

1. T
2. T
3. F
4. T
5. T
6. b
7. c
8. b
9. c
10. b

Lesson 27
Personal Planet

1. F
2. F
3. T
4. T
5. F
6. c
7. d
8. c
9. c
10. a

Assessment Answer Key
ENERGY/MATTER

Lesson 28
Baffling Beads

1. T
2. F
3. T
4. F
5. T
6. b
7. b
8. a
9. d
10. c

Lesson 29
Sound Seeker

1. T
2. T
3. T
4. F
5. F
6. b
7. a
8. d
9. c
10. a

Lesson 30
Liquid Literacy

1. T
2. F
3. T
4. T
5. F
6. c
7. d
8. b
9. b
10. b

Lesson 31
Periodic Puzzle

1. T
2. F
3. T
4. T
5. T
6. c
7. d
8. d
9. c
10. b

Lesson 32
Circuit Tester

1. T
2. F
3. F
4. T
5. T
6. a
7. d
8. a
9. b
10. d

Lesson 33
Shifting Sulfate

1. T
2. T
3. F
4. T
5. F
6. b
7. a
8. d
9. a
10. d

Lesson 34
Cool Coin

1. T
2. T
3. F
4. F
5. T
6. b
7. d
8. b
9. c
10. b

Lesson 35
Burning Steel

1. T
2. F
3. F
4. T
5. F
6. d
7. a
8. b
9. b
10. d

Lesson 36
Flowers & Fumes

1. T
2. F
3. T
4. T
5. F
6. c
7. b
8. d
9. b
10. c

Shopping List

This **"Shopping List"** is provided for your convenience. It contains all the items that are not common classroom supplies (paper, pencil, scissors, etc.) or components found in your Materials Kit.

Please note: There are a few items (like tissue paper rolls) that require advance planning for effective collection.

Lesson 2
Apples
Knife
Lemon juice

Lesson 3
Match

Lesson 4
Gloves

Lesson 5
Bowl

Lesson 8
Cardboard tube

Lesson 9
Plastic cup (clear)

Lesson 10
Aluminum foil
Plastic

Lesson 12
Hammer

Lesson 14
Egg
Sealable bag (large)

Lesson 15
Clear jar

Lesson 16
Weights
Newspaper

Lesson 17
Juice can

Lesson 19
Newspaper

Lesson 21
Shoe box with lid
Paper mache paste
Graph paper

Lesson 22
Propane torch

Lesson 23
Basketball

Lesson 24
Compass
Tape measure

Lesson 25
Foam board
Push pins
White thread

Lesson 26
Plastic wrap
Plastic bucket

Lesson 29
Plastic wrap

Lesson 33
Matches

Lesson 34
Matches
Aluminum pan

Lesson 35
Aluminum pan
Match

Lesson 36
Plastic wrap